# AMERICAN ARTISANS

By Hammer & Hand, all Arts do ſtand

The mighty arm of early American labor. Detail from membership certificate, New York Mechanics Society, 1791. (Courtesy, The Henry Francis DuPont Winterthur Museum)

# AMERICAN ARTISANS

## Crafting Social Identity, 1750–1850

Edited by
Howard B. Rock,
Paul A. Gilje, and
Robert Asher

The Johns Hopkins University Press
Baltimore and London

This book has been brought to publication with the generous assistance of the George Meany Memorial Archives.

©1995 The Johns Hopkins University Press
All rights reserved. Published 1995
Printed in the United States of America on acid-free paper
04 03 02 01 00 99 98 97 96 95    5 4 3 2 1

The Johns Hopkins University Press
2715 North Charles Street
Baltimore, Maryland 21218-4319
The Johns Hopkins Press Ltd., London

ISBN 0-8018-5029-0
ISBN 0-8018-5030-4 (pbk.)

Library of Congress Cataloging-in-Publication Data
will be found at the end of this book.

A catalog record for this book is available
from the British Library.

*To Professor Alfred F. Young*

*in appreciation of his*

*work on and in behalf of*

*the American Artisan*

# Contents

# Acknowledgments

THE ORIGINS OF THIS BOOK were in a conference entitled "The American Artisan," held under the auspicies of and at the George Meany Memorial Archives in Silver Spring, Maryland, on October 11–12, 1990. It was organized by Stuart Kaufman, director of the archives and editor of *Labor's Heritage;* Howard B. Rock, of Florida International University, and Robert Asher, of the University of Connecticut. All of the essays in this volume except those of Tina Sheller and Bruce Laurie were delivered there in a preliminary form.

The editors of this book would also like to thank Jonathan Prude and Thomas Dublin for their helpful readings of and suggestions regarding the essays. In addition Bob Brugger and Miriam Kleiger of the Johns Hopkins University Press gave the most careful attention to the final editing and preparation of the book.

This book is dedicated to Professor Alfred F. Young, now emeritus at Northern Illinois University and the keynote speaker at the original conference. Professor Young is in many ways the godfather of modern artisan studies. Aside from his pathbreaking studies on artisans, he has given selflessly of his time to assist nearly all scholars of this generation who write or wrote on the American craftsman. Advice from Al Young is never cursory; rather, he would devote hours of his time to giving meticulous analysis of the evidence and logic of the work of a young or seasoned historian. If this slowed his steady and ever-increasing output a bit, it has also greatly enhanced numerous studies of early American history. Our dedication is in appreciation of this generosity of spirit as well as Professor Young's gifted scholarship.

# Introduction

## PAUL A. GILJE

## Identity and Independence:
### The American Artisan, 1750–1850

IN 1723 A SEVENTEEN-YEAR-OLD apprentice in Boston broke his solemn agreement with his master and ran away. The young man first went to New York, where he found the prospects unappealing, and then moved on to Philadelphia. In the Quaker City the apprentice labored as a skilled workman—a journeyman. Following a sojourn in London this artisan returned to Philadelphia, set up an independent printing shop, and by dint of hard work, a good marriage, appropriate political connections, and an understanding of the market for printed goods, became fabulously wealthy and retired at the age of forty-two. After the master craftsman hung up the leather apron that had marked his life as a mechanic (*mechanic* was an eighteenth-century term for *artisan*) he gained renown as a philosopher, a man of science and letters, a provincial leader who had transatlantic visibility, a fomenter of rebellion, an author of American independence, and the most venerable of the founding fathers at the Constitutional Convention.[1]

A little more than one hundred years later, another young artisan broke the ties that bound him. This youth worked on the Baltimore docks as a caulker. Excluded from some shipyards because of the color of his skin, he nonetheless hired himself out, earning enough not only to maintain his own independent existence but also to make a profit for his owner. As a slave this man knew both visible and invisible chains. He escaped to the North, stopping, as had the Boston apprentice, in New York, and then moved on to New Bedford, Massachusetts. Despite his skill as an artisan, the racial prejudice of white caulkers made it impossible for him to continue in his trade. He therefore labored at any job that came his way. He was rescued from obscurity by chance, when he was asked to speak at an antislavery meeting about life in captivity. His ability and intelligence quickly attracted attention, and he became one of the foremost abolitionists, an international celebrity, a symbol and a spokesman for his race, and a confidant of presidents.[2]

The careers of Benjamin Franklin and Frederick Douglass can help us begin to define what an artisan was. Both men were skilled workers who labored with their hands, using tools. Before practicing a trade, such workers had to be trained in its "mystery," or "art." In other words, they had to obtain some dexterity in the manual production of goods or the provision of a service. The type of tools and equipment varied from trade to trade. Printing utilized larger machinery than did caulking, and after Franklin's time it became increasingly mechanized, whereas even in the nineteenth century caulking remained more labor intensive and skill based. These two trades, however, represent just a small sampling of the hundreds of artisanal occupations—including carpentry, butchery, carting, shoemaking, and silversmithing—identified in the period 1750–1850. Being an artisan in the eighteenth and early nineteenth centuries meant belonging to a productive, nonfarming class that was society's mainstay.

The standard procedure by which whites obtained this status was to serve an apprenticeship when a youth. During the apprenticeship period, set in a written contract, the worker agreed to labor for no wage; instead, the master provided room, board, clothing, some education, and knowledge of the trade. When the youth reached the age of "freedom," usually twenty-one, he became a journeyman. At that point he could work for whomever he wanted at the going wage.[3] Then, after spending some time acquiring the necessary capital, the journeyman might set up a separate shop to become a master. The progression from apprentice to journeyman to master, however, represented the ideal. The process did not always work out that way. Franklin left Boston long before his "freedom" was due. Most white youths fulfilled their contracts; some eventually became masters, while others remained journeymen all their lives. Black slaves did not serve formal apprenticeships as whites did. Douglass could have labored in Baltimore till he died and would never have been granted freedom.[4]

"Independence"—mainly economic, but more than that—was the goal of almost all artisans. Mechanics sought independence in a variety of ways. Franklin ran away to obtain his freedom and worked hard—or so he repeatedly asserted in his autobiography—to become a master and a gentleman. Douglass gained some autonomy through his work as a caulker, although that autonomy was violated each Saturday when he had to turn over his wages to his owner and report his every movement. Douglass's work as an artisan allowed him to see that the path to freedom lay in escaping to the North. Artisanal identity could thus help an individual transcend the limits of social status dictated by birth.

Artisanal independence, however, did not allow all craftsmen to rise above their status as mechanics. Some artisans managed to become rich, like Franklin, but others suffered poverty. Most workers sought knowledge of a craft in an effort to sustain their social status, not change it. They strove for "a competency"—the ability to maintain an independent household, support a family, and work in one's trade. (This may have been Douglass's ambition when he ran away.) Having a trade enabled an artisan with skill and tools to identify himself as independent and to occupy a middling position in society.[5]  *Schultz*

Indeed, the relationship between mechanic status and social identity linked Franklin and Douglass, and all other artisans in the eighteenth and early nineteenth centuries. Studying social identity entails more than delineating an emerging class consciousness, although that is part of the story. One needs to examine how mechanics' perceptions and self-perceptions changed over time and in various locations. Identity and independence came to have different meanings for different groups of artisans depending on local circumstances and various other developments. Thus, one of the central questions that we need to examine is how groups of workers—such as artisans—identified themselves in relationship to other workers and in relationship to those above and below them on a social scale.

Historians have debated exactly what social position mechanics occupied in the colonial period. Some scholars describe artisans as would-be entrepreneurs; others see them as more akin to common laborers, and as the raw material for the makings of an American working class.[6] No doubt the upper echelons of tradesmen, men like Franklin or Paul Revere, fit the first characterization, while most others fit the second.

In the eighteenth century the gentry denigrated mechanics, granting them little respect in a hierarchical world that prized the gentleman who eschewed all labor. Indeed, the elite defined the term *mechanic* as "belonging to or characteristic of the 'lower orders'; vulgar, low, base."[7] Some artisans may have deferred to people of higher social standing and believed themselves inferior. Other mechanics, however, had already begun to mold a stronger, separate self-image, one inherited from the political upheavals of the seventeenth century, highlighting the artisan's role as a producer. Although this tradition stressed the independence of artisans as individuals, it also fostered a common identity and a sense of mutuality.[8] By the middle of the eighteenth century, the ideals of the Enlightenment had strengthened the mechanic's position, holding up the craftsman as a practitioner of the useful arts. Franklin epitomized and championed this view, espousing a new set of values which emphasized hard work, self-improvement, and the importance of innate ability. The simple tradesman, donning a leather apron and using his skill to produce necessary goods, represented an embodiment of the Age of Reason.[9]

Between 1750 and 1850 two major changes affected the mechanic's world. First, American resistance to British imperial measures brought tradesmen into the thick of the fray. Members of the elite in cities such as Boston, New York, Philadelphia, Baltimore, and Charleston depended upon mere mechanics to form the shock troops of rebellion.[10] It is now impossible to ignore the impact of the American Revolution upon artisans. Participation in crowd politics in Boston, for example, allowed a Boston shoemaker to see himself the equal of John Hancock.[11] In newspaper columns and pamphlets, anonymous authors used the by-lines "Tradesman" and "Mechanic"—conjuring up the image of independent producers who strove for mutuality and the public good—to call for sacrifices in the cause of liberty.[12] The political empowerment that came with this involvement can be seen in the conscious sense of identity and purpose of groups such as the Committee of Mechanics in New York City. That committee, formed in 1774, stood in the vanguard of resistance to Great Britain. The mechanics pushed and prodded the committees dominated by merchants and lawyers to take more radical positions, and issued, in response to the staymaker Tom Paine's *Common Sense,* a call for independence as early as the spring of 1776. Tradesmen thus assumed leadership positions that thrust them into the forefront of rebellion.[13] By the end of the Revolution, the word *mechanic* had taken on a new meaning. Although a handful of Americans clung to aristocratic trappings and still looked askance at tradesmen, the ideals of the Revolution had elevated the common man. It became increasingly difficult to use *mechanic* as a slur word to denigrate men who earned their living by the sweat of their brow. Instead, the positive connotations of the term were paramount, and mechanics were seen as comprising a special segment of society which contributed to the economic and political well-being of the new Republic. Jeffersonian Republicans seized upon this new identity and drew these mechanics into their political orbit in the 1790s by recognizing the artisans' role as part of the independent producing class, ensuring Thomas Jefferson's election to the presidency in 1800.[14]

Yet, just as the artisan took on new political significance and appeared to dominate the American urban scene, large changes in the modes of production began to undermine his position. During the colonial period many artisans had achieved master status, if not the wealth and fame of Franklin; and during the early years of the Republic, a greater demand for goods and widespread prosperity encouraged young men to enter the trades.[15] As they did so, conditions changed. Masters began to cut costs by hiring apprentices and half-trained journeymen. Masters emphasized speed, and the quantity rather than the quality of goods, and eventually brought machinery into the workshop. Ideals of individual enterprise took precedence over the mutuality of the workshop. These changes varied in timing and extent, depending upon trade and location. But by 1850 the percentage of skilled craftsmen in the work force had diminished sharply.[16]

Study of the decline of the artisan's world began in the early twentieth century with an interest in the institutions of labor organization. This early work examined the first journeymen's associations, which were formed in part as an effort to halt journeymen's decline in status and were precursors to labor unions.[17] Recent historians, following the leadership of Herbert Gutman and E. P. Thompson, have concentrated on a more rounded approach, emphasizing the cultural dimensions of the artisan's world and the origins of an American working class. The idea has been to study all aspects of the worker's experience, including the nature of work and home life.[18] For example, the status of shoemakers in Lynn, Massachusetts, declined in the first half of the nineteenth century as a result of mechanization and changing relations of production. These developments led to group coherence, union organization, and the great strike of 1860.[19] Philadelphia workers responded to industrialization in a variety of ways. Some workers held tenaciously to a traditional artisanal culture of drinking, carousing, and violence. Others bought into a new set of values, favoring Christianity, sobriety, and hard work, that was espoused by their middle-class employers. A militant group of workers recognized their own class identity and, when conditions were right, organized fellow workers and led strikes.[20]

Economic change did not affect all craftsmen in the same way. In New York City during the early Republic, for instance, there were several conflict trades—printing, shoemaking, cabinetmaking, construction, and tailoring—in which most of the city's strike activity took place. Other mechanics persisted in their devotion to traditional forms of production and even encouraged municipal regulation.[21]

Artisans shared a core set of values that provided them with a special identity as productive members of the new Republic. While these values had antecedents in the colonial period, they can also be connected to the ideology of the American Revolution and labeled "artisanal republicanism." Indeed, scholars have traced the development of these ideas into the 1830s and 1840s, when they came to form the basis of a "consciousness of class" which viewed labor as "a form of personal property, in direct opposition to capitalist conceptions of wage labor as a market commodity."[22]

Despite the vitality of these ideas among mechanics, there remained much diversity in the artisanal population. Some artisans continued in craft production and occupied an ambiguous class location between those mechanics who were being driven down economically and socially and their counterparts who seized new opportunities and, as masters with capital, became businessmen. Members of this last group formed the nucleus of America's new middle class by taking themselves out of the workshop and assuming positions in which they supervised and coordinated the manual work of others, or sold and distributed goods that they did not make themselves.[23] In Rochester, New York, the entrepreneurial artisans separated themselves from their employees and utilized evangelical religion to replace the paternal guardianship of traditional labor relations.[24]

During the last thirty years, in other words, scholarship on artisans has explored the mechanic's social identity and its connection to the development of both a working class and a middle class. While this effort has been exemplary, it has related only part of the story, because it concentrated on the issue of class formation in the northeastern cities. We need to go beyond this localism and examine artisanal identity and independence in a variety of contexts.

The chapters that follow suggest some of the new approaches to studying this group of American workers. Each chapter stands on its own as a separate creation by a particular author, and the authors are very diverse. Taken together, however, the chapters suggest a broader context of artisanal identity. Several of the chapters are cast within the standard paradigm of class formation but illuminate it from new directions. Others, especially those on the southern artisan, demonstrate the range of the artisanal experience with identity and independence during the period 1750–1850, and examine forces that militated against class conflict.

The first four chapters expand the geographic base of our understanding of tradesmen by centering on artisans in the South. Chapter 1, Christine Daniels's study of craft dynasties in Maryland, reminds us that artisans populated the small towns of the countryside as well as the cities. Indeed, rural mechanics facilitated the finishing and movement of goods in an area devoted to commercialized agriculture. Moreover, Daniels offers us a unique picture of tradesmen across generations. She finds that craftsmanship was most often handed down within families in those trades that required the highest capital output. Since the level of capital investment for some trades changed after the American Revolution, she finds that the trades that stayed within families during the early Republic were different than those that had done so in the colonial period. The ability to identify with a trade across generations and maintain an independent household, therefore, depended on the nature of the craft, the type of tools required, and the capital needed to start up the business.

Tina Sheller, in chapter 2, downplays class identification among mechanics in Revolutionary Baltimore and argues that ethnic, religious, and even political identity united many master artisans and merchants. In fact, the city's elite formed close economic ties to master tradesmen, providing start-up capital and marketing assistance. Although Sheller admits that master mechanics shared an independent identity as craftsmen, and even utilized the term *mechanic* in the names of some of their organizations, there was a wide gap between the masters and those who worked for them. In the new, rough-and-tumble world of Baltimore—which grew from a mere village to a small city in this period—masters relied on a variety of forms of bound labor, thus creating a social wall between themselves and their workers. Only with the decline of the use of bound labor in the 1790s did masters and journeymen begin to identify with each other as mechanics.

The presence of bound labor, especially slaves, had an impact on the world of the southern artisan. In chapter 3, Michele Gillespie finds that slavery did not discourage artisans from flocking to colonial Georgia, setting up shop, and making a living. After the Revolution, the expansion of the cotton kingdom offered some of these tradesmen an opportunity to transcend their mechanic status by investing excess capital in slaves and land. Thus many southern artisans, like their northern counterparts, utilized their trade to obtain a new status and participated in the emerging class system of their region. Instead of maintaining their mechanic identity and becoming part of a new working class or a new middle class, these artisans joined the planter class. Gillespie adds an important temporal refinement to her analysis. As the upcountry of Georgia became more settled, class boundaries became more rigid, and it became increasingly difficult for artisans to become planters unless, like other entrepreneurial planters, they joined the migration of the cotton kingdom into the new lands further west.[25]

As the life of Frederick Douglass illustrates, slaves also labored as artisans. James Sidbury, in chapter 4, provides us with an important portrait of Richmond slave artisans during the years 1780–1810. Sidbury's essay allows us to contrast the experience of these African Americans with that of whites in the North and the South. Slave craftsmen did not enjoy the same opportunities and privileges as their white counterparts, nor can they be said to have shared ideas of artisanal republicanism, yet they did develop their own identity and a degree of independence. Slaves in a city such as Richmond obtained greater control over their lives than was possible in the countryside. They enjoyed a more varied social life, and utilized the urban environment to create private space for themselves. The very developments that northern artisans decried—the creation of larger workshops, and increased distance between master and journeymen—slaves greeted with enthusiasm because it released them from closer supervision by whites. Sidbury also reminds us, however, that as the cotton kingdom expanded and the value of field hands increased, the specter of being sold into the Deep South threatened the destruction of the slave artisan's world.

Whereas the chapters on southern artisans demonstrate the variety of the artisanal experience across time and space; the next three chapters reveal new insights concerning tradesmen in the well-traversed territory of the northeast during the early Republic and the Jacksonian era. Each of these chapters explores how artisanal culture led mechanics into new areas of identity. Ronald Schultz, in chapter 5, focuses his attention on the attraction of evangelical religion. He argues that a sense of community was as important to the artisan as was the ideal of competency. Economic and social change shattered the unity of the community of mechanics in the early nineteenth century, and evangelical religion, rooted in artisanal culture's longstanding religiosity, offered both a fulfilling personal experience and a replacement for the loss of community.

There were many obstacles to the creation of a working-class identity. Schultz believes that religion often served to stifle class awareness. Chapter 6, Teresa Murphy's study of the ten-hour movement in New England, suggests that different interests and identities made it difficult for artisans, semiskilled industrial workers, and women factory operatives to unite in a common cause. In particular, the craftsmen in the building trades, who prided themselves on their independence, could not view workers who were more dependent, especially females, as equals. Gradually the artisans decided to include other workers in the ten-hour movement and even hired speakers to proselytize their cause. Yet persistent prejudices and varying local conditions in the factory towns precluded success. Petitioning emerged as one important vehicle that enabled disparate groups, including propertied artisans, to declare their support for the ten-hour day. Although this method failed to change state policy, the process helped to politicize female factory workers.

Murphy's essay suggests that artisans' sense of identity as "mechanics" had an impact on the politics of the workingman's movement, serving to convince artisans to organize, while creating a wedge between them and less highly skilled workers. Bruce Laurie, in chapter 7, joins political and labor history further by tying artisans' anxiety about their independent identity to their support for third-party politics. Laurie argues that while economic change propelled some artisans into the business world of entrepreneurs and drove other workers into the factory and impoverishment, there remained a large middling element of masters and journeymen who labored in small shops. This group, Laurie believes, occupied a crucial place in the political spectrum and helped mediate class relations. Although artisans never felt entirely secure economically, they strove to retain their independence and their identity as mechanics despite the pressures of change. Rather than pushing persistently for a special class identity as workers, they turned to third-party politics that blamed social problems on an external force—be it privileged masons, immigrants, or the "Slave Power." Because of this search for security, third-party politics thus became an intrinsic component of the political system.

Alfred Young's now-classic story of George Robert Twelves Hewes demonstrated that a close examination of one individual can illuminate a variety of social and economic trends.[26] Gary Kornblith and William Pretzer (in chapters 8 and 9, respectively) follow in this tradition with their detailed studies of the printers Joseph T. Buckingham and William W. Moore. In both chapters we see men struggling to clarify their identity as mechanics while striving for economic independence. We also get a personal view of the middling artisans of the type attracted to third-party politics (as described by Laurie) and the special role they played in forming a bridge between the working and middle classes. Kornblith's biographical sketch demonstrates just how difficult it was for a mechanic to sustain independence by describing how Buckingham moved in and out of the status of master and proprietor of his own shop. More importantly, Buckingham became a crucial spokesman for the community of mechanics in Boston in the 1820s and 1830s and articulated a new definition of independence which deemphasized a reliance upon ownership of property and centered around the ideals of self-reliance, self-discipline, and industriousness within a dynamic market economy.

The careers of Buckingham and William Moore have many similarities. Both men were skilled artisans who hoped to establish independent shops, and both ultimately did not succeed in that goal because of the economic vicissitudes of the early national and Jacksonian periods. Both, too, espoused artisanal values. Moore, Pretzer points out, ultimately found respectability, and independence, not as a master but as a foreman in Washington, D.C., printing shops. In this intermediary position, Moore won the support of those below and above him, while obtaining enough financial security to own a house and participate in several clubs and associations that marked the life of those in the lower middle class. Kornblith and Pretzer thus show the resiliency and flexibility of mechanics' identity and independence during the swirling economic changes of the first half of the nineteenth century.

The final two essays approach the issue of artisanal identity through images and iconography. Howard Rock, in chapter 10, explores artisanal ideals through an examination of symbols utilized by master mechanics in parades and printed matter. He discovers that the iconography portrayed an artisanal republicanism wedded to mutuality and industry, and excluded any representation of the entrepreneurial spirit that created rifts between journeymen and masters in the early nineteenth century. He argues that this iconography depicted a benevolent society that masters, who controlled the creation of these symbols, hoped would minimize conflict within the trades.

Harry Rubenstein, in chapter 11, focuses on the image that individual artisans wanted to project of themselves. He notes that starting at the end of the eighteenth century and continuing through the first half of the nine-teenth century, artisans and other workers eagerly embraced their craft and occupation when they had their image captured by painters or photogra-phers. He believes that this pattern reflected the republican ideal of the pro-ductive citizen. By the second half of the nineteenth century this practice had declined, and almost all Americans went to the photographer dressed in their Sunday best. Respectability no longer belonged to the workplace and its grime; instead, all Americans who could afford to have their pictures taken aspired to a generic middle-class ideal represented by white collars and the sanctity of the family.

Benjamin Franklin and Frederick Douglass were worlds apart, yet were united as independent mechanics. The chapters in this book reiterate this theme. While each artisan may have differed in his ultimate goal, all used their artisanal status to assert their social identity. The essays in this volume do not overturn the main elements of the artisans' story as it has developed. Instead, they add to our understanding of tradesmen, demonstrating that the issues of mechanics' identity and independence encompass more than the rise of artisanal republicanism and the creation of the working and mid-dle classes. Three larger questions emerge from an examination of these es-says. First, we can ask how artisanal workers viewed themselves in rela-tionship to others. Second, with the issue of artisanal identity in mind, we can then address when and how classes developed. Finally, both of these questions allow us to understand not only the instances of class conflict which have been the focus of most studies of labor history, but also what forces militated against class conflict, and what was the impact of those forces on the larger story of the American past. Central to answering each of these queries is the examination of the changes across time and space which affected artisanal identity and independence and reveal some of the varied and complex social experience of American labor.

# PART I

# STUDIES OF THE SOUTHERN EXPERIENCE

# 1

CHRISTINE DANIELS

# From Father to Son:
## Economic Roots of Craft Dynasties
## in Eighteenth-Century Maryland

IN COLONIAL AMERICA, as in seventeenth- and eighteenth-century England and Europe, families and businesses often were entwined in a symbiotic relationship. Business acumen and family strategies complemented each other. Kin connections provided businesses with capital, credit, and contacts. Family firms, in turn, provided kin with employment, training, and opportunities for advancement.[1] Merchants, professionals, agriculturalists, and craftsmen used family firms to their advantage.

Colonial historians occasionally have disagreed, however, on the importance of kin connections in artisanal establishments in early America, and on the possible effects of the American Revolution on artisanal family practices. Some have argued that artisans retained their traditional attachment to craft dynasties until the early nineteenth century. Carl Bridenbaugh, for example, wrote that an intergenerational command of craft skills enabled artisanal families in the eighteenth century "to live in near-baronial style, and to dominate, nay rule over, the social and political life" of an area for generations; and W. J. Rorabaugh has argued that intergenerational craftsmanship was important in all crafts until the 1840s.[2]

Other historians, however, have disagreed. Stephanie Wolf, for example, has asserted that crafts in eighteenth-century Germantown, Pennsylvania, "showed very little tendency for traditional family patterns to develop . . . fathers do not appear to have trained their sons to follow in their footsteps." Wolf attributes the lack of dynasties to the presence of a modern, commercial world view. Most scholars who discuss craft dynasties agree that they declined in importance after the American Revolution, when, presumably, a modern world view became increasingly widespread.[3]

A close examination of this question in Kent County, Maryland, suggests that both groups of historians are partly correct. Craft dynasties were vital to some crafts, but not to others. Practitioners of trades that were capital intensive or required a great deal of start-up capital had often been apprenticed to their fathers' craft. These artisans included millers, brewers, blacksmiths, tanners, weavers, and those who did elaborate woodworking, such as joiners, house carpenters, and shipwrights. Crafts that required a dedicated shop site, such as a smithy, a brewery, or a tannery, usually descended in families. Crafts that did not require expensive tools or a dedicated site did not inspire dynasties.

The likelihood that a boy whose father or uncle practiced a capital-intensive craft would be bound to that craft, moreover, did *not* decrease after the American Revolution. On the contrary, it increased. Regardless of the presence or absence of a modern commercial world view, changes in the structure of certain trades, particularly tanning, made barriers to entry higher than they had been before the Revolution, and family businesses more valuable. This change encouraged the increasing frequency with which family members were apprenticed into these trades.

## The Craft Economy in Kent County

The eighteenth-century records for Kent County include a fine run of orphans' apprenticeship indentures. These contracts were made for children whose fathers had died, and who were bound out through the Orphans' Court to learn a trade, to work in husbandry, or to learn housewifery. A total of 384 craft indentures survive for the period 1675–1810 for orphan apprentices bound to thirty-three crafts.

Not all orphans were bound through the county court, for many men provided for their sons' apprenticeships in their wills. Kent County wills provide information on 120 boys who were bound to trades or who inherited their fathers' tools. These 504 indentures and wills, supplemented by probate inventories, records from Anglican and Quaker churches, genealogies, court proceedings, and four local plantation account books, provide the evidence for the conclusions presented in this chapter.[4]

By the late seventeenth century, the local economy in Kent County supported a number of craftsmen. The county was one of the first places in Maryland or Virginia to engage in intercolonial trade with the West Indies. By the 1680s, Kent County merchant-planters sent timber, hides, provisions, and grain to the West Indies, as well as tobacco to England. The grain trade flourished after 1715, as it did later in other areas of the Chesapeake.[5]

All the products that Kent County planters shipped to the West Indies required local processing, and much of this processing was accomplished by skilled artisans. Carpenters hewed timber, tanners made leather, and millers ground flour. Coopers provided packaging for all goods, while shipwrights built sloops and schooners to carry goods to West Indian ports. As wheat became increasingly important, moreover, the need for skilled workers escalated. Wheat hogsheads were heavier than those containing tobacco; cartwrights and wheelwrights built vehicles to transport them. Wheat also required more extensive processing than tobacco; as a result, bricklayers, millwrights, blacksmiths, and other artisans constructed gristmills.[6]

Increasing commercial activity encouraged the growth of a market town on the county's main river, the Chester, by 1710; by 1750, about thirteen hundred people dwelt in Chestertown. The town flourished from about 1730 to the end of the American Revolution, when it was surpassed by the city of Baltimore. Baltimore's site on the western shore provided access to newly opened western lands and frontier farmers' produce.[7]

Many, but not all, of Kent County's eighteenth-century craftsmen worked in Chestertown. Artisans who made common goods—blacksmiths, carpenters, coopers, tanners, shoemakers, and weavers—often worked out of rural shops as well.[8] Regardless of a shop's location, however, capital-intensive trades were more likely to give rise to craft dynasties than were other trades. The value of a craftsman's tools and supplies determined, to a great extent, whether a son would follow his father's trade.[9]

Whereas all crafts demanded an initial investment, some required only a very small one.[10] Not every artisan, for instance, had to buy or lease a shop. Many craftsmen who did not require a dedicated industrial site such as a forge or a tannery worked from their homes. Rural artisans in Kent County, moreover, were often tenant farmers or overseers for large planters. Overseers usually paid no rent for their quarters, and tenants paid no more for their leases than they would have paid had they not practiced a craft.[11]

In addition, many craftsmen, particularly rural craftsmen, did not maintain an inventory of raw materials or finished goods. They performed custom work for local merchants and planters. The craftsman's clients procured wool, hides, or other goods, had them processed by the artisan, paid him only for his labor, and collected the goods when they were finished. This arrangement was common among shoemakers, tanners, tailors, and saddlers before the American Revolution.[12]

Other craftsmen, however, required a considerable capital investment in order to establish a business. Master artisans in some trades required either a dedicated industrial site, or expensive tools, or extensive supplies, or some combination of these factors to follow their crafts. Table 1.1 describes the mean amount of capital required to follow various crafts in eighteenth-century Kent County. It also indicates whether or not the craft required enough specialized equipment to make a dedicated industrial site necessary. There were, of course, wide variations in the amount of capital craftsmen invested in their businesses, even within the same craft. If a shop was located in

Table 1.1. Capital Required for Various Crafts in Kent County, Maryland, 1675–1810

| Craft | N | Mean Value of Capital[a] Pre-1783 | Mean Value of Capital[a] Post-1783 | Dedicated Site Required |
|---|---|---|---|---|
| Blacksmithing | 23 | 15.60 | 6.30 | Yes |
| Brewing | 2 | 8.70[a] | NA[b] | Yes |
| Bricklaying | 5 | 0.80 | NA | No |
| Carpentry | 7 | 0.70 | NA | No |
| Cooperage | 8 | 1.55 | 2.40[a] | No |
| Elaborate woodworking[c] | 17 | 8.80 | 9.10 | Yes/No |
| Milling | 4 | 90.10[a] | 352.00[a] | Yes |
| Shoemaking | 10 | 0.25 | 0.45 | No |
| Tailoring | 7 | 0.15 | 1.85[a] | No |
| Tanning | 7 | 34.10 | 320.00 | Yes |
| Weaving | 14 | 3.95 | 3.45 | No |

*Source:* Data are from Prerogative Court Probate Accounts and Inventories: Kent County Inventories; Kent County Court Proceedings, 1675–1810; and Account Book, 1716– 50; Sprinkle Collection; as well as from Ledger A, 1718–41, Ledger B, 1725–65, Tilghman Family Papers; Bohemia Accounts, 1735–61; and Bohemia Accounts, Daybook, 1790–1870— the latter group of sources are in Manuscript Collection, Georgetown University Library, Washington, D.C..

*Note:* Capital includes value of tools, raw materials, and finished goods. All prices in this essay have been deflated by the price series developed by Lois Green Carr and Lorena Walsh, and modified by P.M.G. Harris in 1988. Prices are rounded to the nearest shilling. I would like to thank Carr, Walsh, and Harris for sharing their index with me.

[a] Mean based on fewer than three observations.

[b] NA = not available.

[c] Includes cabinetmakers, house carpenters, joiners, turners, wheelwrights, millwrights, and shipwrights.

Chestertown, for example, high purchase or lease prices for the site could send an artisan's costs skyrocketing.

Some crafts, therefore, clearly had higher barriers to entry than did others. Some crafts also paid higher wages to journeymen than did others, however. Journeymen blacksmiths, for example, received a higher daily

Table 1.2. Wage-to-Capital Ratio for Various Crafts in Kent County, Maryland, 1675–1810

| Craft | Mean Wage per Day | Wage-to-Capital Ratio | |
| --- | --- | --- | --- |
| | | Pre-1783 | Post-1783 |
| Blacksmithing | 0.25 | 61.6 | 25.2 |
| Brewing | NA[a] | NA | NA |
| Bricklaying | 0.1 | 8.0 | NA |
| Carpentry | 0.1 | 6.0 | NA |
| Cooperage | 0.15 | 10.3 | 16.0 |
| Elaborate woodworking[c] | 0.25 | 35.2 | 36.4 |
| Milling | 0.55[b] | 163.8 | 640.0 |
| Shoemaking | 0.1 | 2.5 | 4.5 |
| Tailoring | 0.1 | 1.5 | 18.5 |
| Tanning | 0.15b | 227.3 | 2,133.3 |
| Weaving | 0.15 | 26.3 | 23.0 |

Source: The data are from Prerogative Court Probate Accounts and Prerogative Court Inventories for Kent County decedents; Kent County Court Proceedings, 1675–1810; and Account Book, 1716–50; Sprinkle Collection; as well as from Ledger A, 1718–41, Ledger B, 1725–65, Tilghman Family Papers; Bohemia Accounts, 1735–61; and Bohemia Accounts, Daybook, 1790–1870—the latter group of sources are in Manuscript Collection, Georgetown University Library.

Note: Capital includes price of tools, raw materials, and finished goods rounded to the nearest shilling.

[a] NA = not available.

[b] Mean based on fewer than three observations.

wage than did journeymen tailors or carpenters. The wage that a master or merchant paid a journeyman varied according to the craftsman's skill, his possession of tools, the employer's eagerness to increase production at a particular time, and doubtless other factors as well.[13] A mean wage for a particular craft, therefore, will hide many variations in pay. The ratio of the mean daily wage for a journeyman to the mean value of capital required for a given craft, however, can be illuminating. Such a ratio can predict the relative difficulty that journeymen in different crafts would have had in acquiring the capital necessary to equip a shop and carry an inventory. Table 1.2 estimates the ratio between journeymen's wages in several crafts and the capital required to open a shop in those crafts.

## Capital and Craft Dynasties

The higher the wage-to-capital ratio, the more difficult it would have been for a young man to acquire the means to enter a craft. Data from Kent County indicate that, of the apprentices in fields with high barriers to entry, a larger fraction were likely to be boys apprenticed into craft dynasties. More than half of the boys bound as millers, brewers, blacksmiths, tanners, or highly skilled woodworkers had relatives who followed or had followed the trade. In other crafts, only one apprentice in fifteen was bound to a family trade.[14] Table 1.3, below, ranks various crafts according to what proportion of their apprentices were bound to family dynasties and compares these figures to the wage-to-capital ratios for those crafts.

The wage-to-capital ratio necessary to enter a given craft or become a master of it predicted whether a boy would need his family's assistance to do so. Crafts in which the ratio was less than twenty-five to one—that is, crafts in which it cost a journeyman less than a month's wages to acquire the necessary tools and equipment—were open to virtually every apprentice. Men who followed crafts in which one month's wages as a journeyman could not pay for the tools of the trade were more likely to be members of craft dynasties. The need for a dedicated industrial site, expensive tools, or extensive processing supplies made it likely that apprentices would be boys following their fathers' craft.

Millers and brewers were very likely to have been bound as apprentices to the craft practiced by their fathers or uncles; both crafts required a considerable investment of capital. While some men in Kent County worked as journeymen millers, many men who called themselves millers were mill owners as well. Mills had complex engineering requirements and cost considerably more to build than large houses.[15] Equipment for a mill was also expensive. Millstones were not quarried locally but were imported from France.[16] Most boys bound as millers were the sons of millers or of wheat and flour merchants.[17]

A brewer needed equipment that might cost fifteen pounds or more. Commercial brewers were virtually always innkeepers as well. When innkeeper Henry Evans died in 1739, he left his Chestertown tavern to his son, Henry, and instructed his executors that Henry was to have "all my utensills and conveniences in the same house Belonging to and used for the Brewing Business," valued at more than seventeen pounds, as well as two stills.[18]

Blacksmiths, who needed both a forge and expensive tools, were very likely to have sons or nephews bound to follow their trades, particularly before the American Revolution. Complete kits of smith's tools, including an

Table 1.3. Apprentices Bound to Family Crafts, 1675–1810

| | | | | Wage-to-Capital Ratio | |
| --- | --- | --- | --- | --- | --- |
| Craft | No. of Apprentices | No. Bound to Family Craft | Percentage | Pre-1783 | Post-1783 |
| Milling | 13 | 10 | 76.9 | 164 | 640 |
| Brewing | 5 | 3 | 60.0 | NA[b] | NA |
| Blacksmithing | 30 | 17 | 56.7 | 62 | 25 |
| Tanning | 23 | 12 | 52.2 | 227 | 2,133 |
| Elaborate woodworking | 50 | 24 | 48.0 | 35 | 36 |
| Weaving | 48 | 15 | 31.3 | 26 | 23 |
| Cooperage | 25 | 3 | 12.0 | 10 | 16 |
| Shoemaking | 84 | 9 | 10.7 | 3 | 5 |
| Bricklaying | 12 | 1 | 8.3 | 8 | NA |
| Carpentry | 24 | 2 | 8.3 | 6 | NA |
| Tailoring | 39 | 2 | 5.1 | 2 | 19 |
| Other | 73 | 3 | 4.1 | | |
| Total | 426 | 101 | 23.7 | | |

*Source:* Data from indentures in Kent County Court Proceedings, 1675–96; Kent County Bonds and Indentures, 1696–1788; Kent County Indentures, 1788–1810; and provisions and bequests in Kent County Wills, 1675–1810.

[a] Rounded to nearest integer.

[b] NA = not available.

anvil, bellows, hammers, and vises, could cost as much as thirty pounds, and wills frequently specify the disposition of a smith's tools or forge.[19] In 1698 Philip Everitt provided that his executors give "my brother Jeffery . . . all his smiths tooles when demanded by him or his sons," while in 1735 Daniel Greenwood provided that his tools were to go to John, Joseph, and William England, "sons of my motherinlaw [stepmother] Sarah England." Patrick Byrne left his shop and forge "to the child my wife Margret now goes with" in 1740. When James Steele died in 1744, he left "unto my son Hugh Steele my smiths tools." David Boyd of Chestertown specified in 1770 that "all and every of my working tools Iron and Coals," were to go to his son, David.[20]

After the Revolution, however, the blacksmith's trade declined in Kent County and became a less dynastic craft. When Chestertown was a thriving port, blacksmiths performed a myriad of tasks. They did ornamental wrought iron work, repaired guns, made metal gears and other equipment for gristmills, and forged anchors. With the county's economic decline, local smiths performed fewer tasks aimed at a consumer-oriented urban market or mercantile trade; such tasks were increasingly performed across the bay in Baltimore. After 1783, Kent County smiths spent their time in an endless round of sharpening plows and shoeing horses.[21] They kept fewer specialized tools, and smaller and less valuable tool kits. Whereas the average kit of blacksmith's tools was worth £15 12s. before the Revolution, it was worth only £6 6s. by the first decade of the nineteenth century. In part as a result, blacksmithing became less tightly bound to particular families. Before the Revolution, approximately three-quarters of the blacksmith's apprentices in Kent County were members of blacksmithing families; after the Revolution, fewer than one-third were.[22]

Tanners, too, often inherited the tools—or more precisely, the site and supplies—of their trade. Tanyards were dedicated craft sites that included a series of deep pits, expensive to build and maintain, that were used as vats in which to cure hides. A tannery or tanhouse, at least two stories high, covered the vats and provided space for the tanners to clean, scrape, soak, wash, and dry the hides. A boy who inherited such a site would almost certainly follow the trade. In 1733 Thomas Garnett left his son Bartholomew "the lot in Chestertown where a place is digged and designed for a tann house," while in 1766 James Claypoole left his "Tann House Tan Yard and all appurtenances" to his son James. Both boys later worked as tanners in Kent County.[23]

Tanner's tools were less expensive than blacksmith's tools. A tanner might acquire a hardwood currying table, tanning forks, currying steels, fleshing knives, and a bark rake for less than five pounds. A tanner who bought and sold hides before the American Revolution (as distinct from one who did custom work for merchants or planters), however, often invested twenty-five pounds or more in hides, skins, and the materials with which to process them—bark, rosin, lime, oil, blubber, and lampblack.

After the Revolution, moreover, many tanners became hide merchants as well. Replacing the unspecialized merchants who had previously employed tanners for custom work, they hired additional journeymen and occasionally shoemakers and saddlers, and vastly increased their inventory of hides, sometimes to more than one thousand pounds' worth.[24] The burgeoning domestic market for shoes affected leatherworks in Kent County much as it did leatherworks in Lynn, Massachusetts; New York; and other urban areas.[25] Establishing a tannery, therefore, required even more capital after 1783 than it had before. In part as a result, tanning became a more dynastic craft during the early nineteenth century. Before 1783, about 40 percent of the boys bound as tanners were members of craft families. Afterward, 60 percent were. A tanner's apprentice who was not an heir to a tannery, especially after the American Revolution, was unlikely to become a master.[26]

Boys bound to highly skilled woodworkers (e.g., joiners, millwrights, turners, wheelwrights, house carpenters, and shipwrights), whose crafts required more specialized tools than were used by an ordinary cooper or carpenter, were also likely to be apprenticed to their fathers' trades. These men often invested ten pounds or more in woodworking tools, while the tools of a country carpenter or cooper often cost less than ten shillings.[27]

Highly skilled woodworkers were not completely specialized in Kent County's predominantly rural economy. A shipwright, for example, might also make cider barrels because both crafts required a tight—that is, waterproof—fit. But a man who used the craft title *joiner* was no rough carpenter and had the tools to prove it.

Joiners, like blacksmiths, were very likely to provide that their tools should descend to their sons. The joiner Thomas Coursey Brown, at his death in 1755, left his tools to his son Thomas. He asked his wife to keep the boy at school "untill he has education sufficient for Country Business and then to Bind him to . . . learn the trade of a joiner." George Perkins, a "Joyner," left "all my Tools" to his son in 1770, while Robert Taylor left "to Joseph Sill my wifes son all my Joiners tools" in 1785.[28]

The Spencers were an important local woodworking family throughout the eighteenth century and can illustrate the nature of a woodworking craft dynasty in some detail. In 1725 the joiner John Spencer owned a shop in Chestertown and worked as a house carpenter and millwright. Both of these crafts required engineering ability; Spencer had to be able to sink foundations to "support the Edifice," to "place Bearers, where the chief Weight of the Building lies," and to "lay Joists, Girders and Rafters." He also worked as a house joiner, which required a "Nicer Hand, and a greater Taste in Ornament" than did house carpentry or millwright's work. Spencer's skills provided him with more trade than one man could handle; by the late 1720s, he employed at least one journeyman and four apprentices.[29]

Spencer died in 1732, and left his shop, his fiddle, a slave, and "all the Best of my Joyners tools," valued at twelve pounds, to his son, Samuel. He provided that his son be bound "as an apprentice to some good Joyner til he come of the age of 18 yrs and then to be at liberty to act and do for himself." The tools were to be kept by Spencer's executors for Samuel "till he come to the age of 18 yrs and he may then have them into his own keeping to do with them as he shall see fit."[30]

Samuel followed his father's trade in Chestertown, and bound his nephew John as a turner in the late 1740s. Turners worked at "a very ingenious business" and used "an engine called a lathe" to create small wooden articles, such as spinning wheels. A man with such a specialized skill, of course, would have worked at other branches of woodworking as well, as the county's population would support few full-time turners.[31]

At Samuel Spencer's death in 1751, his entire personal estate (valued at forty-nine pounds) comprised expensive clothing and wigs, his father's fiddle and music books, and twenty pounds' worth of joiner's tools and plank. His nephew John worked in Chestertown throughout the 1750s, and John's son Samuel was apprenticed to a millwright in 1775.[32]

Most of those who did elaborate woodworking did not need a specialized craft site, although many worked out of shops rather than their homes. A shipwright, however, might possess a shipyard, which virtually ensured a dynastic craft succession. Moses Tennant had worked as a shipwright in Kent County for at least twenty years at his death in 1766, when he left his house and boatyard on Morgan's Creek, as well as all his "working tools that belongs to boatbuilding," to his son John. Members of the Alford family also worked as shipwrights in Chestertown for at least sixty years and probably longer. At his death in 1774, the shipwright Moses Alford left his two sons his shipyard in Chestertown.[33]

Weavers' sons were also often bound to follow their fathers' trade. A loom was not as expensive as a mill, a brewery, a forge, a tannery, or an elaborate set of woodworking tools. But a journeyman weaver could not acquire his tools over a period of time as a carpenter, a tailor, or a shoemaker might. A loom was a one-time capital investment that, with sleys, harnesses, and other necessary equipment, might cost four to seven pounds. The all-or-nothing nature of this tool made looms an oft-mentioned legacy. In 1735 Abraham Milton left his son Philip "my weavers loom with all the necessaries thereunto belonging." In 1765 Patrick Macatee left his son Andrew "my weavers loom and tackling." George Williamson made the same bequest to his son John in 1771, while in 1776 William McKinney left his son James "the house I now make use of for a weavers shop" as well as his loom.[34]

As Chestertown became a satellite of Baltimore, the number of capital-intensive craftsmen who required an urban market, including cabinetmakers and shipwrights, declined. Those who followed capital-intensive trades but who supplied rural market needs, such as blacksmiths, weavers, and tanners, remained an important part of Kent County's economy. Contrary to most scholars' assertions, however, the proportion of apprentices in these capital-intensive trades who were bound to their fathers' crafts did *not* decline after the American Revolution. The likelihood of a boy's being bound into his family's craft, particularly if the craft was tanning, increased after the American Revolution. Before the Revolution, 44 percent of the boys

Table 1.4. Boys Apprenticed by Fathers' Wills, Kent County, Maryland, 1675–1810

| Decedent's Provision | Number | Percentage |
| --- | --- | --- |
| Boy to choose trade | 40 | 43.0 |
| Executor to choose trade | | |
| Boy's consent and/or talent specified | 19 | 20.4 |
| Consent not specified | 18 | 19.4 |
| Trade specified by decedent | 16 | 17.2 |
| Total | 93 | 100.0 |

*Source:* Data from Kent County Wills, 1675–1810.

*Note:* The group includes one boy apprenticed by a mother's will.

bound to costly crafts were learning their fathers' trades; after the Revolution, 58 percent were.[35]

## The Legacy of Wills

Men whose estates included a considerable capital investment in tools and a shop site sometimes suggested or prescribed in their wills that their sons follow their trades. The fact that a father was an artisan, even an artisan in a capital-intensive trade, however, did not force his son to follow rigidly in his footsteps.[36] The boy's preferences were usually taken into account.

Between 1675 and 1810, the surviving wills of the period include ninety-three references to craft apprenticeships for minor sons. Table 1.4 summarizes the provisions for boys who were to be bound to crafts in accordance with their fathers' wills. The fathers' provisions do not seem in any sense rhetorical. Each will uses highly individual language, and as a group the wills reveal a wide spectrum of provisions for minor sons. These documents, therefore, may be taken as statements of individual fathers' hopes and desires for their sons.[37]

Nearly half of the boys whose apprenticeships were specified in their fathers' wills were to choose their own trades. In 1745, for example, the carpenter William Woodland provided that when his eight children reached the age of majority, they "should be bound out . . . to sutch trade or trades as the said childring shall think proper." The weaver Abraham Milton left his loom to his son Philip, but also provided that "if any of my sons incline to Trades then they may have Liberty to choose a Trade," while the local Quaker meeting was to choose a master. The tanner Oliver Caulk, who died in 1806, stipulated only that his sons be apprenticed to "Godley masters that are of blameless lives and conversation," and that they learn "useful branches of business." In 1748 the cordwainer William Taylor provided that his son was "to be bound out when he comes to age of fourteen to such a trade as he might chuse," while in 1754 John Foreman's sons were to be bound to trades only "if they are willing."[38]

Fathers who worried about the choices of youth sometimes stipulated that older advisers were to help the boys. In 1761, for example, John Hynson's sons were to "bind themselves out . . . by the advice and approbation of my good friends Thomas and William Ringgold if they will be advised by them." In 1768, Samuel White's three sons were to have "the liberty to choose what trades they desire," but White's father, John, was "to assist . . . in the binding out of my children to what trades they should choose and he approve of."[39]

Another one-fifth of boys apprenticed by their fathers' wills were to be bound to trades by their fathers' executors only with the boys' consent, or according to their talents. In 1723 Daniel Ferrill wanted his sons "bound out by there mother to some handycraft Trade such as my sons shall be most Inclined to." John Inch made the same provision in 1735. In 1756 Charles Scott appointed Alexander Williamson, the local Anglican minister, as one of his executors and provided that Williamson should bind out Scott's sons "to the several calings or Businesses which he shall think fit provided the children shall agree to the same." In a few cases, like that of John Kennard, the father's executors were to "have [the son] Taught the calling or Business that he shall appear to them to be the best Quallified for."[40] In nearly two-thirds of the cases, therefore, the boys were to give their explicit consent to a trade.

In eighteen other cases, the boys were to be bound to trades by their fathers' executors, and there was no mention of consent. This does not necessarily imply that such a boy would be bound out without regard to his wishes. While in a few unhappy instances this might have been the case, the choice of executors suggests that the boys' wishes were probably considered.

In six cases, the boys were to be bound out by the local Quaker meeting, usually "to some of the people of the said profession."[41] In such cases, members of the meeting considered the boys' preferences and abilities in determining the trades to which they would be bound. In 1728, for example, James Tibbet, a millwright and miller, left his three sons and two stepsons "to the care of the monthly meeting of the people called Quakers . . . to be educated as they think fit and no otherwise and be bound to trades at their discretion." Four years later, the meeting bound the eldest, Samuel, to the house carpenter William Trew, noting that Samuel was "to learn the trade of a House Carpenter Boatwright or Sawyer which of the three should be easiest to him he being Lame." In 1739 Samuel finished his apprenticeship in "the Trade of a Carpenter it being his own Election."[42] Like his father, Samuel became a woodworker, but the Quaker meeting clearly considered the boy's ability and inclination when it bound him to a trade.

In six cases, a boy was left to the care of a brother or an uncle, who was "to bind him to such trade as he shall judge best for him."[43] Arguably, at least, such family members would be inclined to listen to the boys' preferences.

In the six remaining cases, the boys were left in the care of executors unrelated to them. Even this arrangement, however, did not necessarily mean that the boys' wishes were thwarted. Most fathers selected executors whom they thought they could trust with their sons' futures and happiness. William Hill, a shoemaker, probably spoke for many fathers when in 1705 he left his minor sons in the care of Francis Collins, a fellow shoemaker, "in whose prudence justice and charity I much confide."[44]

In only fifteen cases did fathers prescribe a trade for their sons; one mother also did so. Fourteen of those sixteen cases, or nearly 90 percent, involved a capital-intensive craft. In 1723 John Clark asked that his son be bound out "to learn the arte mistery craft and trade of a joiner and House Carpenter," while in 1729 William Spearman, a planter and carpenter, wanted his son Francis bound out "in order to learn the art and mistery of a Joiner." In 1730 Oliver Higgenbotham, a carpenter, left his tools to his three sons with the provision that "my three boys may be bound as apprentices unto George Moor (a house carpenter)." In 1746 Martha James willed that her two sons were to be bound to James Claypoole to be "brought up in the church and to the trade of a Tanner." Thomas Garnett left his tannery to his son Bartholomew provided he "live with my cousin Joseph Sharp and learn of him the Tanning trade." James Steele left his smith's tools to his son Hugh provided that he "be bound apprentice unto a blacksmith." Aaron Alford left his shipyard to his sons, William and Aaron, provided that "my son William shall take his brother Aron bound to him as an apprentice . . . as soon as my said son William shall be free from his present master."[45]

Not all fathers who followed capital-intensive trades insisted that their sons do so. The tanner Oliver Caulk, for example, asked only that his three sons do useful work. They were to follow trades "of most use in the creation and likeliest to suit their constitutions, such trades as Tanners Joiners Carpenters &c &c." Tanning was, not surprisingly, the first trade that came to Caulk's mind when he considered the trades "of most use in the creation," but he gave his sons the choice of his trade or another.[46]

Not all boys for whom trades had been mandated in their fathers' wills, moreover, necessarily disliked or resented their callings. Samuel Spencer, for example, added to his father's extensive collection of joiner's tools during his career, suggesting that he had a predilection and an aptitude for his craft. Finally, of course, if a boy did not want to follow a given trade he could refuse his inheritance or dispose of it upon reaching his majority. John Spencer's will indicates that if Samuel had not wanted to be a joiner, he was, at eighteen, "at liberty to act and do for himself" and to do with his father's tools "as he shall see fit."[47] John Spencer knew that even with a set of valuable tools and a shop site in Chestertown as an incentive, a father could exert only so much influence from beyond the grave.

Intergenerational patterns of craftsmanship in Kent County clearly ran strongly along the lines of capital investment. Crafts with high barriers to entry encouraged the growth of craft dynasties; those without such barriers did not. The boys entering these trades were not forced into the arrangement against their wills; they usually made the decision to enter the craft themselves. The result of this intergenerational accumulation of capital was the craft dynasties beloved of historians, in which tools and craft skills were handed down from father to son for generations. In some crafts, such as blacksmithing, the tendency to dynasties declined after the Revolution, reflecting changes in the local economy as Kent County became progressively more rural. In other crafts, however, such as tanning, changes in the national market encouraged an increase in family ownership and control of craft sites and tools. The evidence from Kent County indicates that craft dynasties reflected not the absence of a "modern" world view, but the capital requirements of individual crafts and the exigencies of different markets for artisanal products.

# 2

TINA H. SHELLER

# Freemen, Servants, and Slaves:
## Artisans and the Craft Structure of Revolutionary Baltimore Town

THE URBAN ARTISANS of eighteenth-century America have not always fared well with historians. Though much is known about their political activities during the Revolutionary era and beyond, there have been few studies documenting their economic and social behavior during this period. We know something about the trades they pursued and the wealth they did or did not accumulate, but we know little about their shops and those who worked in them, their economic engagements outside of their shops, and the social and economic relationships that defined the craftsman's place in the town social structure.[1] In short, we still cannot answer adequately the basic questions: who was the eighteenth-century urban artisan? and what was the nature of the craft hierarchy in which he worked?

In this chapter I will attempt to shed some light on the issue of mechanics' identity by exploring several aspects of artisanal life in Revolutionary Baltimore Town. I will try to create a comprehensive historical context for understanding eighteenth-century craftsmen by examining the nature of artisanal enterprise and by probing the nature of relationships between mechanics and merchants, and between mechanics and their workers. A consideration of these issues suggests that the study of eighteenth-century artisans has not been sufficiently concerned with the fundamental social divisions of eighteenth-century life, namely those of independence and dependence, freedom and bondage.[2] An appreciation of these essential parameters of eighteenth-century society—that is, a fuller realization of the eighteenth-century social context—is crucial to our understanding of the mechanics of Baltimore and the impact of the Revolution upon them.

## The Town Economy and the Trades

The economy of Baltimore Town was young and relatively undeveloped on the eve of the Revolution. Though founded in 1729, Baltimore grew slowly during the first three decades of its existence. As late as 1752, the town consisted of only about twenty-five houses, a tobacco inspection warehouse, a brewery, a tavern, and a church. Beginning in the early 1760s, Baltimore entered into a spectacular era of growth. This growth derived from the dramatic expansion of the grain and flour trade handled by Baltimore merchants. Between 1765 and 1769, exports of wheat from the well-situated port on the northwest branch of the Patapsco River rose by almost 50 percent, from 194,477 bushels to 288,529 bushels. Exports of flour more than tripled between 1768 and 1770, from 22,800 barrels to 76,200 barrels. The increase of town commerce spurred population growth. A small village of two hundred inhabitants at midcentury, Baltimore Town had mushroomed into a bustling port town of six thousand residents by the time of the Revolution.[3]

Baltimore's role as an entrepot for the grain trade determined its early industrial development. The great bulk and perishability of grain generated a high volume of wagon, sloop, and schooner traffic. As early as 1761, one Baltimore merchant commented on the heavy flow of vehicles into town: "The Demand for wheat is Large, I have Known above three hundred waggons In a week In Town with wheat." The dramatic increase of haulers and shippers bringing wheat to Baltimore gave rise to a "linkage network" of industries and services to facilitate the processing, packaging, storing, and transporting of grain: shipbuilding and its allied manufactures (sailmaking, ropemaking, block making, pump making, and anchor forging), metal forging, flour milling, baking, brewing, leather tanning, cooperage, the provision of food and lodging, and building construction.[4] On the eve of the Revolution, the town landscape featured shipyards, ropewalks, tanyards, breweries, bakehouses, and a distillery. A wide variety of craftsmen produced goods on these sites as well as in small shops. In 1775 Baltimore contained a diverse community of tradesmen, including all types of maritime craftsmen, tanners and curriers, saddlers, wheelwrights, blacksmiths, coppersmiths, gunsmiths, bakers, brewers, distillers, tobacconists, potters, tallow chandlers, coopers, cabinetmakers, silversmiths, clock- and watchmakers, printers, hatters, shoemakers, tailors, staymakers, breechesmakers, house carpenters, stonemasons, plasterers, and painters.

Working within a young, though expanding, economy, town craftsmen struggled hard to obtain a livelihood in Revolutionary Baltimore. Prior to the war, they faced stiff competition from the accomplished artisans of Annapolis, Philadelphia, and London. Fashion-conscious residents of Baltimore purchased luxury goods, such as fancy apparel, fine porcelain and ceramic ware, cabinetware, silver, clocks and watches, and jewelry almost exclusively from the craftsmen in these metropolitan centers.[5] For the supply of essential industrial goods, most notably ship chandlery, town merchants also chose English products over locally made cordage and ironwork, which had a reputation for inferior quality.[6] In general, local artisans supplied residents of Baltimore and the neighboring counties with craft services, such as the repair and alteration of goods, as well as with the more common articles of commerce and everyday life, such as barrels, clothing for children, servants, and slaves, basic pieces of furniture, simple earthenware, crude pots and pans, saddles and harnesses, and soap and candles.[7]

The economy of a small town did not support intensive craft specialization. Most mechanics offered customers a variety of craft services and products. For example, the cabinetmaker Gerrard Hopkins offered his services for chairwork as well as cabinetwork; the saddler John Gordon advertised that he would "carry on the chaise- and chair-making business," as well as the manufacture of saddlery; Thomas Morgan, a watch- and clockmaker, informed the public that in addition to his regular trade he offered his services for the "guilding business"; John and Robert Casey advertised that they made breeches and gloves, and also carried on the "skinning business"; and Francis Sanderson, a coppersmith, advertised that he "also carries on the Tin business."[8]

Artisans could diversify their businesses if they were skilled in more than one trade, as many were; if they entered into a partnership; or if they employed the skills of others. When the tobacconist Robert White announced his entrance into the spinning-wheel business, he advertised that he had "procured some of the best hands could be had." The tailor and habitmaker Richard Burland informed the public that in order to serve women, he had "engaged an extraordinary workman at the staymaking Business." The saddler John Gordon's notice of entry into the chaise- and chair-making business was prefaced by the information "Said Gordon has furnished himself with several good hands." In October 1778, the *Maryland Journal* printer Mary Katherine Goddard advertised that to her printing office she had added a bookbinding room, for which she had engaged "an excellent workman." Most indicative of this practice was the following notice placed by William Whetcroft, a goldsmith and jeweler in Annapolis: "Having purchased the Servants lately belonging to Mr. [William] Knapp [clock- and watchmaker] with all the materials for carrying on the Watch and Clock-Making Business hereby informs the Public, that he Repairs all sorts of Clocks and Watches."[9]

Many artisans were involved in one or more nontrade enterprises. Quite a few craftsmen ran taverns or inns, or took lodgers into their homes.[10] A substantial number owned land and buildings that they rented to others. Perhaps most significantly, more and more tradesmen functioned as retail merchants. The two major cabinetmakers of Revolutionary Baltimore sold goods that had not been produced in their shops. Gerrard Hopkins sold lumber from his yard in Gay Street, while Robert Moore advertised paper hangings and mock India pictures for sale.[11]

During the war, several tradesmen began retailing craft tools and materials. When trade with Great Britain resumed, they also began selling imported articles of their craft even as they continued manufacturing in their shops. For example, the saddler John Gordon came to Baltimore in the early 1770s. By 1780 he was supplying saddlery and nails to his fellow craftsmen. By September 1784 he was advertising "a large neat assortment of saddlery ware, coach, phaeton & chair furniture, best London & Dublin made saddles, etc." The advertisement went on, "He continues, as usual, to make and sell all kinds of men & women's saddles, coach, phaeton, chair & waggon harness, & all kinds of horse furniture."[12] The clock- and watchmakers Gilbert Bigger and Ambrose Clarke, who arrived in Baltimore from Dublin at the end of 1783, informed the public in 1784 that they had mastered every branch of their business, and that they also offered for sale "an assortment of watches, house-clocks, and a fashionable and cheap assortment of jewellry arrived in the last ships from Europe." For some artisans, these expanded retailing activities proved to be the beginning of careers as merchants and the end of their lives in the trades.[13]

## Artisans and Merchants

The craftsmen of eighteenth-century Baltimore worked within a larger town economy dominated by commerce. Artisans' relationships with merchants therefore formed a vital part of successfully establishing a trade. Merchants played a central role in the craft economy as employers, creditors, middlemen, and patrons. Mechanics' ties with merchants, however, were not limited to the marketplace. Traders and tradesmen shared ethnic, religious, and political bonds as well.

Merchant-manufacturers utilized skilled labor for the market-oriented production of rope, iron, rum, beer, and bread.[14] Merchants also employed artisans essential to the conduct of trade. They employed these craftsmen for their own shipping needs, and hired them out as well. The merchant James Nevin, for example, advertised: "He keeps a Cooper at work and will supply all persons that may want Jobs done in that way." Alexander Stenhouse offered "a Variety of Painters Colours" for sale and announced that he had "engaged a young man, completely bred to the different Branches of Painting and Gilding; those who have any thing to do in that Way may depend on having that Business well executed."[15]

In order to secure a first-rate craftsman, a merchant might agree to advance a loan or to set up a shop in return for a term of service and a share of the shop's profits. The firm of Johnson, Johonnot, and Company offered the following terms to lure a journeyman cooper from Philadelphia to Baltimore: "I would propose him a Shop and tools to lay in the Stuff at the lowest rate. he to be charged at that rate for it. He to live with me. paying no more for his Board than he can get it for in the town. and if he does not like my living he may go otherwheres to board he to receive half the Profits arising from his labour. To work for us at least Three Years. to enter into Bonds for that. And the Accounts to be settled twice a Year. we Keeping his Shop book where a fair account shall be kept open for his Speculation at any time."[16] A similar arrangement is suggested in the newspaper notice of Andrew Greble Jr., a cedar-cooper from Philadelphia, who advertised his services "at his Shop, Back of shipping merchant Mr. Melchior Keener's." Also indicative of this practice is the following notice placed in the *Maryland Gazette* in April 1771: "A young man, who has served a regular Apprenticeship to the business of a Jeweller, is willing to article with any Gentleman or Merchant for a term of Years, on advancing some Money."[17]

These arrangements point to another important function of merchants in the artisanal community. Because of their widespread commercial contacts and their access to capital, merchants provided essential business and financial services to artisans. Artisanal enterprise was not limited to the confines of the town and the docks. Craftsmen regularly solicited "foreign orders" and orders from "country shopkeepers" in the widely distributed *Maryland Gazette* (Annapolis) and, beginning in 1773, in the *Maryland Journal and Baltimore Advertiser*. For orders, payment, and delivery of goods, some relied on the mail.[18] Some craftsmen traveled regularly between towns.[19] Still others employed the credit and connections of merchants. A tobacco and snuff manufacturer in Bladensburg encouraged customers "to send or give their Orders to some Merchant in the next adjacent town, or other convenient Landing, who, he hopes, will be thereby encouraged to become a wholesale Customer." A fuller located at a mill outside of Baltimore instructed customers to leave their orders with the merchants Alexander and John McKim. The proprietor of a bleachfield for whitening linen informed the public that linen could be left with any one of a number of merchants in Baltimore Town. The tailor James Cox did work for a number of out-of-town customers from such areas as Goochland County, Virginia; the Eastern Shore of Maryland; and Deer Creek, in Frederick County,

Maryland. While his account book did not always record how payment was made or goods transported, several entries note the name of a Baltimore merchant as responsible for the account.[20]

In addition to assisting in the marketing of craft goods and services, merchants were important sources of credit and capital for artisans. Nowhere was this more evident than in Baltimore's small but growing community of shipbuilders. Mercantile patronage was vital to maritime tradesmen. Owing to the high cost of production, few craftsmen would build a ship without a contract or order from a merchant. Merchants who were themselves involved in maritime industries such as ropemaking or ship chandlery also proved valuable to town shipbuilders. Seeking to create a market for their own goods, they solicited shipbuilding and ship repair business from out-of-town customers for the artisans of Baltimore.[21]

On a smaller scale, merchants extended credit for the purchase of raw materials, food, and imported goods directly to tradesmen whom they knew.[22] In addition, merchants loaned artisans money on bond. The business records of the merchant-ironmaster Charles Ridgely Jr. reveal evidence of numerous small loans to craftsmen. The surviving papers of the merchant Mark Alexander show that in 1775, Alexander gave the master shoemaker John Cannon a mortgage in the amount of fifty pounds, at 6 percent interest. The extant accounts of the tailor James Cox indicate that the merchant-craftsman Richard Lemmon lent the master craftsman Cox seventy-five pounds at 4 percent interest in 1773.[23]

The business ties between merchants and artisans were reinforced by the strong bonds of religion and ethnicity. Both groups were largely members of dissenting Protestant denominations. Many artisans shared the Scotch-Irish heritage of the merchants and worshipped in the First Presbyterian Church. Both traders and tradesmen founded the town's first Baptist and Methodist congregations, while the Society of Friends also included members of both groups. German artisans, merchants, and innkeepers attended Baltimore's German-language Lutheran and Reformed churches. Kinship ties further strengthened the relationship between workshop and counting house. The tailor James Cox and the merchant Mark Alexander were brothers-in-law, as were the prominent hatter David Shields and the merchants Alexander and John McKim.[24]

Another important bond between Baltimore merchants and artisans which frequently, but not always, coincided with ethnoreligious ties was that of politics. Merchants and artisans alike were active in town politics in the Revolutionary era. Together they formed in 1763 the Mechanical Company, a quasi-governmental group devoted to organizing a local militia and protecting the town from fire. They also united in resistance to the Stamp Act, forming the Sons of Liberty, a group largely composed of members of the Mechanical Company. At the beginning of the war, merchants and mechanics served on the Committee of Observation for Baltimore and joined forces in the Whig Club to expel suspected Tories from town.[25]

And what of the bond of craft? To what extent did that bond unify Baltimore's artisans and isolate them from merchants? Scattered evidence from this period indicates that there was clearly a sense of craft identity in the community. Artisans retained their craft titles even as they engaged in many nontrade pursuits. They played an important role in the Mechanical Company, so named in deference to their ample representation in its membership. In 1769 they founded the Mechanical Fire Company, which included the town's leading craftsmen and consisted almost exclusively of members of the trades. And at the commencement of the struggle for independence, they organized their own company of militia.[26] In addition, master craftsmen supported each other economically. They patronized each other's shops, and they assisted each other through the provision of loans and credits, and the sharing of shop space.[27]

Overall, however, there is little evidence of a strong sense of artisanal separateness for this period. No specific trade organizations are known to have existed prior to the Revolution. Baltimore society was too small and undeveloped for such social segmentation to have occurred, and the forces of unity were greater than those of divisiveness. Economic, political, and ethnoreligious bonds were especially strong among merchants and artisans at this time. These ties were reinforced by Baltimore's unique and isolated position in Maryland society and politics. The Scotch-Irish Presbyterian merchants and mechanics of Baltimore were outsiders in the Anglican, agrarian universe of the Chesapeake. Their distinct religious and economic interests clashed frequently with those of politically dominant southern Maryland. Baltimore's political struggles with the planter-dominated leadership in Annapolis served to unify townsmen beginning in the Revolutionary era and extending well into the nineteenth century.[28]

Both merchants and artisans were the founders and builders of the vibrant commercial town of the 1760s and 1770s. With the exception of a few long-established, landed merchants such as the Ridgelys, the Moales, the Philpots, and William Lux and John Stevenson, most of the mercantile community, like the town's craftsmen, arrived in Baltimore in the decade and a half before independence. Though many brought capital and trade connections, they were essentially "new men" attempting to establish businesses in the young port, and in this respect they had much in common with town tradesmen. Substantial workshops and manufactories developed alongside bulging warehouses and dry goods stores. Master artisans as well as merchants emerged as town leaders during the Revolutionary era and beyond.

## Artisans and Their Workers

Whereas a variety of social and economic ties united mechanics and merchants, an enormous chasm separated artisans and their workers in Baltimore on the eve of the Revolution. The master craftsmen were free and independent men; those who labored in their shops were unfree, dependent men and boys, chiefly white servants, but also slaves and apprentices.

Craftsmen employed indentured and convict servants in their shops because such persons were the cheapest and most plentiful source of skilled labor available to them. White servants played a critical role as a major source of skilled labor in the economy of the eighteenth-century Chesapeake down to the time of the Revolution.[29] Colonial records indicate that between 1745 and 1775, almost 20,000 servants, including 10,560 indentured servants and 9,360 convict servants, arrived at the port of entry of Annapolis. Arrivals of servants increased considerably in the years just before the war, from an average of 730 servants per year in 1764–69 to an average of 1,520 servants per year in 1770–75.[30] One merchant involved in the trade estimated that between 1772 and 1774, 6,000 servants from Ireland and England had been sold in Baltimore alone.[31] Numerous advertisements for servant sales in the Baltimore press between 1773 and 1775 testify to the briskness of this business. They also point to the importance of skilled craftsmen in the servant trade. During the three years prior to independence there were sixteen separate announcements of servant arrivals published in Baltimore's newspapers. All but two of the announcements advertised the availability of tradesmen, several specifying the representation of as many as twenty-six different crafts. Eight ships brought servants from England (six from London); six ships brought servants from Ireland; and one ship brought German redemptioners.[32] Merchants offered both indentured (four-year) servants and convict (seven-year) servants for sale.

Bernard Bailyn's recent study of English and Scottish migration to America sheds further light on the prewar servant trade and the prominence of skilled craftsmen in it. In his analysis of a register of emigrants from Great Britain to America between December 1773 and March 1776, Bailyn found that Maryland "was the single most powerful magnet for the emigrants. A quarter of the entire emigration went to this one colony." Of the 2,328 emigrants from Great Britain to Maryland, 2,262 (97%) came as indentured servants. Sixty percent (1,336) of these servants were skilled craftsmen, including 258 artisans whom Bailyn characterizes as "highly skilled" (goldsmiths and silversmiths, clockmakers, gunsmiths, bookbinders, engravers, glassblowers, gilders, and mathematical instrument makers), as well as 433 textile craftsmen, 119 artisans in "service" trades, and 532 "others."[33]

Merchants found a large market for servants among plantation owners and settlers in the backcountry. "Before the W[ar]," the merchant George Salmon explained to a correspondent in 1784, "it was very common for a Man to buy 40 or 50 Servts. out of a vessel and to take them back in[to] the country for sale." A less important but still noticeable clientele for the servant traders was the town mechanics. Describing the fate of convict servants, William Eddis wrote from Annapolis in 1770: "These unhappy beings are, generally, consigned to an agent, who classes them suitably to their real or supposed qualifications; advertises them for sale, and disposes of them, for seven years, to planters, to mechanics, and to such as choose to retain them for domestic service." And again, with regard to redemptioners, Eddis noted: "As soon as the ship is stationed in her berth, planters, mechanics, and others repair on board."[34]

Newspaper advertisements further point to the use of white servants and slaves in artisans' shops. The Annapolis goldsmith and jeweler William Whetcroft, as noted earlier, advertised the acquisition of servants in the clock- and watchmaking business. The clock- and watchmaker David Evans announced that he employed "workmen trained in London," who were most likely servants.[35] Artisans' advertisements for runaway skilled servants, for the sale of the time of skilled servants, and for the sale of businesses whose property included servants and slaves provide scattered but concrete evidence of the composition of craft shops. The shipbuilder George Wells offered a reward for the return of four indentured servants, including two sawyers and a ship carpenter; the cabinetmaker Robert Moore advertised for a runaway servant who was "by trade a looking glass frame maker, but since his arrival in Baltimore, has been chiefly employed at cabinet work"; the tailor Cornelius Garritson sought the return of two servant tailors; the shoemaker Andrew Davidson advertised the sale of "the time of a Servant Man, a Shoemaker by trade"; the boatbuilder James Collins offered the handsome prize of one hundred pounds for the return of a "runaway apprentice boy from Cork Ireland" who had been at the boatbuilding business three years; and the silversmith Christopher Hughes placed a notice for a runaway servant silversmith. Baltimore County records reveal that the blacksmith John McClellan, the watch- and clockmaker John McCabe, the tailor James Cox, and the painter John Proctor each purchased a convict servant in 1773.[36]

Black slaves also worked in craft shops, though they seem to have played a lesser role during this period. The 1776 census for Deptford Hundred, better known as Fells Point, Baltimore's shipbuilding center, for example, enumerated the presence of forty-two servants in the households of eleven maritime craftsmen. These eleven craftsmen owned a total of only six slaves.[37] Other evidence of slaves in town workshops is scattered. The sale of a smith's shop included "bellows, anvil and a young Negro Man that has been used to work at the smith's business"; the sale of a tobacconist's property included "two Negro Men, used to said business"; and the saddler John Gordon and the ropewalk owner Thomas Worthington both advertised for runaway slaves.[38]

Contemporary observations offer further testimony regarding the nature of Baltimore's workforce. In December 1766, Governor Horatio Sharpe reported to the Board of Trade that "most" of the "Manufacturers" of Maryland were "Servants from G. Britain dispersed over the Province." Ten years later, John Adams wrote that the inhabitants of Baltimore Town "hold their Negroes and convicts, that is, all laboring people and tradesmen, in such contempt that they think themselves a distinct order of beings."[39]

The presence of white servants and slaves in the workshops and shipyards of Revolutionary Baltimore is suggestive of the texture of relationships in the eighteenth-century trades. It would be difficult indeed to characterize the craft hierarchy in terms of "cooperative labor wherein master craftsman, journeyman, and apprentice were bound together in service to themselves, each other, and the community."[40] In Baltimore, servants were "bound" to their masters, but their masters were certainly not "bound . . . in service" to the servants. Both servants and slaves were legally chattel property, and the artisan could dispose of their labor as he pleased.[41] Craftsmen's continual placement of runaway servant advertisements in local newspapers testifies to the fact that the way in which mechanics employed their workers was hardly guided by an ethic of "cooperative labor."[42]

## The Impact of the Revolution

Let us return to the questions posed at the beginning of this essay—who was the eighteenth-century urban artisan, and what was the nature of the craft hierarchy? In answering this question, it is important to clarify what Richard Dunn has called "the basic facts of laboring life in eighteenth-century America."[43] The chief social distinction between artisans in Revolutionary Baltimore was not based upon the individual's level of skill and experience, as were the distinctions embodied in the traditional craft hierarchy. The definitive factor in the lives of mechanics, as in the lives of many others, was legal status—whether one labored in freedom or bondage.

The free artisan of Baltimore Town was, in general, either a small proprietor or, if in the building trades, an independent contractor. Like the town merchant, he was a rational man of business struggling to achieve a livelihood in the young, but growing, town economy. Toward that end, he employed the cheapest skilled labor available, offered a variety of goods and services to meet the demands of the local market, and invested his earnings in land and buildings. The independent craftsmen of Baltimore, like the mechanics of Charleston, were "ambitious, ever watchful of [their] interests and always ready to improve and extend them."[44] Though hardly the greedy, unbridled capitalists well known to the nineteenth century, they were clearly not the guardians of an anticapitalist ethic. They were vital and active participants in the expanding marketplace of Baltimore. The economic interests, ethnic and religious backrounds, and political goals of artisans tied them more closely to town merchants than to those who worked in their shops and shipyards.

The unfree craftsmen of Revolutionary Baltimore were largely indentured and convict servants, and to a lesser extent, slaves. We know little about their lives, although runaway servant advertisements and John Adams's observation of the "contempt" in which townsmen held "their Negroes and convicts" suggest that those lives were not easy. White servants represented a temporary labor pool, rather than a group of aspiring artisans. Most seem to have left town either before or after their indentures expired.[45]

If we comprehend that the most salient feature of artisanal life in Baltimore prior to the Revolution was legal status, we can gain some sense of the magnitude of the changes brought on by the Revolution. The war forced a fundamental reorientation in Baltimore's workforce by eliminating white servants from the town's labor market. With the commencement of armed conflict in 1775, the extensive servant trade ground to a halt. At the same time, many of the servants bound to Baltimore artisans fled the town to join the state and Continental armies. As a result, master craftsmen faced a critical shortage of labor. They responded to this shortage in two ways. Wealthy artisans who had extensive labor needs—for instance, masters in the shipbuilding trades—replaced their white servants with black slaves. The slave population of Baltimore's shipbuilding center, Fells Point, increased dramatically in size, from 65 in 1776 to 276 in 1783. Whereas in 1776 eleven major artisans in the shipbuilding and shipfitting trades owned a total of six slaves, by 1783 eighteen such tradesmen owned a total of 119 black bondsmen.[46]

Other craftsmen who required fewer workers looked to apprentices and free white journeymen to take the place of servants. This was evident in the increasing number of notices placed in the town newspapers for journeymen and apprentices. It was also evident in the rising number of apprenticeship indentures recorded by craftsmen in the clothing and building trades. (See table 2.1.) Between 1778 and 1781, mechanics recorded forty-nine apprenticeship indentures with the Baltimore County Orphans Court. Nineteen (39%) of the indentures were registered by craftsmen in the clothing

Table 2.1. Apprenticeship Indentures by Craft in Baltimore, 1778–89

| Craft | 1778–81 | | 1782–83 | | 1784–86 | | 1787–89 | |
|---|---|---|---|---|---|---|---|---|
| | No. | % | No. | % | No. | % | No. | % |
| Clothing production[a] | 19 | 39 | 25 | 30 | 37 | 32 | 31 | 37 |
| Building construction[b] | 8 | 16 | 30 | 36 | 33 | 28 | 11 | 13 |
| Food processing and packaging[c] | 2 | 4 | 10 | 12 | 19 | 16 | 13 | 15 |
| Leatherworking[d] | 9 | 18 | 4 | 5 | 4 | 3 | 5 | 6 |
| Shipbuilding[e] | 1 | 2 | 5 | 6 | 5 | 4 | 3 | 4 |
| Metalworking[f] | 5 | 10 | 4 | 5 | 9 | 8 | 13 | 15 |
| Luxury goods production[g] | 4 | 8 | 3 | 4 | 3 | 3 | 7 | 8 |
| Others[h] | 1 | 2 | 2 | 2 | 7 | 6 | 1 | 1 |
| Totals | 49 | 100 | 83 | 100 | 117 | 100 | 84 | 100 |

*Source:* Baltimore County Register of Wills, Orphans Court Proceedings, vols. 1 and 2 (1777–87; 1787–92), Maryland State Archives, Annapolis.

[a] Includes tailors, hatters, shoemakers, breechesmakers, and weavers.

[b] Includes house carpenters and joiners, bricklayers, stone masons, plasterers, and painters.

[c] Includes coopers, bakers, millwrights, and butchers.

[d] Includes saddlers, tanners, and curriers.

[e] Includes ship carpenters, joiners, sailmakers, and blockmakers.

[f] Includes blacksmiths, nailmakers, tinworkers and coppersmiths, and gunsmiths.

[g] Includes cabinetmakers, silversmiths, clock- and watchmakers, and coachmakers.

[h] Includes wheelwrights, barbers, potters, tallow chandlers, and soap boilers.

trades (tailors, hatters, shoemakers), and eight (16%) were registered by artisans in the building trades. In the shipbuilding trades, only a single ship carpenter took an apprentice. During the following two-year period, 1782–83, the number of indentures filed with the court rose by more than two-thirds, to eighty-three. Twenty-five (30%) were registered by craftsmen in the clothing trades, while thirty (36%) were assigned to artisans in the building trades. Together, these two industries accounted for two-thirds of all indentures contracted during the last two years of the war. These totals contrast significantly with the five indentures (6% of the total) registered by artisans in the shipbuilding trades. Clearly, craftsmen in the shipbuilding trades were obtaining their workers from a different source than were those in the building and clothing trades.

The labor recruitment patterns established during the war years persisted into the postwar era and beyond. During the 1780s, maritime craftsmen con-

Table 2.2. Slaveholdings in Baltimore, 1790

| | No. of Slaves Owned | | | |
| --- | --- | --- | --- | --- |
| | 1–3 | 4–9 | 10+ | Total |
| Merchants (N = 39) | 15 (38%) | 19 (49%) | 3 (8%) | 37 (95%) |
| Artisans (N = 102) | 42 (41%) | 12 (12%) | 2 (2%) | 56 (55%) |

Source: Heads of Families at the First Census of the United States Taken in the Year 1790: Maryland (Washington, D.C., 1907), 17–22.

tinued to use slaves in their shops and shipyards. Though slaveholding declined with the postwar contraction of the shipbuilding industry, several craftsmen maintained significant numbers of slaves. The largest slaveholder in Baltimore in 1790 was the shipbuilder David Stodder, who owned twenty-five slaves. Altogether, in 1790, fourteen known maritime tradesmen owned a total of seventy-one slaves.[47]

Most other town artisans, even those with large shops, utilized various forms of white labor. Apprenticeship, as table 2.1 demonstrates, remained an important source of workers for the clothing and building trades. A second important source for all of the crafts was the resuscitated servant trade, revived on a large scale immediately after the war. The flow of servants, however, lasted only a few years.[48] By the end of the Confederation era, free white journeymen assumed a greater presence in craft shops.

Substantial slaveholding was not prevalent among nonmaritime artisans during the Confederation era. Those who did own slaves typically possessed no more than three. Even tradesmen with large households (those with more than sixteen members) owned no more than three slaves each.[49] The minor role of slaves in the craft labor force can be illuminated by placing artisans' ownership of slaves within a larger context. Table 2.2 compares the slaveholdings of the largest master craftsmen (including maritime artisans) with those of Baltimore's most prominent merchants. Almost all (95%) of the town's leading merchants owned slaves. Half (49%) of them owned between four and nine black bondsmen. In contrast, a bare majority (55%) of Baltimore's major artisans owned slaves, and most of these slaveowning tradesmen possessed no more than three such workers. A very few mechanics had free blacks living in their households. In the above group of 102 mechanics, only seven (7%) had free blacks in their households.

Why did slavery take hold in the maritime trades and not in other town crafts? The organization of production, it would seem, was a critical factor, at least during the war years. The maritime trades were highly centralized, controlled by a small group of well-to-do craftsmen.[50] These craftsmen had large labor needs and possessed sufficient wealth to purchase slaves. Most other town trades were less centralized. They were characterized by smaller units of production—that is, in the nonmaritime trades there were larger numbers of independent craftsmen, who controlled smaller groups of workers. Artisans in these trades had less wealth with which to purchase slaves; and because production units were smaller they had less need to resort to this form of labor.

By 1790, however, the scale of production in several crafts, including boot- and shoemaking, hat making, clothing fabrication, nailmaking, and cooperage, had expanded considerably, and still artisans in these trades owned few slaves.[51] How can this be explained? A second critical factor in the labor recruitment patterns of the postwar era may have been the availability of skilled slaves. Shipbuilders and shipfitters may have resorted to slave labor because of the existence of a population of slaves skilled in these trades. During the colonial period, shipyards in South Carolina and Virginia employed slave labor extensively in skilled work.[52] The disruption in shipbuilding occasioned by the war in these states, which sent such Virginia shipbuilders as David Stodder north to Baltimore, may also have made slave maritime tradesmen available to the shipbuilders and shipfitters of Baltimore. In contrast, other crafts may not have had a sufficient body of skilled slaves available to them in the region. The planters of the colonial Chesapeake, as David Galenson has shown, employed their slaves largely in unskilled labor. Because of the extensive importation of skilled white servants into the Chesapeake and the high relative cost of slaves, these planters relied heavily on white servants for skilled labor for the first three-quarters of the eighteenth century. By the time of the Revolution, they had not developed a large workforce of skilled slaves as the planters of South Carolina and the West Indies had done. The artisans of Baltimore, unlike those of Charleston, did not face competition from skilled slaves owned by local planters and other town residents.[53] The peculiar nature of the labor system of the Chesapeake, with its racial division of skilled and unskilled labor, therefore, as well as Baltimore's proximity to the free-labor regions of western Maryland and Pennsylvania, may well have been responsible for keeping slavery out of the majority of Baltimore's trades.

Baltimore's increasing reliance on free workers and its movement away from indentured labor after the Revolution meant that the town's system of craft labor would come, in the nineteenth century, to resemble that of the North more closely than that of the slaveholding South. The transition

Freedom, supposedly the reward of enterprise. Detail from New York Master Sail Makers Society membership certificate, 1793. (Courtesy of The New-York Historical Society, New York City)

from a system heavily dependent upon bound labor to one that emphasized free labor in Baltimore resembled a similar change in the nature of the work force which had begun to the north in the more mature economy of Philadelphia twenty years earlier. The use of slaves and indentured servants in the Philadelphia trades had declined considerably following the Seven Years' War. Slaves had disappeared from craft shops owing to Quaker attacks on the institution of slavery, and a sharp drop in the supply of slaves in the 1760s. The decrease in artisans' purchases of indentured servants was, as in Baltimore, a result of changing economic conditions brought on by war —a slowdown of the servant trade, an increase in the available supply of free labor in the city, and the growing desirability of maintaining a flexible, non-permanent labor force during frequent periods of economic instability.[54]

In Baltimore, as well as Philadelphia, the shift from an unfree workforce to one that contained both free and bound workers created new problems and tensions within the town crafts. Master craftsmen of the early Republic had to forge new relationships with their free workers. At the same time, free journeymen had to struggle to define their rights in the workshop, and that struggle was hampered by the presence of a large bound work force in their midst. The formation of trade organizations of masters and journeymen in the 1790s represented the process of coming to terms with the new social, political, and economic conditions of the workshop in the post-Revolutionary era. These organizations did not challenge the decline of an existing traditional, cooperative craft hierarchy. The crafts in Revolutionary Baltimore, as we have seen, functioned in neither a traditional nor a cooperative manner. Instead, craftsmen struggled to create a craft structure that could accommodate the interests both of artisan-proprietors and of their growing numbers of free workers.[55]

# 3

MICHELE K. GILLESPIE

# Planters in the Making:
## Artisanal Opportunity in Georgia, 1790–1830

COMPETITION WITH SLAVE CRAFTSMEN during the colonial era did not prevent the emergence of a substantial group of white artisans in Georgia after the American Revolution.[1] Instead, many artisans thrived during the early Republic.[2] The rise of staple-crop economies, the availability of inexpensive land, and limited competition from skilled urban artisans provided migrant white artisans with new opportunities for economic and social mobility in a slaveholding world in the burgeoning cotton South. As a result of these structural realities, a number of skilled white men from the North and Europe found work and established shops in the port city Savannah and the upcountry trade center Augusta between 1790 and 1820. Many of these artisans subsequently acquired capital, land, and most importantly, slaves, transforming themselves into planters.

Entry by artisans into the planter class in Georgia began to wane only with the maturation of the cotton economy, the extensive settlement of the upcountry, and the flood of low-priced, northern-made goods into the urban markets of the South. Although in the 1830s and thereafter a few successful master craftsmen continued to transform themselves into planters, by that time most white artisans, particularly journeymen, were failing to experience much upward mobility. Some men tacitly accepted this situation, continuing to seek work as small proprietors and journeymen in the largest towns and cities in Georgia; others chose to move westward, as itinerants, to the newest settlements on the cotton frontier, a pattern that replicated the earlier movement of artisans to Georgia.

Southern artisans, especially those seeking work in the emerging cotton economy, experienced a set of circumstances very different from that experienced by their northern counterparts.[3] Although the lower South felt the impact of the commercial revolution, and to a much lesser extent the transportation revolution, the industrial revolution made limited headway in the region before 1860. While the transformation of master craftsmen into planters in Georgia during the early Republic mirrored the transformation of master craftsmen into entrepreneurial employers in the North, the resemblance ends there.

The marginal place of free labor in this slaveholding world discouraged class consciousness and class formation. Unlike the fledgling middle class in the North, which fostered the creation of a working class, the planter class in the South found little reason to press for the establishment of more wage labor in a slave-labor economy. Moreover, those master craftsmen who had become planters, as well as master craftsmen and journeymen who hoped to become planters, conceived of themselves as members of the "ruling race."[4] They participated fully in the slave economy, relying upon slave labor as much as free labor in their shops and using slave labor exclusively in their homes and fields whenever their financial resources allowed. In addition, even as opportunities for upward mobility for artisans dwindled in the early nineteenth century, masters and journeymen did not experience the blanket devaluation of their skills which transformed northern artisans into wageworkers. The growth of the traditional staple-crop economy and the slave labor system created unique opportunities for skilled, free white men to accumulate capital, land, and slaves. These sets of realities not only prevented the formation of a working class in Georgia and fostered the transformation of artisans into planters; they encouraged skilled white men to believe that they too could share in the rewards of the slave economy.[5]

## Migrant Artisans in the New Cotton Economy

Geographic, demographic, and economic shifts already in progress greeted migrant artisans upon their arrival to Georgia in the late eighteenth and early nineteenth centuries. Although lowcountry economic patterns had remained virtually the same since the colonial era, because seacoast planters continued to rely on extensive slave labor to cultivate staple crops of rice and indigo, great change was under way in the upcountry.

A series of treaties nefariously negotiated with Native Americans opened up greater and greater expanses of the Georgia Piedmont to white settlement. The headright system of land distribution, bounty grants, and eventually a lottery made cheap, fertile land readily available to adventurous settlers. While some white migrants contented themselves with subsistence farming, others harvested cash crops. Tobacco prevailed during the late eighteenth century in the upcountry, but the fall in its market price, the invention of the cotton gin, and the rise of cotton prices ignited widespread interest in short-staple cotton during the first decades of the nineteenth century.[6]

The transition to a cotton economy increased the rate of settlement in the hinterland, nearly quadrupling the state's white population between 1790 and 1820.[7] Unlike lowcountry planters, whose enormous profits mandated extensive investments in capital, land, and slaves, upcountry farmers collected small-scale but respectable returns from tobacco and cotton, despite limited capital and labor. Farmers quickly realized, however, that the introduction of slave labor to their farms brought them even greater gains. By 1820, four out of five Georgia slaves toiled in the upcountry, a remarkable transformation from 1790, when the great majority of Georgia's slave population had lived and worked on lowcountry plantations.[8]

These structural changes provided white artisans with opportunities unavailable to them in the older cities and towns along the Atlantic seaboard and in Europe. Disheartened by the existence of established proprietorships and manufactories in these places and frustrated by job competition, hundreds of men from Europe, New England, the mid-Atlantic region, the upper South, and even nearby Charleston made their way to Georgia between 1790 and 1820.[9]

The trades these migrant artisans practiced were as diverse as their origins, according to the advertisements they placed in local newspapers. In Augusta, the painter William Anson announced his arrival from London, the blacksmith F. R. Gaddy told prospective clients about his Richmond experience, the jeweler Jeremiah Andrews described his Philadelphia training, the gardener John Barberon emphasized his experience in the West Indies and France, and the tailor Joseph Sudor respectfully informed the public of his recent arrival from Charleston.[10] In Savannah, the watchmaker Thomas Lee claimed a Liverpool background, the baker Francis Herbert Berry his experience in a Charleston shop, and the hairdresser Lewis Cuigno his training in Bordeaux.[11]

Artisans practicing commonplace trades such as blacksmithing and baking were just as likely to relocate to Georgia as were artisans in luxury trades such as furniture making and silversmithing. A master tailor, for example, advertised his ability to hire plenty of newly arrived journeymen from cities stretching up and down the Atlantic coast.[12] The vernacular architecture of Savannah—New York-style stoops and dormer windows, Rhode Island gambrel roofs, and New England porticoes built in the wake of the Savannah fire of 1796—attests to the presence of northern-born carpenters from a variety of locales.[13] Although artisans in ordinary trades often lacked the resources, family connections, and training characteristic of luxury craftsmen, they too chose to make their way to Georgia despite limited capital and an uncertain future.

The experience of the tanner Reuben King indicates that relocation to Georgia was often as much a last resort as an adventurous act. After finishing his apprenticeship in Connecticut on his twenty-first birthday, King settled his debts and "against the advice of my best friends . . . although I was steadfast in my opportune undertaking" headed for Pittsburgh by ship, stage, and foot during the summer of 1800. Upon reaching his destination, his savings having been exhausted by his travels, King found work with a succession of local shoemakers. Unable to set up his own shop, without any capital, and discouraged by too much competition, King walked to Baltimore, collecting enough money from day jobs and shoe sales along the way to buy his passage to Savannah, where he arrived in the spring of 1801, only to travel further south to the remote settlement of Darien.[14] Eventually, propitious circumstances enabled King to establish a tanyard, although he suffered a series of setbacks along the way. Yet his experience was not unlike that of many other artisans who migrated to Georgia hoping to establish shops of their own.

Artisans who arrived in Georgia during the early Republic were generally fortunate in this regard. The growth in the size and wealth of the state's white population generated rising consumer demand for a wide variety of local artisanal goods. Increasing emphasis on the production of staple crops encouraged the expansion of marketing and transport facilities in Savannah and Augusta. This development in turn produced more service-oriented artisanal work.[15] Furthermore, the availability of cheap upcountry land meant that artisans could choose alternative or supplemental livelihoods if their craftwork failed to generate steady demand.

Savannah, the largest export center south of Charleston, provided the greatest number of migrant artisans with work opportunities.[16] The busy port shipped rice, indigo, sea-island cotton, and lumber from the lowcountry, as well as tobacco, upland cotton, grains, and hides from the upcountry, to distant markets by way of the Atlantic. Coastal planters who brought their wealth-producing staples to Savannah, merchants who arranged the sale and shipment of these crops, and other urban dwellers spent their profits on consumer goods and luxury items too costly or too fragile to import. Such select items included clothes, furniture, silver, and carriages copied from European styles—all produced for well-to-do clients by local master craftsmen in the elite trades. Other artisans provided planters and merchants with luxury services such as house building, painting, paper hanging, and watch repairs.[17]

While the livelihoods of artisans who catered to the consumption patterns of the planter and merchant elite in Savannah tended to be more secure than the livelihoods of artisans in more commonplace trades, the needs of the city dwellers generated a fairly steady demand for nonluxury goods and services as well. Thus, white artisans in ordinary trades in Savannah could usually find jobs as journeymen, though they might have had more difficulty than their fellow tradesmen in Augusta in setting themselves up as masters.

The town of Augusta, though half the size of Savannah and more remote, also attracted migrant artisans. This thriving entrepot connected the vast upcountry of Georgia and South Carolina to Savannah by way of a 120-mile stretch of the Savannah River.[18] In the late eighteenth century, farmers who marketed their staples through Augusta relied on local artisans' skills to outfit them with the few necessities they themselves could not produce. But as some of these formerly self-sufficient farmers transformed themselves into planters through the sale of tobacco and cotton, they began to purchase luxury items, as did their wealthier counterparts along the coast. Like the changes taking place in Savannah, these changes under way in Augusta and the surrounding countryside fostered the demand for luxury and nonluxury goods and services alike.[19]

Records of master craftsmen's experiences with their clients disclose the extent of artisans' dependence upon consumers whose fortunes rested on the successful sale of staple crops. Economic changes that occurred outside the regional economy, including drops in European prices for staples, increases in the availability of northern manufactured goods, and the national depression in the wake of the War of 1812 affected consumption patterns. In addition, a disparate array of local factors, ranging from the impact of a drought to planters' prioritization of debt responsibilities, shaped consumer demand, as well as payment practices.

Artisans certainly recognized their dependence on the planter class. As a "Mechanic" claimed in a letter to the editor of the *Columbian Museum and Savannah Advertiser:* "The planter takes his money, buys more negroes, goes on a frolic to the northward," but when the carpenter he hired requests his wages for work performed, the planter puts him off. When the carpenter seeks legal redress, he discovers that "the courts are tedious and will tire the carpenter out before the planter."[20] Sometimes payment occurred only after a client's death. Fairly typical was the experience of a Savannah cabinetmaker owed more than $250 for work completed in 1802 and 1803; he received his due only upon the settlement of his patron's estate in 1805.[21] While such payment practices did not undermine the businesses of successful master craftsmen, they did prove disheartening to young craftsmen.

John Richards, an Augusta gunsmith forced to divide his last twelve hundred dollars among his creditors, poured out his financial woes in an unusual advertisement attesting to his sterling character. "Assiduity has been my study, and fidelity my prop. Fortune's frowns are daily crowding in upon me. . . . I hope my creditors will take one serious moment to deliberate upon my indigent circumstances at present, and be so amicable as to withdraw their suits against me."[22] He then recommended that young artisans who hoped to avoid his misfortune invent a cotton machine "that shall work without the impelling power of water, fire, beasts, or humans."[23] Richards clearly recognized that an artisan's success was linked to his ability to meet the new demands of this cotton economy.

Reuben King found himself in similarly desperate straits when, after working industriously for several years at his tanyard, he was unable to collect monies owed him. "I am now all Most discouraged," he recorded in his journal. "I am without Money without Credit and Nothing to Sell."[24] As both Richards and King had discovered, the fortunes of Georgia artisans were inextricably tied to the production of staple crops, the vagaries of the world market, and ultimately, the spending power, consumer habits, and payment practices of wealthy whites—usually planters. Fortunately, during the late eighteenth and early nineteenth centuries, occasional setbacks caused by tardy customers were generally offset by the growing world market for the staple crops, particularly cotton, which spurred local consumer demand for artisanal goods and services. Most artisans, as long as they could weather some occasional hard times, benefited from these developments. Indeed, Reuben King's business, like so many other artisanal concerns, apparently recovered despite the realization of his worst fears.[25]

Evidence of growing artisanal wealth as a result of these market changes can be found in the Chatham County General Tax Returns for 1798 and 1799. Out of 1,301 returns in 1799, representing those Chatham County residents prosperous enough to own taxable property (houses, lots, stock in trade, carriages, slaves, etc.), mechanics' returns comprised a respectable 16 percent. By contrast, planters' returns comprised 13 percent; merchants' returns, 14 percent; and shopkeepers' and professionals' returns the bulk of the remainder.[26]

The tax digests also demonstrate rapid growth in the number of taxpaying artisans in luxury and nonluxury trades over a single year's time. The number of taxpaying tailors and butchers, for example, more than doubled between 1798 and 1799; the number of taxpaying luxury tradesmen also grew substantially. Overall, the number of taxpaying artisans increased 29 percent (see table 3.1).

Savannah master craftsmen in a variety of trades providing products to planters, as this evidence suggests, did make money, as did Augusta craftsmen. Like artisans everywhere, they used their new wealth to expand their shops and add labor in the form of apprentices and journeymen.[27] But even more important, in a distinct departure from craft tradition elsewhere, these men also used their capital to buy slaves and land, thus beginning their transformation into planters.

Table 3.1. Artisans Listed as Taxpayers in the Chatham County, Georgia, Tax Returns, 1798 and 1799

| Type of Artisan | Number | | | | Number | | |
|---|---|---|---|---|---|---|---|
| | 1798 | 1799 | Change | | 1798 | 1799 | Change |
| Tailor | 16 | 34 | +18 | Carpenter | 58 | 69 | +11 |
| Butcher | 5 | 15 | +10 | Printer | 0 | 8 | +8 |
| Jeweler/silversmith | 2 | 8 | +6 | Lumberman | 0 | 4 | +4 |
| Tanner | 0 | 3 | +3 | Hairdresser | 0 | 3 | +3 |
| Gunsmith | 0 | 2 | +2 | Baker | 3 | 6 | +3 |
| Tinsmith | 0 | 1 | +1 | Cooper | 1 | 2 | +1 |
| Currier | 0 | 1 | +1 | Shipwright | 0 | 1 | +1 |
| Bookbinder | 0 | 1 | +1 | Pilot | 0 | 1 | +1 |
| Brickmaker | 0 | 1 | +1 | Blacksmith | 3 | 4 | +1 |
| Tobacconist | 0 | 1 | +1 | Cotton ginner | 0 | 1 | +1 |
| Wheelwright | 0 | 1 | +1 | Wharfinger | 0 | 1 | +1 |
| Cabinetmaker | 5 | 4 | −1 | Hatter | 2 | 2 | 0 |
| Ship carpenter | 4 | 3 | −1 | Saddler | 5 | 4 | −1 |
| Shoemaker | 14 | 12 | −2 | Barber | 3 | 1 | −2 |
| Painter | 5 | 2 | −3 | Trunkmaker | 2 | 0 | −2 |
| | | | | Chairmaker | 7 | 4 | −3 |
| | | | | Bricklayer | 12 | 5 | −7 |
| | | | | Total | 146 | 205 | +59 |

Source: Chatham County General Tax Returns 1798, 1799, microfilm, GDAH.

Artisans in a number of trades in both Savannah and Augusta frequently took on apprentices shortly after arriving in Georgia. The inclusion of an apprentice in a new craftsman's shop provided him with relatively inexpensive help, broadcast his confidence in his ability to support another household member, and gave him legitimacy as a master competent enough to train a young man in "the mysteries of the trade."[28] Likewise, the hiring of journeymen also signaled a master craftsman's confidence in his skills and the future success of his shop. Shortly after his arrival in Georgia in 1795, Edward Griffith advertised for "one or two journeymen silversmiths" to whom he would pay twenty dollars per month plus board and lodging. A boot- and shoemaker sought several journeymen and apprentices after setting up a small workshop in 1797.[29] The Savannah artisan John Gardiner sought "3 or 4 journeymen who are good workmen." The Augusta me-

chanic William Savel announced the success of his business while also noti-
fying the public that he had acquired "a number of workmen."[30]

## White Artisans and Skilled Black Labor

Throughout the early Republic, master craftsmen sought help from apprentices and trained journeymen in many trades, ranging from printing,
tailoring, and tin plating to coach trimming, bricklaying, and plastering.[31]
Artisans who took on apprentices and hired journeymen in Georgia emulated the traditional craft practices of artisans in Europe and the northern
United States. At the same time, they used the acquisition of this labor to le-
gitimize their authority as craftsmen.

Whereas master craftsmen's reliance on apprentices and journeymen
was an important stage in establishing themselves as bona fide artisans in
their new locations, their growing reliance on slave labor marks an even
more important development in their adaptation to this slaveholding world.
The use of slave labor by white artisans, while not unheard of in northern
cities during the late eighteenth century, was becoming increasingly atypical
during the course of the early nineteenth century. The staple-crop economy in the slaveholding lower South, in contrast, encouraged urban towns-
people as well as planters to hire and buy skilled and unskilled slaves (and to
a lesser extent, to hire free blacks) throughout the antebellum era. Artisans,
like most other men with capital in a staple-crop region, chose to participate in the slave economy.

Unfortunately, it is difficult to determine precisely how many white artisans owned or hired slaves (and what kinds of slaves they owned or hired)
during this period. The available evidence suggests that an individual artisan's ownership of slaves provided a strong indication of his rising economic and social status, regardless of whether or not the artisan purchased
skilled slaves, who were more costly. Male field hands sold for approximately $450 in 1800—as much as a modest town house and lot—and slave
artisans and trained domestic slaves generally proved more expensive.[32]

Most migrant artisans spent some time accruing enough capital to afford an unskilled bondsperson. A skilled slave artisan or domestic servant required even greater investment. Thus, although the silversmith Devine
Lambertoz arrived in Savannah in 1795 and immediately sought an apprentice, a full eight years elapsed before he acquired his first slave, a domestic.[33] Likewise, Joseph Rice, who appeared in Savannah in 1787, quickly obtained apprentices, then "excellent workmen," but some years passed before
he acquired "a valuable young Negro man," presumably a skilled slave.[34]
The acquisition of slaves demonstrates the degree to which these artisans

adapted to the social, cultural, and economic realities of the slaveholding world around them.

This was no easy task. While a significant social distance separated master craftsmen such as the silversmiths Lambertoz and Rice from their skilled slaves, this was not always the case for white journeymen in non-elite trades who lacked the capital to establish their own shops and buy slaves. Skilled white and black laborers worked alongside each other in a variety of situations. The brickmaker George Miller employed ten white men and six of his own slaves at his Savannah brick factory. The Chatham Steam Saw Mill operated with the assistance of three white sawyers and eight slave sawyers, as well as two slave women and four slave children. Four white men, two slave men, and two "boys," the race of the latter unclear, ran a Chatham County iron foundry. The L. Baldwin Company's candle- and soap-making establishment employed three white men and one slave.[35] Yet while these sources demonstrate that whites and blacks, free and unfree laborers, worked together in early-nineteenth-century Georgia shops, it cannot be determined whether workers shared the same tasks and skills or were assigned them according to a racial hierarchy. White men working in these situations must have been aware of the lack of boundaries separating them from the slaves with whom they worked. In a society that degraded the kinds of labor that slaves performed, it must have been important to these white journeymen to set up a social distance based on a conception of racial differences. This experience may also have compelled them to hire and buy slaves of their own when the opportunity presented itself.

Newspaper advertisements seeking the return of skilled runaway slaves, along with occupational information from registries of free blacks, make it clear that master craftsmen consistently relied on skilled black labor that they owned or hired. In the majority of runaway advertisements in Savannah newspapers, lowcountry planters reported that their skilled slave artisans had fled to Savannah and sought urban work while pretending to be free.[36] Many of these runaway slave artisans were well known in the city, much to their masters' chagrin, and knew how to find work and hide themselves from their masters in the relative anonymity of this urban world.[37]

Of course, not all slave artisans who worked in the city were runaways. Many slave artisans had leave to find work in Savannah during dull periods on the plantation. Other slave artisans belonged to local residents, including merchants, shopkeepers, and artisans. On the whole, nevertheless, slave artisans appear to have represented a relatively small proportion of the city's slave population and tended to be clustered in labor-intensive and low-status trades such as brickmaking and construction.[38]

Augusta's population of slave artisans appears to have been even smaller

Table 3.2. Populations of Savannah and Augusta, 1800–1830

|  | % White | % Slave | % Free Black | Total |
|---|---|---|---|---|
| *1800* | | | | |
| Savannah | 51 | 46 | 4 | 5,146 |
| Augusta | 52 | 46 | 2 | 2,215 |
| *1810* | | | | |
| Savannah | 47 | 42 | 10 | 5,215 |
| Augusta | 45 | 53 | 2 | 2,476 |
| *1820* | | | | |
| Savannah | 51 | 48 | 1 | 7,523 |
| Augusta | 48 | 51 | 1 | 4,000 |
| *1830* | | | | |
| Savannah | 48 | 47 | 5 | 7,776 |
| Augusta | 50 | 49 | 1 | 5,500 |

*Sources: Second Census of the U.S.; Aggregate Amount of Persons Within the United States in the Year 1810; Census for 1820; and Fifth Census; or Enumeration of the Inhabitants of the U.S.*

[a] Figures are estimates. Manuscript census returns did not distinguish between town and county. Percentages are rounded to the nearest whole number.

than Savannah's. Though Augusta whites hired groups of slaves for heavy, monotonous work such as felling timber and attending cotton gins, little evidence exists to suggest widespread reliance on the work of slave artisans. An examination of local newspaper advertisements reveals that in Augusta few runaway slave artisans attempted to pass themselves off as free blacks or as slaves permitted to hire out their own time, though this was a common-place practice in Savannah.[39] In fact, most runaways from the Augusta countryside bypassed the upcountry town to head to Savannah or Charleston, where larger black communities, more job opportunities, and more anonymity awaited them.[40] Furthermore, slave artisans were simply rarer in the upcountry, and therefore were less likely to be hired out in Augusta during the off season, as their talents often proved too specialized for the small-scale upcountry plantations and farms that prevailed there.[41]

Upcountry plantation development also discouraged the establishment of a significant skilled free black population in Augusta. Between 1800 and 1830, the free black population never exceeded 6 percent of the total population in Augusta; Savannah's free black population exceeded that figure only once, in 1810, when it rose to 10 percent of the city's inhabitants (see table 3.2).[42]

Table 3.3. Occupations of Free Blacks in Savannah and Augusta

| Occupation | Savannah (1817) | Augusta (1819) |
|---|---|---|
| Tailor | 12 | 0 |
| Carpenter | 10 | 12 |
| Barber | 5 | 1 |
| Apprentice (craft not named) | 5 | 0 |
| Cooper | 4 | 0 |
| Butcher | 3 | 0 |
| Shoemaker | 2 | 0 |
| Bricklayer | 1 | 0 |
| Rigger | 1 | 0 |
| Ship carpenter | 1 | 0 |
| Blacksmith | 0 | 1 |
| Harnessmaker | 0 | 1 |
| Millwright | 0 | 2 |
| Saddler | 0 | 2 |
| Sawmill attendant | 0 | 2 |
| Total | 44 | 21 |

*Sources:* Chatham County Court of the Ordinary, Register of Free Persons of Color, 1817, microfilm, GDAH; Richmond County Court of the Ordinary, Register of Free Persons of Color, 1819, *AC,* Mar. 31, 1819.

The existence of a registry of free persons of color for Chatham County (Savannah) in 1817 permits some speculation about the degree of competition between white journeymen and free black artisans in this port city during the latter days of the early Republic. Twenty-one percent (forty-four) of the adult free black men on the registry listed artisanal occupations. The nine occupations that these forty-four men claimed can be collectively characterized as commonplace trades. Half of the men worked as either tailors or carpenters. Likewise, the 1819 registry for Richmond County (Augusta) listed twenty-one artisans, all of whom worked in nonluxury trades, half as carpenters. While Savannah free blacks worked in artisanal occupations that were generally considered distasteful, dirty, or servile (i.e., butchering, bricklaying, and shoemaking), it is interesting to note that several Augusta free blacks worked in relatively elite trades such as harnessmaking and saddlery. This suggests that the predominance of white journeymen in Savannah discouraged white masters from hiring free black artisans, while the lack of competition in the smaller town of Augusta allowed free black artisans entry into more select trades (see table 3.3).[43]

While white journeymen in elite trades suffered little or no competition from free black artisans, these registries point out that competition must have existed between white journeymen and free black artisans in the non-elite trades of carpentry and tailoring. While white carpenters and tailors may have felt squeezed by the presence of a small number of skilled, free black artisans in Augusta and Savannah, white artisans in most other trades apparently did not have free black competitors. Yet little evidence of white resentment of free black competition appeared in either Savannah or Augusta during this period. Although migrant journeymen faced some competition from blacks, they could not protest this competition too vociferously in a staple-based, slaveholding economy.

The extant records indicate that master craftsmen in a number of trades owned slaves. White journeymen seeking employment from such masters, and hoping to become masters themselves, could not afford to voice their antagonism regarding black competition. White journeymen carpenters, for example, were forced to compete with slave carpenters because many master carpenters owned slaves. Although the Augusta carpenter William Dearmond was not a wealthy man at his death, his estate included "negroes" as well as "horses, hogs, household and kitchen furniture, carpenter's tools, etc."[44] Another Augusta carpenter, James Harrison, was much better off. In addition to two town lots and many upcountry acres, he owned 11 slaves, at least some of whom must have helped him at his trade.[45] The Savannah carpenter Asa Hoxey owned 10 slaves by 1820.[46] While the hard labor and seasonality of the carpentry trade made the use of slave labor an obvious choice for masters, many artisans in other trades were equally dependent upon slave help. The Augusta baker J. B. Larey owned 3 slaves, the Augusta shoemaker Reed Collins owned 12 slaves, the Savannah shoemaker John Miller owned 6 slaves, and the Augusta blacksmith Lud Harris owned 3 slaves.[47] The Augusta cabinetmaker John Harwood owned 5 slaves in 1809, and the Savannah cabinetmaker Benjamin Ansley owned 14 slaves in 1812, according to his estate records.[48] White journeymen seeking positions were forced to accept the predominance of slaveownership among master craftsmen. Accordingly, journeymen appear to have worked to take advantage of new opportunities for social mobility by directing their energies toward becoming independent artisans and eventually planters, and modeling themselves after other artisans who had made this transition.

## Artisans as Planters in the Making

Holland McTyre was one example of a successful artisan turned planter. He first advertised his carriage-making shop in Augusta in 1795. Two years later he owned three slaves, but no other taxable property. By 1809 he had acquired approximately four hundred acres in Richmond County, some four hundred upcountry acres elsewhere, and eleven slaves. McTyre continued to add slaves to his holdings, owning twenty-three by 1818.[49] Nicholas Long's career resembled McTyre's. The Augusta coachmaker owned no real estate in the mid-1790s but possessed three slaves. By 1808, he held close to four hundred upcountry acres and eleven slaves. Twelve years later, he possessed more than eight hundred acres in three upcountry counties, twenty-three slaves, and a carriage.[50]

Other artisans in luxury trades patronized by rich planters and merchants worked to achieve the accoutrements of planter status, though their gains were more modest than those of McTyre and Long. The riding-chair maker Joshua Pharoah, after twelve years of residence in Augusta, owned 100 Richmond County acres, a house, two thousand dollars in inventory, two unimproved lots in nearby Harrisburg, a carriage, and one slave. The cabinetmaker William Barnes owned approximately 150 upcountry acres, eight slaves, and a carriage by 1812, while the Savannah chairmaker Henry Densler owned more than 100 upcountry acres, along with five slaves.[51] H. Bunce, a clock- and watchmaker, owned four slaves and more than 200 acres in Richmond County within eight years of his arrival in Augusta.[52] William Allen, a cabinetmaker and upholsterer, acquired more than 900 acres in Burke County between 1789 and 1795. In his will, drawn up in 1795, he bequeathed to his brother three slaves, 300 acres on Butler's Creek, and "his horses, cattle, hogs, plantation tools, and household furniture."[53] As these examples suggest, during the early Republic master craftsmen in luxury trades could accumulate land and slaves and thus build their own plantations.

Yet artisans in trades that did not cater exclusively to the planter elite and that did not produce high-priced goods could also hope to acquire land and slaves. The potter and tile maker Nathaniel Durkee owned virtually nothing in 1800.[54] By 1818, he claimed four hundred acres in Wilkinson County, four slaves, six hundred dollars worth of town lots, and one hundred dollars' worth of inventory.[55] Jacob Dill, a blacksmith, came to Augusta in 1807 and bought a house within two years of his arrival. By 1816, he owned nearly two hundred upcountry acres, twelve hundred dollars in inventory, six slaves, and a carriage, as well as his home. By 1830, Dill's property included seven more slaves.[56] The stonecutter Garret Laurence, who arrived in Augusta in 1811, owned six slaves, one hundred acres in Richmond County, and more than two thousand acres in Wilkinson County by 1818. Within twelve years, he had acquired three more slaves.[57] Even women artisans occasionally appear in the records as planters in the making. The Augusta mantua maker Mrs. Jones owned a female slave in 1820.[58] Jane Whiteford, a Savannah milliner, acquired four hundred upcountry acres in Washington County in 1788.[59]

Artisans in elite and non-elite trades alike became planters. They generally followed a prescribed set of patterns to achieve this status. Upon arrival in Augusta or Savannah, they hired apprentices and journeymen as soon as they could afford them. As they accrued capital, they hired and bought slaves, working to increase their slaveholdings over time. They also invested in town lots and upcountry land—real estate usually destined for residence but sometimes purchased for speculation. It would be misleading to suggest that all artisans made the financial and social headway indicated by the evidence here. Nevertheless, it is clear that many artisans in a wide range of trades hoped to become independent planters. Although in 1820 not one of a group of Augusta and Savannah artisans (a bricklayer, a stonecutter, an artist, a potter, a bookbinder, a herald painter, and two watchmakers) owned a single slave, each possessed between fifty and three hundred upcountry acres.[60] The acquisition of upcountry land often marked the first stage in the transition from artisan to planter.

Still, some journeymen experienced few gains after years of toil. The clock- and watchmaker John Cortelyou arrived in Augusta in 1803. Six years later he owned no property and managed to pay only his poll tax. The Augusta bookbinder Peter Browne, the cabinetmaker James Alexander, and the blacksmith Gideon Sealy also proved unable to accumulate capital over a similar time span, although Browne eventually acquired one hundred upcountry acres in Franklin County.[61] These men had to hope that the future would bring them better fortune.

Competition from free black and slave artisans must have lessened the opportunities for upward mobility for some white journeymen in non-elite trades such as tailoring and carpentry. By the 1820s and 1830s, the growing availability of ready-made clothing from New York City, ready-made boots and shoes from New England, and ready-made cabinets and furniture from the North would also serve to discourage artisans in luxury and nonluxury trades alike. The end of the land lottery system in 1832 added yet another roadblock to artisans' hopes for prosperity.

As late as the 1830s, the southern slaveholding world encouraged artisans to believe that despite dwindling opportunities they too could share in the prosperity of the slaveholding South. Accordingly, when artisans failed to find work in Savannah or Augusta, many did not despair but turned to the countryside instead. Skilled men found employment on plantations as itinerant carriagemakers, carpenters, wheelwrights, and blacksmiths. They followed speculators to fledgling towns such as Milledgeville, Athens, and Macon, where they set up their own shops with little or no competition from other craftsmen. And some artisans headed to the newest frontiers.

The Savannah resident William Harris Garland, unable to find a position in this port city, resigned himself to work as a mechanic on a "sailboat" that traveled the Altamaha and Ocmulgee Rivers to the new cotton town of Macon. William Talmage, a New Jersey–born blacksmith, took a five-month tour through several hundred miles of isolated land in western Georgia and Alabama; along the way he picked up steady work and earned high wages for doing machine repairs and making parts. At journey's end, he used his savings to buy his own shop, along with four slaves, in Athens, Georgia. Ironically, despite the fact that by the 1830s they were increasingly excluded from the planter class, Georgia artisans continued to apply traditional artisanal work patterns to an expanding slaveholding economy in the hope of transforming themselves into planters.[62]

During the early Republic, first-generation urban mechanics secured places for themselves in Georgia's slaveholding world. They used their artisanal skills to accumulate capital, which many exchanged for land and slaves. By taking advantage of widening economic opportunities, these artisans adapted themselves to the peculiarities of this slaveholding society by turning themselves into planters.

While capitalist transformation in the Northeast was beginning to divide artisans into two distinct classes, wage-earning journeymen and entrepreneurial master craftsmen, economic transformation in Georgia allowed the most successful artisans to enter the planter class. The expanding upcountry and the market for short-staple cotton, along with the increasing entrenchment of the slave-labor economy, stimulated urban development and planters' consumption of goods and services. Some artisans benefited from these developments, although they did not use their new wealth to pursue entrepreneurial activities as their northern counterparts did. Instead, they acquired the trappings of the dominant men of the southern social order.

Even artisans who failed to accumulate substantial capital and were unable to transform themselves into planters were not losers. The expansion of the cotton economy generated work for them as itinerant mechanics and small-town master craftsmen. Migrant artisans, whether planters in the making or struggling journeymen, accepted the economic realities of the lower South during the early Republic. Unlike their counterparts in the North, where a working class was in the making, skilled white laborers in the South adapted their experience in a traditional craft economy to a slave-labor world.

4

JAMES SIDBURY

# Slave Artisans in Richmond, Virginia, 1780–1810

SKILLED SLAVES fit awkwardly into the existing literature on the history of artisans in America. Virginians had been engaged in large-scale production for distant markets since the 1620s. During the first half of the eighteenth century slaveowners began to have their bondsmen trained to work in crafts that supported the region's staple-crop economy, especially carpentry and cooperage.[1] Relationships between skilled slaves and their masters—a word with far different connotations for historians of slave societies than for historians of free artisans—had long been unequal, paternalistic, and conflict ridden. As the nineteenth century commenced, northern journeymen faced increasingly long odds against their rising to the status of master, but slave artisans had never enjoyed legitimate aspirations to that status or to any public voice.[2] All of these differences have led historians to conclude that slaves sought to increase the social and cultural space that separated them from their masters.[3]

Several historians working within this tradition have explored the anomalous position of slave artisans in southern societies. Gerald Mullin argues that rural slave artisans became "marginal men" in eighteenth-century Virginia: by learning a trade they acculturated to the white world but also gained increased social space between themselves and their masters and a greater chance for escape, which helped compensate for the loss of their African cultural heritage.[4] Barbara Jeanne Fields and Richard Wade discuss urban slavery during the antebellum period; both see slavery "disintegrating in Southern cities."[5] Historians who have written about eighteenth-century slave artisans, however, have rightly focused on rural artisans, and historians of urban slavery have generally limited their studies to the forty years preceding secession.[6]

However, artisans also lived in communities outside Boston, New York, and Philadelphia at the turn of the nineteenth century. Following the American Revolution the Chesapeake region underwent an important urban boom. Baltimore came to monopolize Maryland's urban functions and came to dominate that state's economy. No single Virginia city rivaled Baltimore's growth, but five towns grew substantially during the twenty-five years following the Peace of Paris. By 1810 a total of almost thirty-five thousand people lived in Richmond, Norfolk, Alexandria, Petersburg, and Fredericksburg. Among these people were more than twelve thousand slaves and more than four thousand free blacks.[7] These towns were not identical. Petersburg, for example, served as the center of Southside Virginia's thriving tobacco economy, while the grain trade fueled Richmond's growth. Each town, however, served as a processing center for an agricultural hinterland and as an outlet into the Atlantic economy. To fulfill these functions each town became a center of artisanal activity. Enslaved artisans did much of the skilled work in these urban centers.

This chapter analyzes the experiences of slave artisans in Richmond from 1780 to 1810. During those three decades Richmond became Virginia's capital and grew into the largest urban center in the new state. A town of little more than 1,000 people in 1782, it included almost 4,000 in 1790 and almost 6,000 in 1800. By 1810 it contained 9,735 residents, half of whom were black. Three-quarters of these black Richmonders were slaves. During those three decades the town developed a diversified economy that rested on mining coal, making iron, milling grain, and processing tobacco. It was well on its way toward becoming the "the most industrialized of southern cities."[8] Thus, of all Virginia cities Richmond probably had the greatest experience with the kinds of changes affecting northern cities during the first decades of the nineteenth century. The city therefore provides a promising opportunity to evaluate the lives of slave artisans in relation to the more extensively documented experiences of free artisans in the North.[9]

Inquiring into the nature of artisanal slaves' lives in early Virginia towns also calls into question the relevance of traditional definitions of artisanship for slave societies. Many Richmond slaves worked in carpentry, brick masonry, blacksmithing, and other trades traditionally deemed artisanal. But the widely accepted definitions according to which artisans were workers who owned their own tools and engaged in petty commodity production would obviously exclude all slaves, for they did not even own themselves. White Virginians did refer to slave craftsmen according to the skills they possessed. But patterns of race relations within Richmond suggest that the most important variable for classifying different occupations held by enslaved urbanites was the degree of personal autonomy the job afforded. Artisanal slaves used the high demand for their labor to win autonomy. Semiskilled urban slaves who drove carts and drays or worked at the town's warehouses and tobacco factories also escaped some of the burdens of close white supervision and achieved similar levels of autonomy. Thus a taxonomy of slave occupations should group the jobs of several types of worker traditionally labeled semiskilled—carters, draymen, warehousemen, stevedores, sawyers, messengers—with traditional crafts. Some traditionally "white-collar" jobs held by black Richmonders—clerks, storekeepers, and physicians—should also be included. Unlike artisans in free states, enslaved skilled workers could not, of course, lead public movements in defense of their rights; instead, they sought to protect their families and their abilities to work and worship as they chose. In short, they struggled to protect their private lives, not to enhance their public standing.

## Demographics and Working Conditions

Before examining the lives of skilled slaves in early Richmond, some might find it helpful to know how many there were, what they did, and the conditions under which they worked. Early Richmond records allow only broad and general approximations of the number of slave craftsmen who worked there. A 1784 city census that listed free residents' occupations indicates that 41 percent of free white men (123 of 302) had skills. Twenty-two artisanal occupations were represented in this census, and households headed by white craftsmen included 34 percent of the small town's enslaved men.[10] Some highly specialized artisans (a goldsmith, two silversmiths, two chairmakers, and two watchmakers) worked in Richmond, but masons, woodworkers, tailors, and shoemakers predominated. Masons, joiners, and carpenters—construction workers who built the rapidly growing town—owned 62 percent (34 of 55) of the adult male slaves possessed by white artisans. Some of the slave men owned by artisans definitely shared their masters' skills, but the census did not list slaves' occupations, so it provides no way to determine how many did so. Attempts to estimate the total number of slave artisans are further complicated because not all slave artisans belonged to free craftsmen: in 1806 George William Smith, a prominent Richmond attorney, offered ten slaves for hire; they included a carpenter, a house servant, a stonemason and road paver, and a boy with experience in a tobacco factory. Clearly, some professionals invested in (or perhaps inherited) skilled slaves whose labor they hired out.[11] Assuming that the skilled slaves owned by non-artisans canceled out many of the unskilled adult male slaves owned by free craftsmen, the total number of slave craftsmen in Richmond might have very roughly approximated three-quarters of the total number of adult male slaves owned by free artisans in 1784. If these assumptions are correct, slaves comprised about 25 percent of Richmond's skilled labor force in 1784. This number would probably be much higher if semiskilled workers such as carters, draymen, and warehousemen were included.[12]

Though the 1784 Richmond City Census allows only crude speculation about the number of slave artisans at work in the city, it permits reasonable inferences about the various strategies chosen by free craftsmen to organize their labor forces and the uses they made of slave artisans. Wealthy building contractors invested in skilled bondsmen and built large work forces on whose expertise they could rely. Dabney Minor, a joiner, headed a household of fourteen adults. Three of them—his wife Anne and two slaves named Amy and Liddea—were women. Of the men, two were white apprentices, and eight were adult male slaves. Presumably Minor could lead a substantial ten-man gang to construction sites, or split up his force to work simultaneously on separate projects. As long as his slaves did not run away, Minor had a large, stable, and presumably skilled labor force. Similarly, the brick mason Henry Anderson's twelve-person household included at least ten people who probably worked at construction sites: Anderson himself, four white apprentices, a wagoner, and four adult male slaves. Anderson also owned a twelve-year-old slave boy who may well have been an apprentice. The carpenter Anderson Barrett paid personal property taxes on sixteen adult slaves in 1800.[13]

Other craftsmen chose different strategies. The joiner Samuel Ford headed an eleven-member household in 1784. He owned six slaves, but only one was an adult male. Unless his two slave women did carpentry work—and no evidence of female carpenters has survived in the Richmond records—then the five-man crew Ford probably led to construction sites included four white apprentices and his slave Ben. Ford invested far less than Minor in his labor force. Ford was also relatively free of the economic exposure that Minor faced if a valuable slave carpenter ran away or died. Perhaps he also faced fewer difficulties associated with forcing unmotivated laborers to work. On the other hand, his work force, composed predominantly of apprentices, must have been far less skilled than Minor's, and he periodically must have faced the frustration of replacing skilled workers in labor-poor Richmond.

Slaves who lacked craft skills also played important roles in artisanal household production. Some white craftsmen probably invested in slave women to increase their work forces. John Selate, a tailor, probably could not have afforded to invest in four skilled slaves, but he did own a woman named Molley. His household also included a journeyman and at least two, probably three, apprentices.[14] Catey Selate, John's wife, might not have been able to keep up with the demands of a household that included her husband, two young children, and four other males. Molley no doubt contributed greatly to the gardening, spinning, sewing, washing, marketing, and cooking, thus making it possible for the household to include several additional male artisanal workers.[15]

Slaves worked in a wide array of artisanal jobs in early Richmond. In 1784 enslaved men were included in households headed by tradesmen practicing thirteen different crafts. These crafts ranged from building trades (carpentry and masonry) to metalwork (blacksmithing and goldsmithing) to shoemaking, tailoring, and baking.

As Richmond grew, its economy developed, and the number of crafts practiced in the city increased. In the absence of city directories or censuses that listed occupations there is no way to know exactly how many occupations slaves pursued in the town. The court records and newspapers of Richmond from the period 1780–1810 specifically mention 183 male slaves, who among them practiced thirty-four different skilled occupations. Slaves worked at crafts that ranged from the quite specialized—sailmaking, making hats, and painting carriages—to the more basic (blacksmithing, carpentry, and driving wagons).[16] Many slaves had mastered more than one craft.[17]

Though Richmond slaves practiced a wide variety of crafts around the turn of the nineteenth century, they were not evenly distributed among those crafts. More than half of the identified slave craftsmen worked in the construction trades (carpentry, masonry, and related areas), in transportation (as sailors, wagoners, and draymen), or as coopers. While some slaves may have worked in high-prestige artisanal jobs such as goldsmithing or cabinetmaking, the records of personal property taxes paid by free Richmonders reinforce the data derived from newspapers and local court records. The largest slaveholder in Richmond in 1800 was the James River Canal Company, which paid taxes on thirty-three adult slaves. Many of those slaves may have worked at unskilled jobs, but digging the canal must have required many wagoners to haul dirt, as well as a corresponding number of carpenters to build locks, and wheelwrights and blacksmiths to keep equipment in working order. The next largest Richmond slaveholder was Moses Bates, a building contractor who paid taxes on twenty-nine bondsmen, most of whom surely worked on major building projects. Other large slaveholders included the building contractor Anderson Barrett (who owned sixteen slaves), the miller Joseph Gallego (who owned ten), and the blacksmith Richard Young (who owned twelve). Men pursuing more specialized crafts generally listed fewer slaves: the coppersmith John Taylor paid taxes on five slaves, the wheelwright Nathaniel Sheppard listed four, and the watchmaker William Richardson listed three.[18] Some of those slaves may have been coppersmiths or watchmakers, but many probably worked as domestic servants. The vast majority of slave artisans in Richmond at the turn of the nineteenth century, like the majority of free artisans, worked in basic construction, transportation, and clothing trades.

Slave artisans' working conditions in early Richmond are almost as obscure as their numbers. The composition of artisanal households recorded in the 1784 census indicates that most slaves working in the building trades worked at racially integrated sites alongside white artisans. Surviving records of early Richmond building sites ratify this finding and indicate that free black artisans worked at the same sites. When John Mayo rebuilt the bridge across the James River in 1800 and 1801, he employed a mixed labor force that included two slave "Masons, Sam and Harry," whom he hired from a Richmond widow; the carpenter "Frank Sheppard the [free] yellow man"; and the white plasterer Frederick Ayton.[19] Mayo's Bridge was an exceptionally large construction project—on one particular day, "70 hands [were] at work"—but integrated labor forces also built the houses and workshops that were the primary product of Richmond's construction industry. In 1801 Anderson Barrett contracted to build a shop for the hatters John and Jacob Fackler. As already noted, Barrett paid taxes on sixteen slaves in 1800, so slaves certainly helped with the "801 feet of shelving" used "in fitting oute a store room" and other jobs. But Barrett's slaves could not do all the work, so he also hired "Mr. [Ninian] Wise," a white craftsman, "for stone work," and the free black "John Sabe for plastering and whitewashing" and "for Iron work."[20] Similarly, in 1805, when the white carpenter Robert Means subcontracted work to the carpenter John P. Gordon, a mixed work force carried out the job. Gordon charged Means for "sawing out a parsel of window frames . . . at my Pit," for his own labor, for cash he paid Solomon "for 3 days work," for one day's "work of Gordon['s] Bob," and for several days' labor by white workers.[21]

Little surviving evidence sheds light on the quality of race relations at these integrated construction sites, but free and slave craftsmen probably worked together relatively harmoniously. Employers sometimes included among their building expenses cash spent on liquor.[22] Slaves, free blacks, and whites often drank together in Richmond's shops,[23] so it seems likely that they shared a few drinks during breaks from their work. Perhaps the most convincing evidence that free workers and slaves coexisted peacefully in Richmond's construction industry is the absence of any record of conflict. In eighteenth-century Charleston, South Carolina, by contrast, a wide assortment of white artisans left a clear record of opposition to slave artisans.[24] White Richmond shoemakers proved similarly willing to oppose the employment of black artisans: during the 1790s the self-styled "Journeymen Cordwainers of the City of Richmond" refused to work "for any person who had negro workmen in [his] employ." In 1802 the journeymen placed an advertisement in the *Virginia Argus* announcing their refusal to work for "John McBride . . . in consequence of his importing Boots, and employing Negroes . . . to the prejudice of our trade."[25]

The cordwainers' complaint may explain why white journeymen in some trades accepted slave co-workers while the shoemakers did not. Their complaint was not, after all, limited to McBride's employment practices. They also charged McBride with importing shoes "of an inferior quality, manufactured in New York."[26] Richmond grew rapidly between 1780 and 1810, and the housing needs of the growing population—combined with public construction projects (including the capitol and the state penitentiary), large commercial projects (including Mayo's Bridge and several merchant mills), and the need to rebuild houses that burned in the town's periodic fires—probably created greater demand for building tradesmen than town residents could meet. A similar situation probably prevailed among coopers. Richmond became a major center of Virginia's burgeoning grain trade during the last decades of the eighteenth century. The flour produced at the mills owned by Joseph Gallego and Thomas Rutherfoord had to be shipped in barrels. The demand for barrels was met by shops like that run by Michael Grantland. In 1798 Grantland advertised his desire to "hire . . . six or eight Negro Coopers and four or five Journeymen coopers."[27] Grantland expected slaves and white journeymen to work together in his shop. Doing so may well have been easier because of the brisk demand for barrels. The shoemakers, by contrast, worked in one of the first crafts to be heavily capitalized, and they faced competition from New York and Boston capitalists as well as from slave craftsmen.[28] As the demand for local shoemaking decreased, slave shoemakers became increasingly dangerous competitors, and white journeymen sought to exclude blacks from shoemaking. They also sought to discourage "journeymen from the North or from anywhere else" from moving to Richmond for fear that the "Town . . . [would become] greatly overstocked with Journeymen Shoemakers."[29] Racial antagonism among artisans appears to have hindered on-the-job cooperation between white and slave artisans only when work was scarce. That occurred in few trades around the turn of the nineteenth century, when Richmond was growing rapidly. This pattern suggests that early opposition to integrated artisanal work sites in Richmond grew out of straightforward fears of competition rather than concern that slave (or black) participation in a craft degraded that labor. That pattern would, of course, change during the course of the nineteenth century.

## The World View of Slave Artisans

More important than the conditions in which slave artisans worked are the ways in which they perceived the world they inhabited. Historians of early American labor have argued (or sometimes assumed) that preindustrial artisans identified with their crafts. Northern craftsmen took pride in their skills and in the things they produced. While they were journeymen they perceived themselves to be on a career path that would allow them to accumulate enough capital to open shops and become their own masters. Northern artisans developed an ethic of producerism and a world view that glorified personal independence. Their ideology eventually led them to support Jeffersonian Republicanism.

Few historians have searched for artisanal republicanism in states south of the Potomac.[30] Richmond's free white journeymen probably shared much of their northern brethren's world view. The city census takers in 1784 distinguished among masters, journeymen, and apprentices when listing the occupations of free residents. That contemporaries deemed such distinctions worth noting strongly implies an assumption that craftsmen could progress through the prescribed levels to master status. The "Journeymen Cordwainers of the City of Richmond" provide explicit evidence that at least some town artisans subscribed to the basic tenets of artisanal republicanism. The shoemakers had formed their organization "for the purpose of regulating the prices of work, Board, etc." In 1803 two charter members who had accumulated enough capital to open their own shops tried to hire journeymen at rates that undercut those set by the organization. The journeymen took out an advertisement expressing their disdain for the traitors as "men who have no Object beyond the accumulation of money."[31] These journeymen had a sense of community in their craft; they accused their former co-workers of having betrayed the brotherhood.

There is little reason, however, to suspect that enslaved artisans participated in this vision of artisanal republicanism. Propertied independence and republican citizenship remained beyond their reach. The 1784 Richmond census did not note which slaves worked as journeymen or were training as apprentices, because slaves could not follow the standard progression to master status. Artisanal slaves did, however, gain real advantages from their skills, and at least a few slaves rooted part of their personal identities in their occupations. Dick, a "good carpenter" who ran away from Dabney Minor, took "a band saw, jack and long plane," suggesting that he intended to continue working at his craft when free.[32] Naming practices provide clearer evidence of slaves' construction of personal identity, but they suggest a tenuous link between identity and occupation. Occasionally slaves took last names that reflected their work. One of the leaders of Gabriel's Conspiracy in 1800 was Jack Ditcher, a ditcher by trade.[33] More frequently, however, those slaves who took last names that have survived in the records appear to have taken the names of prominent white or free black families. The scanty surviving evidence strongly suggests that slaves used work skills to gain autonomy from their masters' households. Slave artisans could not head productive households built around artisanal shops. Instead, they used their skills to increase the social distance that separated them from their masters. That distance allowed Richmond-area slave artisans to take advantage of social and cultural opportunities offered in the growing town.

The first object pursued by many enslaved Virginia artisans during the post-Revolutionary era was to move to a growing town. Richmond served as a processing and transportation center for a large agricultural hinterland. The large mills, warehouses, wharves, and tobacco factories that grew up in town became centers for much work that was once done in the countryside. As the town grew, it absorbed many slave artisans from the surrounding countryside.[34] Some of these slave artisans belonged to master craftsmen and had moved to Richmond as part of established households. Others were hired out by rural masters to urbanites who needed skilled workers. Still others won the privilege of self-hire; they got to move to town and find their own housing, food, and work in return for a set weekly wage.[35]

Rural slaves had little control over the economic forces that pushed skilled workers into Virginia's growing towns, but they sought to use those forces for their own benefit. As Richmond grew it developed a great need for carters, wagoners, and draymen to transport goods to and from warehouses and wharves. Obviously, slave wagoners played only an indirect role in creating this need. Nonetheless, Bob, a Goochland County slave who belonged to Thomas Woodson, used the demand for wagoners to his advantage. Bob was, according to Woodson, an "honest and cerfull felow," and "as good a wagoner as any in richmond." In 1800, perhaps after taking some of Woodson's wheat to market, Bob reported to his master that he could "get 6 or 7 Dolers per month" working in town. He would also be able to live with his Richmond wife. Woodson needed money more than he needed Bob's labor on the farm, so he allowed Bob to hire out his own time. This arrangement was illegal, so Woodson asked a Richmond friend to "stand as marster" for Bob; but that only entailed collecting Bob's wages and keeping the slave from "being interupted when at his bisiness." Unfortunately, Bob was not "cerfull" enough: the Richmond authorities caught him, and the Hustings Court ordered that he be sold by the sheriff. As usually happened in these cases, however, the court rescinded the order to sell and "award[ed] the discharge of B[ob]" after he spent a month in jail.[36] Bob's story shows how slaves could make use of the urban demand for transport workers to influence where they were allowed to live, but it also reinforces the fact that skilled slaves remained slaves and subject to white power. Many other slaves from the Richmond area did the same thing as Bob; only a small minority were caught, and the court rarely sold those who were caught.[37]

Artisanal slaves' preference for urban life grew out of the greater opportunities for autonomy that the town offered. Virginia plantations were relatively small, and the number of slaves who lived on a single quarter rarely exceeded twenty or thirty. In Richmond, in 1800, more than two thousand black people lived within a little more than one square mile. Richmond authorities left ample evidence of the unease caused by slaves exploiting the social opportunities created by this demographic concentration. Richmond grand jurors complained of free blacks running disorderly houses, tippling houses, and gambling houses that catered to slaves. They pointed out the "evils" that resulted from "the toleration of such a number of vagrants, beggars, free negroes, and runaway slaves as daily infest[ed]" Richmond's streets. They decried the "negro dances where persons of all colors . . . too often assembled." They sought remedies for the "great disorders" caused by "negroes . . . who behave[d] in a very riotous manner, particularly on the Sabbath day," and for the "numerous collections of negroes and other persons" who gathered "(almost) every Sunday in the Street near such Houses (as we believe) supplies them with Spirits," and "engaged in Gaming, fighting and other disorderly Conduct." By 1799 disorderly people assembling "for the purpose of dancing at night" had "become very common throughout the City."[38] In short, urban life offered slave artisans more excitement and variety than did rural life. This excitement created among Richmond-area rural slaves a "custom to visit" town "every Saturday night."[39]

Implicit in white authorities' complaints about black behavior in Richmond is the assumption that slaves were insufficiently supervised. White authorities' fear of the lack of supervision had two related sources. Historians of slavery have long recognized that plantation slaves and masters struck an implicit bargain that respected the relative autonomy of slaves' communal life in the quarters.[40] On the one hand, slaves' freedom in town was no different from that in the countryside: when not working for their masters, their time was their own.[41] On the other hand, however, town life offered many new opportunities, and masters feared that unoccupied slaves could cause far more trouble in town than they did on the plantation. More important, whites feared the cumulative effect of so many slaves gathering together at night to drink, gamble, and dance. Grand jurors' complaints represent a fear for the maintenance of "proper order," but there is little evidence that the slave property of many masters was threatened by the autonomy of Richmond blacks' night life.

What then, did slave artisans seek to gain when they won the right to move to town? They certainly enjoyed urban social life, but town life offered enslaved urban artisans more than the opportunity to drink, dance, and gamble, as the story of John Russell illustrates. Russell, a slave carpenter, belonged to a New Kent County planter named Armistead Russell. In 1805 and 1806 Armistead Russell hired the slave to Anderson Barrett, the Richmond building contractor. When Barrett returned John Russell to his master on December 25, 1806, the slave ran away. He returned to Richmond ("where he [had] . . . a wife") and sent word to Armistead Russell that he would not willingly live outside of town.[42] Armistead Russell gave in and hired out John Russell to Barrett for a third year. At the end of 1807, John and Armistead Russell played out the same drama once again. Barrett returned John Russell, who promptly ran away. Armistead Russell advertised for his runaway slave. Unfortunately, the outcome of this struggle is unrecorded.

John Russell's story provides a rare glimpse into the inner world of a Richmond slave artisan. He was a carpenter. Given Anderson Barrett's apparent zeal to retain his services, he was probably highly skilled and industrious. But no matter his skill and industry, John Russell could not have risen any further as a carpenter. He used his skill to influence his master's choice of whom he would work for, but he would always work for someone. The opportunity to become an artisan-entrepreneur remained completely beyond the reach of slave craftsmen.

Armistead Russell's advertisements suggest that John Russell focused his ambition toward other kinds of independence. John Russell may well have enjoyed the active urban social life that Richmond offered slaves. Armistead Russell obviously suspected, however, that it was his slave's wife, more than the town's night life, that attracted John Russell. According to the second advertisement, John Russell's Richmond wife was "a free mulatto woman."[43] John Russell had married a free black woman and presumably had begun to raise a family of free children. Slavery prevented him from becoming the master of an artisanal workshop but perhaps not from becoming the patriarch of a free black family.

Marriages like John Russell's were, of course, extralegal, and there is no way to determine how common they were.[44] Other evidence shows that some Richmond slave artisans used their skills (or good relationships with their masters) to protect and stabilize families in the growing town. Many slaves who won their freedom while manumission was legal in Virginia used the money they earned through their skills to buy family members.[45] Nathaniel Anderson, a freed blacksmith who acquired his son Charles from Thomas Nicolson, set the young man free in 1804 as thanks for "exemplary faithfulness and industry and great good conduct."[46] The free black barber

John Kennedy manumitted Sally, a twenty-one-year-old woman, in 1792, and in 1796 the free black blacksmith Thomas Gibson freed Lucy, whom he owned "by virtue of a sale from . . . John Gibbons." Peter Hawkins, a free black man and early Richmond's only dentist, emancipated his "wife Rose . . . and . . . child called Mary" as a token of his "love and regard."[47] That slave artisans who won their freedom placed a high priority on protecting their families is shown by their buying and freeing their spouses and children.

Numerous advertisements seeking the return of runaways illustrate that family and friends were also important to black artisans who remained enslaved. "Bob a black smith by trade" left his Buckingham County master for "Richmond since he has relations there."[48] Ransom, a literate "tailor by trade," ran away to the place where "his father lives."[49] George, "by trade a blacksmith," belonged to Susanna Crenshaw. For several years prior to 1799 he was hired out in Richmond. Crenshaw then hired him out to a Hanover County man, but George ran back to Richmond, where he was "suspected . . . [of] lurking," presumably with his friends.[50] Conversely, town life might have little appeal to slaves forced to leave their families to work in the city: Lewis, a sixteen-year-old barber, ran from Richmond back to his home in King and Queen County, where "he ha[d] a mother."[51]

Some slave artisans, perhaps more ambitious, sought to escape slavery entirely, while others sought to improve their lives as slaves. A few fled from Virginia, usually by water. Richard James expected the "Mulatto Man" Jim Stovall, "a rough carpenter and coarse shoemaker," to "make his escape" from Richmond "by water."[52] Robert Gamble believed that his "BLACK MAN named Jackson, a House Carpenter," planned to use "false papers of freedom" to make "his way to the eastern states."[53] Others planned to pass as free within the state: David Logan felt certain that Robert, "a mulatto man . . . [and] a shoemaker by trade," had "procured a forged pass or free papers."[54] At least one slave blacksmith named Davy rejected the fugitive life of a runaway passing as free; he struck an agreement with a white "villain" with whom he had become "too familiar." Davy ran off with the villain, chose a new master for whom he preferred to work, and allowed himself to be sold.[55]

Advertisements for the return of runaways provide the clearest available evidence of slave artisans' values and goals, but they defy efforts to make simple generalizations. Runaway artisans pursued a wide range of goals; there is no clear distinction between their goals and those pursued by other runaway slaves.[56] In fact, what is most striking about the behavior of artisanal slaves in the Richmond area is the modest degree to which their skills shaped their outlooks.

Urban slave artisans, like other Virginia slaves, appear to have focused principally on family and, if the evidence from Gabriel's Conspiracy provides a key,[57] on religion, rather than on work, when constructing their personal identities. Urban social conditions offered many opportunities that rural slaves lacked; slave craftsmen used their artisanal skills to improve their chances to get to the city and enjoy those opportunities. But skilled slaves remained slaves, and lacking realistic opportunities to pursue advancement through their crafts, they developed an instrumental attitude toward their skills.

This does not mean that slaves failed to develop their skills, or that they took no pride in their work. One need only visit the capitol building in Virginia—a building that the slave carpenters discussed in this essay helped to build—or one of many other eighteenth- and nineteenth-century structures in Richmond to see that enslaved Richmonders displayed great mastery of their work. Nor should one assume that slave craftsmen lacked pride in their work. On the contrary, Richmond artisans were infamous among area whites for their haughtiness: one master explained that "as [his runaway shoemaker was] a proud negro, it is probable he may make for Richmond."[58] Similarly, some slaves derived satisfaction from their work: a runaway named Davy was described as "a very good blacksmith" who would probably seek employment "in that business as he was more fond of that than any other occupation."[59] But even very skilled artisans such as Davy apparently developed competence in several crafts. Slaves mastered as many skills as they could to make themselves as valuable as possible and thus to gain greater bargaining power against their masters. They used that power to win greater autonomy from whites, autonomy they used to pursue their private goals.

## Conclusion

How then do skilled slaves fit into the developing dominant interpretation of early American labor history? To a large extent, they do not. Northern artisans focused much of their energy on the public realm. They marched in parades, formed unions, joined parties, and insisted on their place in the young Republic. When the effects of economic development began to close down their access to social advancement and personal independence, they protested. As this essay shows, slave artisans did not—could not—do these things.

Richmond's slave artisans used their skills, and the bargaining power they gained because their skills were in short supply, to enlarge the private sphere. Theoretically slaves were mere extensions of their masters' wills; as chattel property they had no legitimate private realm. But the reality in all American slave societies proved more complicated. Slaves and masters struggled with each other to develop conventional boundaries to slaves' private lives. These bounds were not always respected, but slaves exacted a toll when masters violated them. The bounds also varied over time and space. Cities and towns, with their highly concentrated black populations and their high demand for short-term labor, enhanced skilled slaves' power in this unequal struggle over autonomy. Between 1780 and 1810 Richmond slave artisans used their enhanced power to carve out greater social space in which to raise families, worship their God, and develop a social life independent of their masters' supervision. On one level this says no more than that slave craftsmen retained greater kinship with unskilled slaves than with northern artisans. On another level, however, it can contribute to ongoing attempts to broaden historical understanding of the varied experiences of skilled working people in early America.[60] Skilled slaves were, after all, a major component of early America's skilled work force, but their experience of the social and economic changes affecting the United States in the early nineteenth century must have been very different from the experience that historians generally ascribe to northern free craftsmen. Slave artisans very likely welcomed the changes associated with the development of large-scale artisanal workshops. Unlike free artisans, they lost no avenue to social advancement, and they had long valued the increased social distance between journeymen and masters which came with large workshops.

Economic development also encouraged western expansion, another process that affected slave artisans much differently than it affected their northern counterparts. In the North, new territory offered new opportunity, and artisanal republicanism could easily develop into Republicanism based upon free soil for free labor. Opening the virgin cotton land in the southwest spelled disaster, however, for slave artisans. The South's cotton would be tended by slaves; after 1808 the slaves who were to work on the southwestern plantations legally could only come from the eastern slave states. When the price of cotton rose, even very skilled slaves became more valuable as plantation field hands than as urban craftsmen.[61] And, of course, when that happened slaves were ripped out of the autonomous worlds they had struggled to build in cities such as Richmond. Slaves caught in the brutal interstate slave trade suffered through forced family separations and horrifying uncertainty about the nature of the masters into whose power they or their family members would be sold.[62] The urban artisans who were sold to cotton planters also must have suffered through the loss of the social space that they had created within Virginia's towns. Labor historians must continue to expand their focus beyond northern seaboard cities in order to develop a fuller and more nuanced view of the lives of American artisans.[63] They must pay attention to the ways in which northern craftsmen differed from other American working people, in order to understand what working people shared. For despite all the differences between northern artisans and slave artisans which this essay reveals, important underlying similarities remain. Work skills comprised the most important possession of both free and slave artisans. Both groups sought to use those skills to gain a measure of control over their own lives, even though the contexts within which they did so were radically different. Paradoxically, the process that helped skilled slaves—the expanding scale of artisanal production—hurt northern artisans, while the opening of the West helped northern artisans but hurt slaves. Both groups struggled to determine their own destinies, and both groups increasingly lost those struggles as they came under the sway of large socioeconomic forces beyond their control.

# PART II

# EXPLORATIONS OF
# CLASS AND POLITICS

# 5

RONALD SCHULTZ

# Alternative Communities:
## American Artisans and the
## Evangelical Appeal, 1780–1830

O F THE MANY PARADOXES of the post-Revolutionary era, none touched the lives of American artisans more than the simultaneous rise of evangelical and working-class movements within the craft communities of the new nation. From the end of the Revolution to the beginning of the industrial era, Presbyterian, Baptist, and Methodist evangelists competed fiercely with the organizers of the nation's first working-class movements for the allegiance of America's artisans, calling on each craftsman to make his choice between God and the community of workingmen. The choice was not an easy one. On the one hand, the artisan's deep commitment to craft and small-producer traditions seemed to point almost naturally toward some kind of collective organization in defense of ancient rights and prerogatives. On the other hand, the compelling logic of evangelicalism focused the artisan's attention on personal redemption and the spiritual well-being of his fellow converts, leaving little time for other organized activities. Caught between these competing appeals, American artisans responded with a vigor that surprised many contemporaries and revealed the deep-rooted moral and religious commitments of the artisanal community. Drawing from their indigenous small-producer and religious traditions, early-nineteenth-century artisans forged their commitments to the evangelical community of faith or the community of class, but seldom both. This essay seeks to explore the reasons why this was so.

## The Moral Traditions of the Artisanal Community

In reality, two sets of moral traditions informed artisanal life in the late eighteenth and early nineteenth centuries. One was a tradition of small-producer thought which American artisans had inherited from their English predecessors; the other was a tradition of artisanal religiosity which historians have only begun to explore. During the years of colonial settlement and social consolidation that marked the seventeenth and early eighteenth centuries, these traditions intersected and supported one another, mutually reinforcing what were often similar doctrines in secular and religious forms. But with the gradual breakdown of America's craft communities in the aftermath of the American Revolution, and the arrival of an intensely competitive revivalism in the late eighteenth and early nineteenth centuries, common religious and temporal understandings were called into question, and the tenets of the small-producer and evangelical creeds became increasingly incompatible in the minds of a growing number of artisans. Thus, to understand the centrifugal pull of these competing claims on the artisan's post-Revolutionary allegiance, we must begin with the traditions themselves.

I have dealt with the question of artisanal moral precepts at some length elsewhere, but it is worth recalling that American artisans entered the post-Revolutionary world armed with a vital and well-articulated set of moral principles which guided their passage through America's age of transition. Having their immediate origins in the capitalist transformation of sixteenth- and seventeenth-century England, the artisans' small-producer traditions emphasized four interconnected precepts.[1] At its core was a simple statement of the labor theory of value, or more appropriately for the time, the social value of labor. As early as the twelfth century, English and European craftsmen had advanced the claim that their labor was alone responsible for the fabrication of the myriad goods upon which civilized society depended.[2] Placing themselves, in this way, at the center of national and community life, by the mid–eighteenth century artisans could claim with utter assurance that their labor represented the true axis of society and the very foundation of community well-being. The artisan felt pride in his labor because his work was indeed vital to the prosperity and proper functioning of his, and all other, communities in the developing nation.

Closely connected to the craftsman's idea of his own social importance was his claim to full political citizenship. English artisans had raised the issue of political inclusion during the popular phase of the English civil war, and as Edward Thompson has shown, the struggle for citizenship rights continued to be an integral part of the Anglo-American artisanal inheritance.[3] American artisans embraced this tradition with unbridled enthusiasm during their own Revolutionary era, and by the 1820s artisans in nearly every state had extended this tradition to include manhood suffrage and the right to hold elective office. Following the example of their counterparts in England, American artisans remained at the forefront of democratic movements well into the industrial era.[4]

As important as citizenship and labor were to artisanal thought, however, the centerpiece of the small-producer tradition was competency. Simply put, competency was the promise of moderate comfort and lifelong economic independence—the guarantee of a middling position in society— which an artisan expected to receive from his early acquisition of a skill and the lifelong practice of his trade. In a very real sense, an artisan who entered a trade felt himself to be entering into a moral covenant with his community; a covenant in which his life of productive labor would be rewarded by an independent position in the community and a life free from the social stigma of poverty and economic dependence. Competency was, in short, the just reward of skilled labor, diligently practiced in the interest of family and the local community.

The final component of the small-producer tradition was community. For the artisan, the virtues of labor, competency, and citizenship were scarcely imaginable without the existence of close-knit craft and local communities. In an era when markets were local and production was mostly for known customers rather than anonymous ones, the custom and clientage of the community lay at the very heart of the artisanal way of life.

Although every craftsman recognized the communal basis of his trade, artisanal ideas about community went well beyond the everyday experience of the shop and neighborhood to encompass more abstract notions of right. For artisans, a good society was like a well-adjusted trade: it required the subordination of individual self-interest and personal acquisitiveness to the collective well-being of the whole. Just as artisans expected a corporate ethic to govern affairs in the shop, so too they expected it to prevail in the community at large. A virtuous community was one that was governed with a spirit of fairness and equity; a place where each individual labored not only for himself but, in the end, for the collective benefit of all.

Down through the early nineteenth century, American artisans lived out their lives informed by these small-producer precepts and applied these precepts within the immediate context of a close-knit community that provided a livelihood, a source of credit, a sense of collective identity, and help whenever death, illness, or hard times struck. As first revolution, and then the growth of commercial and industrial capitalism, disrupted the lives of these artisans, it was to their communities and their distinctive value system that they instinctively turned for understanding, support, and immediate relief. Yet even as they turned to the prodigious resources of their communities and to those communities' critical moral code, American artisans also drew upon a less secular tradition.

A distinctive artisanal religiosity had emerged from the ferment of church reform and popular religious dissent in late medieval England. Beginning in the late fourteenth century, John Wycliffe's indictment of unreformed priests and the hierarchical church quickly attracted an artisanal following and helped establish Lollardy as the popular foundation of English Dissent. Repression drove the Lollard tradition underground during much of the fifteenth century, but as episcopal court records in the south and east of England reveal, craftsmen formed the largest group of those caught up in the church's anti-heretic campaigns.[5] The equation of artisans and religious radicalism continued into the sixteenth century, so that by the time Elizabeth ascended the throne in 1558 the main tenets of the nineteenth-century evangelical program—free-will Arminianism, individual reading and interpretation of the Bible, and the holding of conventicles among the converted—were already well-established hallmarks of a characteristically artisanal religious tradition.[6] The seventeenth-century Baptists, with their large artisanal following and notoriously heretical opinions, were merely consolidating a tradition when they chose separatism over "a national church tainted with relics of popery and too lax in its admission of the ungodly to communion."[7]

These ideas found their way to America in the minds of immigrating artisans who brought their small-producer and dissenting traditions with them to the New World.[8] Although the seventeenth and eighteenth centuries remain a dark age in our understanding of artisanal religiosity, ample evidence survives to indicate a continuing religious tradition among America's urban craftsmen in the colonial era.[9] Certainly many religious controversies of the era, such as the Keithian dispute in late-seventeenth-century Pennsylvania and Leisler's rebellion in turn-of-the-century New York, were fueled by artisanal religious partisanship; and the remarkable success of George Whitefield's eighteenth-century urban revivals would not have been possible without heavy artisanal support.[10] At a more mundane level, at the end of the eighteenth century, a period well before the rise of serious urban proselytization, more than three-quarters of the recorded marriages in Philadelphia's Lutheran churches involved men of artisanal rank. And in the city's three Presbyterian churches, more than half of the identifiable congregants were craftsmen in the manufacturing trades.[11] If artisans were not always church members during the seventeenth and eighteenth centuries, religion nonetheless played an important role in their moral lives.

Perhaps the most important, and unnoticed, indication of artisanal religiosity was the ubiquitous and detailed knowledge of the Bible and biblical themes found among all ranks of American craftsmen. Biblical themes and references dominated the primers that were used to educate children in New England, and the Bible itself was a favorite text for teaching basic literacy throughout the colonial and early national periods.[12] Indeed, it was this widespread knowledge of Christian principles among American craftsmen that helped make Paine's *Common Sense* a popular success in 1776 and caused his public downfall when he renounced Christianity in *The Age of Reason* nineteen years later.[13]

## The Response of Artisans to the Evangelical Appeal

When Baptists, Methodists, and evangelical Presbyterians made their distinctive appeals to the nation's artisans in the early national period, it was to a people already well prepared. Preaching in storefront churches, in rented meeting halls, and on local street corners, urban evangelists carried the message of Christ to the nation's craftsmen. Drawing on the simple and direct style developed by George Whitefield in his celebrated revivals of the 1740s and 1750s, these urban itinerants met with comparable success a half century later. It was with a feeling of moral righteousness and religious vindication that growing numbers of early-nineteenth-century evangelists looked out on congregations swollen with men and women from the nation's laboring classes.

This heartfelt response of America's artisans ran the geographic gamut from Baltimore, where by 1815 nearly two-thirds of the men in the city's Methodist congregations were artisans and journeymen, to New York City, where mechanics formed a majority of men within Methodist congregations as early as 1786.[14] Only Boston escaped the spreading wave of evangelical enthusiasm, allowing the shoemaking town of Lynn to become the center of early New England Methodism.[15] The reasons for the lack of evangelical enthusiasm on the part of Boston artisans are themselves instructive, and had little to do with religious indifference. As Aaron Hunt, an early Methodist preacher, explained, the Methodists' lack of success among Boston artisans had its roots deep in the religious culture of New England: "We were opposed [in New England] by infidels and Universalists, but also by our Calvinistic brethren, who considered us intruders, warning their people against us as deceivers, frequently after our preaching, and sometimes interrupting us while preaching."[16]

The Congregational establishment especially sought to exclude evangelical interlopers from Boston, and from New England as a whole. In 1793 a locally prominent Congregational minister offered this typically condescending advice to Thomas Ware, a Methodist itinerant on the Pittsfield circuit. "My advice to you sir," the minister admonished, "and to your itinerant brethren, is, to desist from disturbing the order of things among us. We want none of your instruction; and, indeed, you are not competent to instruct us. We have learned and able ministers, and all the necessary means of grace among us, and we do very well without you."[17]

If Boston and much of New England followed their own religious traditions, however, turn-of-the-century enthusiasm gained in force throughout the rest of the country. By the 1820s not only the Methodists, well known for their aggressive proselytizing and the active involvement of the laity in propagating the movement, but also the Presbyterians and Baptists, supported churches in laboring-class districts. As with the Methodists, working craftsmen made up the majority of men in these newly formed congregations.[18] In Philadelphia, to take only one example, the proportion of workingmen among males in the city's New Light Presbyterian congregations grew from slightly less than 40 percent in 1804 to a dominant 77 percent during the 1830s, a proportion only slightly below that of Quaker City Methodists in the latter decade. In America's cities, artisans, journeymen, and mariners were a powerful force in the creation of the evangelical movement.[19]

## The Power of the Evangelical Appeal

This evangelization of turn-of-the-century artisans has generally been explained in one of three ways. In one view, more closely associated with the English than the American case, artisans turned to evangelical religion as a kind of spiritual compensation for the declining fortunes of the craft system and the precipitant decline of their unique way of life. In this sense, early-nineteenth-century Methodism represented what the late Edward Thompson termed a "chiliasm of despair."[20] In the second, largely American, view, enterprising artisans saw in evangelical religion both a warrant for upward mobility and a badge of entrepreneurial "respectability" in the early industrial age.[21] And in the third view, evangelical religion is portrayed in a dual light, not only as a cultural quiescent imposed on American craftsmen by employers in search of a pliant workforce but also as a tool used by the middle-class generally, as a potent means of disciplining the growing numbers of "masterless men" created by the early phases of commercial change and industrialization. From this perspective, religion served to reestablish social control in an age when family and traditional social bonds were in an active stage of decay.[22]

There are elements of truth in all of these positions, and together they point to the complexity of evangelical sentiment in an age of fundamental social transformation. Yet they also miss the heart of the matter. Absent from these views is the perspective of the artisan himself and, most importantly, an understanding of the complex interaction between the indigenous culture of America's artisanal communities and the new evangelical movements of the early nineteenth century. Evangelicalism might have been a source of spiritual compensation and a justification for social control and upward mobility, but it could have been none of these things without the moral foundations provided by the artisanal community itself.

The artisanal community and the small-producer and religious traditions that provided its moral underpinnings are central to any understanding of artisanal evangelicalism in the early industrial era. The half century between 1780 and 1830 was an age of intense cultural experimentation, when new ideas flourished and old ideas were refurbished or summarily discarded. The Christianization of the American people was, as Jon Butler has pointed out, one of the greatest of these experiments.[23] Following the lead of the ever-present Baptists and Methodists, established denominations such as the Presbyterians created evangelical wings, while new sects such as the Churches of Christ and the Mormons competed with one another to bring ordinary Americans to God's table.[24] The resulting complexity of religious confession was at times numbing, as old and new congregations split over seemingly trivial matters of doctrine, and breakaway ministers sought to build whole new denominations on the bedrock of voluntary baptism, universal salvation, or even the existence of distinctive male and female deities.

Yet through all of this diversity, two approaches addressed the latent religiosity of America's artisanal communities. One approach appealed to the intellectual side of artisanal culture and offered a religious rationalism stripped of the burden of election and eternal damnation that had driven so many away from Calvinistic Protestantism, not only in New England but in the mid-Atlantic and western states as well. Emerging in rural New England during the height of the Revolutionary crisis, this anti-Calvinist path was best represented by the early Universalists.[25] As Universalist churches emerged in America's urban centers at the turn of the nineteenth century, artisans and journeymen flocked to hear their message of democratic salvation and to embrace the Universalist image of a tolerant and benevolent God. Rational and humane yet firmly Christian in spirit and doctrine, the Universalists offered an alternative to old-style Calvinism and radical Deism which resonated deeply with the small-producer tradition and the diffuse Christianity of the artisanal community.

We can see this appeal most clearly in the Universalist hymnody, a body of song which was at once an expression of religious sentiment and a vehicle of spiritual instruction. One of the hymns it contained, Abner Kneeland's "Invitation to the Gospel," captures the laboring-class voice of early Universalist hymnody with special poignancy.

Hear ye that starve for food,
By feeding on the wind,
Or vainly strive with earthly good,
To fill an empty mind.

The Lord of Love has made,
A soul reviving feast,

And lets the world, of every grade,
To rich provision taste.[26]

With their imagery of sufficiency and social leveling, hymns such as this held an obvious attraction for urban craftsmen caught in the uncertainties of the declining craft system and searching for a friendly acknowledgment of their most pressing concerns. Yet the Universalists went further than this diffuse populism, directing many of their hymnodic messages to the artisan's distinctive moral code. Elhanan Winchester's popular "America's Future Glory and Happiness," for example, focused on the artisanal notion of competency and economic independence.

No more the labour'r pines, and grieves,
For want of plenty round;
His eyes behold the fruitful sheaves,
Which make his joys abound.[27]

In the end, what the Universalists offered was a community of love which in many ways echoed the solidarity of the nation's developing journeymen's benevolent societies, as well as the traditional mutuality of the larger craft community. It was here that Universalist hymnody best mirrored the contemporary sentiments of American artisans and gave a new voice to their most deeply held values.

How sweet is the union of souls,
In harmony, friendship and love;
Lord help us, this union to keep,
In *union* God grant we may meet.[28]

This was written at a time when the nation's journeymen were hotly debating the value of trade union organization, and the idea of union expressed here effectively linked together the three communities of craft, church, and early trade union.

In Philadelphia, the Universalist appeal went deeper still, moving beyond ideology toward organization. In the early nineteenth century, Quaker City Universalists drew much of their laboring-class support not only from their willing acceptance of and participation in artisan culture but also from their support for the emerging workingmen's movement.[29]

Almost from its inception, Philadelphia's First Universalist Church had been a meeting ground for the early leaders of the city's laboring-class movement. For the next thirty years, the city's two Universalist churches regularly opened their halls to journeymen, inviting them to discuss the pressing economic and political issues of the day and providing them with meeting rooms for their weekly society meetings. It was only fitting that when the militant Philadelphia shoemaker William Heighton preached his vision of a citywide trade union and a workingmen's party that would restore American artisans to their former power and independence, he did so from the meeting room of the Southwark Universalist Church. In a very real sense, rational religion was the handmaiden of the formation of Philadelphia's working class.

In Philadelphia, the workingmen's movement drew together the older elements of small-producer thought and artisanal religiosity to create a new community patterned on the traditional values and substance of the past. By accepting the essential lineaments of this community, Universalism was able to give new form and direction to the religious sentiments of the city's artisans and transform rational anti-Calvinism into a reservoir of support for the emerging working-class movement.

The rational religion of the Universalists was not the only path that American artisans followed to salvation, however. Equally prominent was the alternative offered by urban evangelism. In the postwar years, Baptist, Methodist, and Presbyterian evangelists opened the doors of Christian brotherhood to America's working people with a degree of success that would have been scarcely believable only a generation before. What accounted for such quick success on the part of America's evangelicals? Or put alternatively, what kept the bulk of American craftsmen from finding religious brotherhood among the Universalists, whose doctrines and demeanor so closely paralleled their small-producer creed?

The answer is as complex as artisanal religiosity itself. One part of the answer lies in the pessimism and anxiety that Max Weber long ago noted as an essential consequence of Calvinism.[30] By the end of the eighteenth century, the notion that the majority of humankind faced perpetual damnation had lost its moral force; in fact, to many, the idea of eternal damnation itself ran counter to the republican and democratic notions of the age. As a popular doctrine, predestination had begun to unravel in the revivals of the 1730s and 1740s, and it left a populace with vivid notions of brimstone and damnation, but with strongly individualistic notions of the mechanics of salvation. In 1792, to cite but one example, the Methodist itinerant William Colbert found Arminian beliefs and anti-Calvinist attitudes widespread among the common people of Pennsylvania and New York. Many along his circuit subscribed to the unsettling idea that no one would be condemned who had experienced a true personal conversion, and many more agreed with a Pennsylvania man who declared that "there was no such thing [as perfection] in the world [for] none could live without sin."[31]

It was from these disintegrating remnants of Calvinist predestinarianism that evangelicals built their popular appeals. In doing so they drew upon lingering fears of damnation and the promise of personal salvation; but mostly they drew upon experience. Whether educated or simply unlettered, newly certified evangelical preachers such as George Peck were counseled "not to mind principle but to preach experience" and to use the "aphorisms and sarcasms [that] were more telling upon common minds than the severest logic."[32] The kind of religion that the evangelists offered was laden with wondrous experience, at times even bordering on the supernatural. In the 1790s, for example, it was widely believed that the Methodist preacher Valentine Cook had "the power of enchantment" over people, and indeed one Methodist itinerant described the "strange tremor [that] pass[ed] over him" as Valentine sang to his congregation. "There," he wrote in terms that remind us that, in the popular mind, religion and the occult had not yet parted company, "the witchery is coming."[33]

The real power of evangelicalism, however, came not from residual occultism but from the evangelical movement's emotional connection with artisanal religious sentiment. The tradition of artisanal dissent, reinforced by the power of the eighteenth-century revivals, had taught artisans to demand an intensely personal and emotional religious experience. As one Methodist recalled, people expected "tornadoes," and if a preacher "did not break down everything before him" he would not long have a congregation.[34] Sometimes this was meant literally, as when the New York itinerant "Father Turck" would "clap his hands, and lift up his chair and dash it down on the floor, and call for the power until he made everything move."[35] Most often it meant a class meeting where the committed made "considerable noise" in praying, singing, and shouting, and followed their testimony with a love feast or collective dinner.[36]

Thus, for the urban artisan, post-Revolutionary evangelicalism held forth the prospect of a new kind of community, one that could address the emotional anxiety fostered by uncertain times while it supported traditional concerns about social status and respectability. Class meetings, love feasts, and spontaneous testimony gave workingmen and their families the freedom to express their deeply felt apprehensions about the declining craft system, at the same time that they provided a positive experience of solidarity and mutual assistance which the craft community found harder to supply.

More than anything else, what artisans sought in evangelical religion was what was missing from their daily lives: a community that offered them mutual support and a sense of purpose as they worked out the increasingly difficult details of their everyday lives. In the end, the sense of personal connection and mutuality that was absent in the new capitalist workplace might be recovered in the congregation and the weekly class meeting. A nineteenth-century mariner described the personalism of the evangelical appeal with great poignancy: "When a man is a-preachin' at me," he told an itinerant evangelist, "I want him to take somert hot out of his heart and shove it into mine,—that's what I calls preachin'."[37] It was by creating a profoundly personal experience of redemption which both encompassed and redefined traditional notions of community and religious life that urban evangelists drew artisans into the evangelical fold. By offering a collective setting for an otherwise individualistic religious experience, evangelicalism created an alternative community that drew from the traditional artisan community at the same time that it formed its very antithesis.

In the end, this search for personal redemption and renewed collective identity went far toward explaining the power of the evangelical appeal. As the nation's craft communities divided into entrepreneurial and working-class factions, and as mounting immigration ignited racial and ethnic strife, evangelicalism offered a way out. By redirecting popular fears and religious sentiments into strict denominational channels, the evangelical movement created communities of faith potentially as powerful and cohesive as the artisanal communities of the past.

## The Conflict between the Evangelical and Workingmen's Movements

This evangelical commitment, of course, came at a price. By forging its own community bonds, evangelicalism drove a wedge into existing artisanal communities. The easy coexistence of small-producer and dissenting traditions which had characterized the seventeenth and eighteenth centuries came apart in the early nineteenth century, driven asunder by the force of ideological competition. Firmly rooted in the moral traditions of the artisanal community, the evangelical and trade union movements arrived at opposite destinations during the 1820s. Fixing their attention on secular concerns—work stoppages, wage reductions, and political representation—the trade union movements of the 1820s admitted religion as an important but subordinate partner. For trade unionists such as Philadelphia's William Heighton, religion was indeed an essential component of the workingmen's movement, but only a Christianity that was rational, nondenominational, and untainted by evangelical aloofness would do.[38] The emotional appeals of city evangelists were, for him, only self-serving abstractions that had little to do with the concrete problems of the nation's workingmen.[39] Rationalist ministers were a welcome part of the movement because they had a vital moral role to perform. But the competitive denominationalism of Methodist, Baptist, and Presbyterian evangelists threatened to divide the working-class community and dilute the power of the workingmen's movement in the process. The workingmen's movement could accommodate religiosity, but not the divisive demands of early evangelicalism.[40]

The reason for this growing incompatibility lay in the nature of the evangelical movement itself. Unlike the more established evangelicalism of subsequent years, the early-nineteenth-century movement demanded near-total commitment on the part of its adherents. For the artisanal convert, the most important thing in his life became his faith, his conversion, and his fellow confessionalists. For the moment, at least, little else mattered. The evangelical focus on eternity did not leave much room for the concerns of the moment, and the convert's world soon became bounded by an epochal contest between God and Antichrist. This was especially true for the Methodists, for conversion was never permanent, and the snares of sin and temptation lay everywhere. Like Christian, the seeker-hero of *Pilgrim's Progress,* the evangelical artisan walked an exceedingly narrow path through an increasingly hostile and degenerate world. With his eyes fixed firmly on the path of righteousness, he had little time for politics, the tavern, or especially, the journeymen's society and the trade union. The end result was the kind of divided community that Heighton and other labor leaders feared. Trade unionism and emotional religion would walk separate paths during the early decades of the nineteenth century, and in so doing they would deprive American artisans of the united community they so earnestly desired.[41]

In the generation after 1830, the fires of spiritual awakening that had animated the early decades of the nineteenth century succumbed to the power of middle-class respectability, organization, and institutionalization. The evangelical landscape of the antebellum years continued to be marked by enthusiasm; but for the most part its early, rough-hewn passions had been effectively channeled and controlled. In this atmosphere of diminished spontaneity, Philadelphia evangelists won growing numbers of working-class men and women to their quiescent vision of community, hobbling the city's labor movement in the process.[42] New York City witnessed a brief revival of rational religion among the city's journeymen and small masters at the end of the 1820s, but the evangelical temperance movement of the 1830s had a larger and more powerful appeal.[43] And during the 1830s and 1840s, New England working people found in antebellum evangelicalism a challenge to traditional authority, but also discovered that it sanctioned long hours and exacting factory discipline.[44] Thus did the early-nineteenth-century contest between the nation's artisanal and evangelical communities continue to cast its shadow across pre–Civil War America.

# 6

TERESA MURPHY

# The Petitioning of Artisans and Operatives:
## Means and Ends in the Struggle
## for a Ten-Hour Day

IN THE SUMMER OF 1844, the Mechanics Association of Fall River, Massachusetts, gave Simon Hewitt one hundred dollars to tramp the countryside of New England, arousing support for a ten-hour day. As Hewitt moved through Essex County and the Blackstone Valley of Massachusetts; around Narragansett Bay, in Rhode Island; and along the Connecticut River Valley to New London, he encountered a variety of laboring conditions and responses to his call for both a shorter workday and a regional convention of workingmen. Workers in the building trades, shoemakers, and textile operatives, he found, lived in very distinct social and economic environments. One of the most important challenges in organizing a regional labor movement lay in devising methods of communication and strategies of action which could successfully unite all groups. Labor activists were divided on at least three levels. Not only were local patterns of industrialization different, but skilled workers did not view semiskilled industrial workers as their equals. This latter distinction, moreover, was strongly reinforced by differences of gender.

Bringing these different groups together was not inconceivable, however. Artisans and factory workers had united a decade earlier in the New England Association of Farmers, Mechanics, and Other Workingmen; and in many ways, the organization of the 1840s was its direct descendent. Local organizing took place by community rather than by trade, for example, except in the big cities. Good moral character rather than wage-earning status was the primary requirement for membership. And criticisms of economic exploitation were closely linked to questions of cultural control. Nonetheless, there were some important innovations in the later movement. The New England association of the 1830s had tried to organize a regional strike, but had failed; the New England Workingmen's Association of the 1840s es-

chewed strikes and focused instead on petitioning. The regional organization of the 1830s had been exclusively male; that of the 1840s was a coalition of men and women. Indeed, the ability to build a coalition across gender lines was closely related to the strategy of petitioning. Petitioning
campaigns did not provide the dramatic and confrontational street theater
of a strike, but the form had become increasingly radicalized and politicized
as a result of the antislavery petitioning campaigns of the 1830s. More important, the meaning of petitioning could vary depending on whether one
was petitioning for oneself or for others and whether the petitioner was a
man or a woman. During the 1840s, as labor protest became a full-fledged
wing of the reform impulse, the labor movement inherited this complex
perspective on petitioning. These varying interpretations of petitioning
were particularly important for labor organizing because they provided
enough elasticity to allow groups that otherwise would have been divided
to work together.

## Confronting Local Differences

In April 1844, approximately 250 carpenters and masons in Fall River
agreed to work on a ten-hour system. They formed a Mechanics Association and started a labor newspaper, the *Mechanic.* Their group may have included some contractors as well as wage earners, but it seems to have been
confined to the building trades in its early days. Building trades workers in
Fall River were particularly sensitive to the length of their workday that
year, and were in a position to do something about it. The town had burned
down the year before, and a massive building campaign was under way. Carpenters and masons were being pushed to work more than usual, but they
also held more bargaining leverage than was common. This position of
economic strength no doubt aided them in taking a strong position against
strikes and physical coercion. They argued that they were merely honoring
a pledge not to work more than ten hours a day and that they were committed to principles of moral suasion. But the commitment to moral suasion was more than a rhetorical ploy.

Concern for both morality and salvation was to pervade the language of
labor organizing in Fall River. Thus, when the tools of "all day" men re-
cruited from Maine mysteriously ended up in Mount Hope Bay, the Mechanics Association vociferously condemned the perpetrators. One of the
resolutions that were passed stated: "We will be bold and uncompromising
in advocating the cause in which we are engaged, claiming for ourselves the
use of that MORAL POWER which is mighty to overturn long cherished systems of oppression and wrong, and to tumble into dust those false gods to
which the rights of many are offered as sacrifice." They also went on to sug-

gest that the destruction had come from those opposed to the association, "in order to cast a stigma upon the upright, manly and straight forward course which we have thus far pursued."[1]

However, this moral reform strategy provided a model for exclusion rather than inclusion. Implicit in the organization of the Mechanics Association was the exclusion of factory workers, whose yearly contracts and company housing made taking the ten-hour pledge far more devastating economically. In part, the reluctance of the mechanics to embrace factory workers may have been dictated by practical concerns: the need for carpenters and masons to rebuild the town gave members of the building trades a leverage that factory workers did not have. But it is also clear that the artisans regarded factory workers as a dependent population that was incapable of helping itself, the antithesis of those pursuing an "upright, manly and straight forward course." An editorial in the *Mechanic* noted that many operatives in Fall River had complained that the shorter workday was limited to members of the building trades. "It is to be regretted that it is so. But who is to blame?" the editor pointedly asked the factory workers.[2] "P.," who wrote to the *Mechanic* during the summer of 1844, asked, "Is there not some American Sadler, Oastler or Ashley who will rise and defend the factory woman and child? Among the factory owners are there no American Woods and Fieldings, who, though interested in the factory system, will come out nobly for a ten hour's rule?"[3] He was, of course, referring to the English reformers. Mechanics throughout New England had followed the British factory debates that were reprinted in labor newspapers such as the *Mechanic,* and had cheered the benevolence of the men who had striven to limit the workday of factory operatives. They were also quite aware of the portrait of factory workers which had emerged in these debates: one of immorality, helplessness, and dependence. In a series of articles run by the *Mechanic,* "N.N." drew a similar portrait of factory operatives in the United States. He described the factory girl as "a wasteful, tawdry, slatternly person." Faced with reproach from local operatives, he warned them "not to demand proofs of the defects in their education; these are too obvious to be denied."[4]

There was a recognition among many mechanics in Fall River that factory owners controlled the building trades as well as textile production; but this did not lead the mechanics inevitably to embrace operatives as partners in the struggle for a shorter workday. In the early phases of their movement the mechanics sought a coalition with masters rather than factory workers. "P.," for example, claimed that the mechanics knew that "their greatest enemies are the corporate companies." However, rather than turning to operatives to form a coalition, he claimed that he "had hoped that some of the petty boss carpenters, for whom the ten hour system would have wrought real good, would have embraced the opportunity of elevating themselves. But, *slave like,* they kiss the hand that smites them."[5]

Although the mechanics in Fall River did not extend their demands to include operatives, they still sought operatives' support—unsuccessfully. Ruby Hatch, the wife of Gideon Hatch, called the women of the town to her house on May 7 to form an auxiliary, the Fall River Ladies Mechanic Association, "for the benefit of the Ten Hour system in this place." Placing an ad in the *Mechanic,* she urged all the women in town to join, particularly "those who work, or ever have worked."[6] Many women responded to the invitation, but not all. Whereas family members of artisans were anxious to join, female operatives were not. "Onward," who attended the first meeting, tried to garner the support of wage-earning women after the first meeting by asking, "Who . . . in this wide world, can sympathize with the ten hour man in his struggle to breathe—a *freeman*—if you cannot?"[7] Apparently it did not occur to "Onward" to ask the artisans if they could sympathize with operatives, who might also want to breathe; his assumption was that the movements must be carried on separately.

This relationship (or rather, lack of one) between artisans and operatives would be challenged as the mechanics began to interact with working people from other towns. The Mechanics Association issued a circular in June 1844 to other artisans in New England, calling for a regionwide convention that would "point out a 'more excellent' system of labor." It was at this point that they hired young Simon Hewitt, who was in between careers as a phrenologist and a Universalist minister, to promote their cause.[8] With one hundred dollars to pay for his expenses, Hewitt began his tour, speaking on the importance of a ten-hour day specifically, and the need to improve the condition of the laboring classes generally. Hewitt's background as a popular lecturer would serve him well, but he may have had a broader vision of the movement than did some of the mechanics in Fall River. Hewitt was a Fourierist, and for him the ten-hour day was but one step toward greater world reform, a reform that would touch everyone.

The reception Hewitt received varied tremendously from place to place. In the missives he sent back to the *Mechanic* in Fall River, Hewitt tried to make sense of the different intellectual and economic conditions he encountered while carrying the gospel of the Fall River mechanics. In the process of give and take which accompanied this exchange, working people throughout New England attempted to incorporate many of the ideals espoused in Fall River, while the mechanics who had sent Hewitt out were forced to confront different forms of industrialization as well as different types of organizing.[9]

One of the first stops Hewitt made was in Lynn. The Mutual Benefit Society of Journeymen Cordwainers in Lynn had corresponded with the Mechanics Association in Fall River and had invited the association's representatives to attend the society's meeting at the beginning of August. The society's initial letter had suggested a movement with similar moral inclinations. William A. Fraser, who was president of the Young Men's Total Abstinence Society as well as corresponding secretary for the Mutual Benefit Society of Journeymen Cordwainers, sent an enthusiastic response to the call for a regional meeting. "We are engaged in a highly important work, a work which recommends itself to every philanthropist," he claimed, "a work which will if carried out, help to redeem the world from poverty and all the vices now existing which arise from poverty." Defending the right of the shoemakers to be heard in their struggle, Fraser continued, "They claim the just and moral right, (a right, given them by their maker,) to live, move and have a being; a right to fair and honest compensation for their labor."[10]

What Hewitt found in Lynn, however, was a movement radically different from the one shaping up in Fall River. The cordwainers in Lynn were pieceworkers who had little to say about a shorter workday. Their demands centered around higher wages, tighter control of apprenticeship, and an end to the order system. And far from eschewing strikes, they were in the process of trying to organize one (an attempt that would ultimately fail). Given both the means and the ends chosen by the shoemakers, it is not surprising that Hewitt was a bit uncomfortable with the movement. He reported to the mechanics in Fall River with some concern that he had attended a convention in Lynn which had been called "for the special purpose of securing the interests of the craft," an approach that Hewitt implied was selfish and retrograde. He tried to alleviate concern by speculating that "at the same time a higher principle than mere interest seemed to lie at the foundation of the movement."[11] Still, in regard to the resolutions passed by the cordwainers, Hewitt was less than enthusiastic. Refusing to endorse them as "*absolute* truth or right," Hewitt nonetheless did find the measures "*expedient.*" Moreover, the shoemakers were ready to do what they could to support a regionwide movement. With this in mind, Hewitt tried to justify the activities in Lynn to his readers back home. "When we consider the disadvantages under which this class of Humanity are, and have for ages been laboring, we are not to feel surprised at all if in an assemblage of men like this, much is said and done which will not commend itself to the judgement of those who have enjoyed greater advantages."[12] It is not clear which disadvantages Hewitt was referring to, though he may have been alluding to the fact that shoemakers made less money than did building trades workers and thus had to pay more attention to wage issues.

The shoemakers pressed unsuccessfully for a strike during the summer of 1844, eventually gaining the support of about one-third of the male cordwainers in Lynn. As hopes for a strike began to fade in the fall, the moral reform rhetoric of the Fall River mechanics and the emerging New England Workingmen's Association began to assume more prominence. "Centre St.," for example, wrote an article for the *Awl* in November about how the truth and justice of their cause proceeded from God, but the article's religious content was very vague. The following week, an article was reprinted from the *Boston Laborer* which suggested that individual thought and investigation were prerequisites of effective action, a prescription that suggested a process similar to that of conversion. "Union is necessary, combined action is necessary, but this cannot be had, without unity of thought and feeling, and this can only be brought about by individual investigation."[13] A contributor named Depot made a similar point, as he tried to turn the failure to stage a strike into a success, or at least a cloud with a silver lining:

> More than six months since, we commenced a work of reform in this town, and believing a strike was necessary, we resolved upon that measure. But finding it imbossible [sic] to enlist a majority in this movement, and seeing at the same time it was only acting upon the effect, while the cause remained, we have abandoned the idea and resolved to strike deeper, at the root of the evil. Our object, be it understood, is *Moral* and *Social Reform*—to show up society and its evils in all its rottenness.[14]

As part of their attempt to create a moral reform movement, the cordwainers appealed for female support intermittently, and received it—intermittently. Like the mechanics in Fall River, who wanted the support of female operatives, journeymen shoemakers encouraged female shoebinders to attend their meetings and cheer them on. They did not, however, intend to fight any economic inequities the women faced.[15] The journeymen made a couple of appeals for female support early in the summer, perhaps in imitation of the Fall River organization, but after receiving no response they ignored the women during the next couple of months as they tried to organize a strike.

On August 17, the cordwainers voted "that each member be requested to bring a lady."[16] This move finally paid off in mid-September, when "Centre St." reported: "I was much gratified, on last Saturday evening, to see so large an attendance of *ladies* at the Town Hall. This is right; for certainly the females are as much interested in any undertaking, which has for its object the bettering of the condition of the males, as the males are themselves."[17] As in Fall River, women from Lynn focused on planning social activities during the winter months to raise money and build morale. During the course of the year, a large number of women gave their names and their time to the planning of festivities, which were well attended by the men and women in the town. Many of the women on the arrangements committee were probably wives, daughters, or sisters of the men in the organization, though actual linkages are difficult to establish. However, given the occupational homogeneity of Lynn during this time, there probably were not too many women outside the merchant class who did not have a husband, father, brother, or sweetheart employed in the shoe trade.[18]

While women joined the labor movements in Fall River and Lynn as auxiliary members to support a male cause, a very different relationship emerged between men and women in the labor movement in Lowell. Both men and women had signed the ten-hour petitions from Lowell which were sent to the Massachusetts legislature in 1843, but there is no evidence that they were part of the same movement (or that much of a movement existed, for that matter). Agitation started again in the spring of 1844, when workingmen in Lowell began meeting at about the same time as their counterparts in Fall River. Goodwin Wood was president of a meeting held on May 16 at the Lowell City Hall, in which the example of working men elsewhere in the state was declared a model for the mechanics in Lowell in their search for a ten-hour day. Moral suasion was important here, as in Fall River, for it was resolved "that we, in carrying out the 'Ten Hour System,' must act with moderation, kindness and love, yet decidedly and energetically; while our object should be in all possible ways to ameliorate and elevate the condition of those who have too long been oppressed by the heartlessness and avarice of combinations and individuals, we should not forget that we are dealing with men & brethren, whose errors we are not to imitate, but to reform."[19]

It is not clear whether or not women were present at this meeting. But at a meeting held in Anti-Slavery Hall in Lowell on July 9, women were explicitly invited to join. Moreover, they were welcomed not as family members who would be supporters of the male struggle, but as working women who had their own set of grievances. The idea of a household economy in which male and female workers were united in a common interest simply could not be sustained in a town where such a large part of the work force consisted of single, wage-earning women who were unrelated to the men in the work force. One of the resolutions passed by the men stated,

> We regard the present system of *piece-work* as practiced in our Factories, as unjust to the Operative, uncalled for by the present good times, and high dividends; and designed cruelly to hoodwink, oppress and grind the faces of the poor. And further resolved, that as the females in the Mills are our fellow sufferers, in this respect, we hereby invite them to co-operate with us in this glorious work of reform.[20]

Tying the issue of piecework to the ten-hour day, they further resolved "that we seek only that which is just and right, when we ask for a reduction of laboring hours to ten per day, and a corresponding advance on, or a total abolition of, this infamous system of *piece-work.*" In making this proposal, the workingmen no doubt intended to relieve any fears that female piece-raters might have had about the effect of a shorter workday on their monthly earnings. This concern for the wages of women may have had another source as well. According to *Vox Populi,* corporations in Lowell restored wages of male operatives to the level of two years earlier in March 1844, but did not do the same for women. This attempt to split the work force along gender lines may have been part of the problem the workers in Lowell were confronting.[21]

When another meeting of the Lowell Association took place at City Hall on July 30, women were present. They continued to attend local meetings and soon constituted a majority of the membership. Mike Walsh reported speaking to "a full audience of factory girls and workingmen, in the large Free Will Baptist Church, on the 22nd of October."[22] "D," a correspondent from Fall River, visited Lowell in November and reported that almost two thousand members, of whom three-quarters were women, belonged to the association.[23] In December, the movement split. The women formed their own organization and faced a precipitous decline in membership.[24] As Sarah Bagley later reported: "We had several [caucus] meetings, and the first week in January organized our association and adopted our Constitution. We then had two members besides our officers, which are thirteen in number, viz: a President, two vice-Presidents, Secretary, Treasurer and eight Directors. Since that time we have been gradually increasing and now number three hundred and four."[25]

For reasons that are not clear, the single-sex organization had to struggle in its early months to attract a following. Its members were dispirited and beleaguered according to "Juliet," who wrote in the *Voice of Industry* a year and a half later that "in Dec. 1844, a few humble individuals were seated in a badly lighted room, reviewing the past, and looking into the fearful future.—Sadness added to the gloom, and a storm raged without." Their reduced numbers may have been due less to their new form of organization than to outright intimidation by management. According to the reporter to the *Mechanic,* "the work of proscription has commenced and I know not where it will end.—The first victim was their worthy President, a man highly esteemed as a man and a christian." He had been fired for talking "ten hours too much among his fellow workmen." Employers also may have directly intimidated the women: when they met for their second meeting, "the number had lessened, for threatnings and fear had taken possession of their roving minds, and altho' they saw the right, those lacking moral courage could find an excuse to desert a cause, where there was little prospect of any compensation." It was apparently at this time that the group adopted the motto "Try again." Although the number of women officially enrolled in the Lowell Female Labor Reform Association was small, their petitioning campaign garnered a large number of names.[26]

The different kinds of support which women were willing to provide, indeed, their very presence, provoked problems for many of the men. Simon Hewitt had to learn very quickly not to take female support for granted, or to assume that women would naturally subordinate their interests to those of men. In Pawtucket, Rhode Island, for example, he issued circulars inviting the men of the town to hear him talk at the American Hall. He was disappointed to find, however, that although a good number of men turned out to hear him speak, women did not. Since he had seen women present at the Fall River meetings of the Mechanics Association, he was surprised to find that women elsewhere might not feel themselves included in an invitation addressed to men. Hewitt was most anxious that women should attend, "for females, in general, work harder than males," and he defended his omission by arguing, "I certainly supposed the *women* would feel themselves included, inasmuch as the 'woman is of the man' and not the man of the woman, and therefore I made no allusion to them." Hewitt assumed that women would occupy a subordinate position in the labor movement. Whether women in Pawtucket wished a place that was equal to or merely different from that of the men is unclear, but they seem to have been making a point about Hewitt's generic use of *man* and demanding separate recognition of their presence and support.[27]

The involvement of female operatives in places such as Lowell may have been one of the most important influences on the attempt that finally did develop among the Fall River Mechanics Association to try to attract mill workers. When the *Mechanic* announced that Simon Hewitt would speak in Fall River, it addressed the working women as well as the working men and cited the example in Lowell as inspiration. "It will be seen by the doings of the meetings in Lowell, which we copy from the Lowell *Operative*, that the people of that place have commenced the work in right earnest. We trust the laborers and operatives of Fall River will not be behind them, in preparing for the great contest which is to take place between Labor and Capital."[28]

"A Ten Hour Woman" suggested that the wives of Fall River mechanics might extend their concern in this direction as well, since many might have children who worked in factories. "This is a subject in which *mothers* should feel a deep and thrilling interest," she argued, raising the specter of factory employment. "There are few mechanics in our community whose children are not obliged to engage in a species of labor as destructive to the physical as it is crushing to the intellectual energies of their nature." Making a final plea to maternal instincts, she concluded, "Where is the mother of such a family whose heart has not ached for her little ones, as she calls them at early dawn, while they plead for a little more sleep."[29]

Asa Bronson, minister of the Baptist church, also gently nudged the Fall River mechanics to open up in July, but apparently to no avail. "Let me respectfully enquire," he began, "whether it would not be best, in order to accomplish these desirable ends, and reach these important objects, to so alter the present Constitution of the Society already formed, as to embrace all that are friendly to the *Ten Hour System* in and around this village, whether they can at present reduce that system to practice or not." If membership rules could not be bent, he suggested the creation of a companion organization to cooperate with the Mechanics Association.[30] In this vein, Simon Hewitt would also urge "upon the Mechanics and Laborers, now employed in the mills, to come together and form themselves into an Association, and help each other to better their condition."[31]

By the end of the summer, with mill workers responding elsewhere, several members of the Fall River Mechanics Association tried to form an Industrial Association. Inviting women as well as men to join, and calling themselves the Workingmen's Reform Association, they put forward a constitution allowing anyone to join who would pay twenty-five cents and sign the constitution. In an address to the workingmen of Fall River the following week, supporters of the movement stressed their growing recognition of a need for unity. Bad working conditions existed, they pointed out, "because we have not, hitherto, been united; and in this has been our weakness. We have neglected to commune with each other upon the subject of our wrongs, and upon the best means of obtaining our *rights*. . . . A portion of the workingmen of Fall River have resolved to act, and to all others we would say, will you act with us?"[32] The movement never got off the ground. While mechanics in Fall River were interested in unity, they did not specifically address the problems that might be peculiar to some of the factory workers. There was no discussion of the effect of a shorter day on piece rates, for example, as there had been in Lowell.

The mechanics in Fall River were haltingly coming to terms with the significance of factory life in shaping their artisanal experience, a significance that became more apparent as they attempted to interact with mechanics in towns that were less industrialized or had different patterns of industrialization. Simon Hewitt ran into problems in several places. In Worcester, only about 50 people showed up to hear him talk, and none of those would speak at the meeting. In New London, where a ten-hour day already prevailed, Hewitt found a great deal of apathy among workingmen "in regard to the higher objects of our movement." Although he had written to veteran labor reformer Charles Douglass to let Douglass know of his arrival, no meeting hall was made available to Hewitt. The shoemakers of Milford, Massachusetts, a farming and shoemaking community, also showed little enthusiasm for the cause. About 125 people attended Hewitt's lecture, but they voted not to act. Hewitt found them far more "independent" in their working conditions than he had supposed. They worked "by the *job*, and pretty much as they please, as respects the *hours* of labor," Hewitt reported, a fact that would have kept him away had he known it previously.[33]

Another Fall River emissary, David Pierce, encountered similar problems in Maine when he tried to forge an alliance with artisans at the Mechanics Convention being held in Portland, Maine. What he found there was a group committed to education only, and opposed to the movement growing in southern New England. Indeed, when Pierce presented the Fall River circular, and one of the Maine delegates proposed to send representatives to the regionwide convention in Boston, the group voted the proposal down during their afternoon session. The question was brought up again in the evening and tabled.[34]

Pierce discovered in the course of these meetings that not only were most Maine mechanics opposed to the ten-hour movement, some of them even doubted the truth of the grievances. Abner R. Hallowel, of Bangor, who spoke in the afternoon, "opposed ten hour associations and combinations of Laborers for the purpose of having their wages advance &c. because they had too much the appearance of monopoly and he wished to keep aloof from that great evil." The president of the convention (probably Oliver Gerrish of Portland) became quite disturbed about the "Massachusetts question" and suggested that the writer of the circular had simply had a bad day at work. According to Pierce, "He thought the writer of that article, at the time of writing it, had his passions very much excited, and selected all the grievances he could find and committed them to paper, while in that agitated state of mind."[35]

Pierce made a final attempt at reconciliation by stressing their shared cause, *"the elevation of the laborers,"* even though their means might be different. This calmed things down a bit, but the Maine convention remained opposed to collective action of any sort. Pierce concluded that one of the fundamental reasons for this difference in consciousness was a difference in market conditions: "the employers of Maine (in general) are not so overbearing as they are in many places, and the employed are not so overworked in that State as they are in this."[36]

No doubt it was discouraging reports such as this which led the editor of the Boston *Laborer* to urge a postponement of the regionwide convention that the Fall River Mechanics Association had originally proposed for the autumn.[37] The *Laborer* was overruled on this issue, in part because not all of the news was bad. Although Hewitt had been unable to obtain a meeting hall in Stonington, Connecticut, he had successfully organized street meetings two nights in a row. With the support of ministers in Woonsocket, Rhode Island, and Waterford, Massachusetts, Hewitt had been able to address large audiences. Even David Pierce found some success in Maine when he left the mechanics in Portland and moved on to the factory town of Saco. Although the initial responses in Worcester and Milford had been disappointing, word soon arrived that organizations had been formed. Meetings also took place in Andover, North Andover, Concord, Marblehead, Woburn, Haverhill, and Newton Upper Falls, inspired by word of these larger organizations. The last-named town sent in sixteen subscriptions to the *Mechanic* early in September. On the evening of September 6, a Friday, the mechanics in Newton Upper Falls held a meeting that filled the hall to overflowing even though no public notice of the meeting had been given.[38] A "Mechanics, Manufacturers and Laborers Association" met in Dover, New Hampshire, at the beginning of August. Its name suggests that employers were present, which might not have been the case elsewhere. In early September, mechanics and laborers in Manchester finally succeeded in forming a Mutual Benefit Association, after being addressed by Mr. Hatch of Lowell.[39]

Many of these associations sought female support and attempted to include women in their organizations. In Woonsocket, the Mechanics Association not only encouraged workingmen to attend their meetings but extended a special invitation to women: "Ladies, to you we appeal! you, in all ages, have ever raised your voices against oppression, come forward and join us! for you, too, suffer the pangs of unceasing toil."[40] The Milford Workingmen's Union, which opened its ranks to anyone "engaged in useful, productive industry" who would sign the constitution and pay a twenty-five-cent initiation fee and six cents per month, admitted women and children for half price.[41] In Manchester, J. C. Stowell conflated the examples of women in Fall River and Lowell to urge the "female portion" of the community to attend future meetings, arguing that no one would benefit more from these reforms than factory operatives. "The ladies of Fall River, Lowell and other places have taken hold of the work; and we see no reason why the operatives of this place should not feel more engaged in the present movement among the industrial classes." Calling for both the "influence" and the "co-operation" of the women, he concluded, "Keep the fires burning upon our altars, and suffer not this heaven-born enterprise to fail its object."[42] When workingmen in Fitchburg formed an organization at the end of the year, they also invited women to join. At one of the first meetings of the Workingmen's Association of Fitchburg it was resolved "that as the present evil state and organisation of society tends to abase & destroy the social & intellectual happiness of *woman*—we wish it to be distinctly understood that the doctrine of equality embodied in the principles of this Association extends to her the privilege of giving in her testimony in the deliberations of our meetings."[43]

At the regionwide fall meeting, delegates from many of these local organizations were present, and they created the New England Workingmen's Association. Wednesday, October 16, had been designated as the time, and Boston as the place. All of the delegates were male. Most were from Massachusetts: shoemakers, carpenters, machinists, molders, and shipworkers trying to work out a way of discussing their problems beyond the craft level. In addition, they rubbed shoulders with men such as George Ripley, from Brook Farm, and George Henry Evans, the land reformer from New York City. No women were present at the meeting, though the "ladies association" of Fall River did supply a banner that stated, "Union is Strength." As Thomas Almy, the editor of the *Mechanic,* later pointed out, "We met with views as to the means of accomplishing our end as dissimilar as are the conditions of society."[44]

Despite their different viewpoints, the delegates managed to create the New England Workingmen's Association, to beat back the attempts of George Henry Evans to press his land reform cause, and to summon support for a petition campaign urging the legislature to reduce the hours of labor in corporations to ten. The resolution to petition the legislature was the most controversial resolution at the meeting.

## Petitions and the Mediation of Difference

Prior to the nineteenth century, petitioning had been a deferential act, a request for the ruler of a country to intervene on a supplicant's behalf. For many white men of the nineteenth century who had other forms of political expression available to them, petitioning carried connotations of submissiveness which rendered it distasteful. For some of the most radical reformers, it represented an interaction with a corrupt government and was thus morally unacceptable. For women, however, petitioning meant something different. Linda Kerber has pointed out that in the eighteenth century petitioning was one way in which women could approach the government; consequently, women used the petition for a variety of personal causes which might border on the political. By the early nineteenth century, particularly in the wake of the antislavery petitioning campaigns, petitioning had become an important political act for women. They signed their individual names in support of or in opposition to moral causes, and this act of signing their names, particularly in the case of slavery, had significant political ramifications. As Angelina Grimké would write publicly to Catherine Beecher, it was woman's only political right.[45]

Since women were not present at the Boston convention, their views on petitioning were not discussed. But for male delegates petitioning raised many problems. Some of the delegates thought it useless to petition, whereas others seem to have found it too submissive an act for men who were citizens. One delegate from Marblehead defended petitioning as a demand on the part of mechanics to protect the poor who had been wronged by the legislature when the corporations were originally created. Solomon Cooper of Fall River provided a more political interpretation by suggesting that petitioning could be an avenue into party politics. Both interpretations would make the activity more manly. After extensive debate, the motion to petition the legislature was carried.[46]

Petitions from five towns remain: one each from Lynn, Fall River, Worcester, and Andover, and two from Lowell. In Lowell and Andover, women as well as men signed. Perhaps for different reasons, each group of petitioners made sure that it was petitioning for someone else. Men may have wanted to distance themselves from the subservient act of requesting what they believed to be their rights, and women may have wanted to demonstrate their moral benevolence at the same time that they exerted a "political" right.

In Fall River, Lynn, and Andover, the introductory language of the petitions was virtually identical; they focused their demands on the regulation of corporations. Arguing that the legislature had a particular responsibility in this area, they pointed out, "You have the power to regulate all corporate bodies which you have created." They stressed the particularly taxing nature of mill work, saying "that to work more than ten hours per day, *especially in factories,* is injurious to the physical and mental power of man—thus debasing his intellect—cramping his energies, and paralyzing his strength—that it deprives him of the opportunity of cultivating his mind and of raising himself to that high rank and station in society for which God designed him." All three concluded by "respectfully" petitioning that a law be passed "constituting Ten Hours a days work in all corporations, created by the Legislature of this State," with the Lynn petition referring even more specifically to "manufacturing corporations."[47] Though many of the petition signers in Andover worked in factories, few worked in factories owned by corporations. In Fall River, where most factories were incorporated, few mill workers signed. And in Lynn, almost all of the signers were shoemakers.

In Lowell, where a large number of operatives working at incorporated factories signed the petitions, the opening language asked for a much more broadly based ten-hour law. The shorter petition, signed by about three hundred men and women, requested the legislature to "enact a Law making ten hours a *day's work*—where no specific agreement is entered into be-

Nineteenth-century American carpenters and joiners believed that their labor and skill were "indispensable for the advancement of civilization." A banner displayed in an 1841 parade in Portland, Maine, sponsored by the Maine Charitable Mechanic Association. (Maine Charitable Mechanic Association)

tween the parties interested." The longer petition referred more specifically to corporations but still sought a broad-ranging law. Noting that they sought "a redress of those evils, daily strengthening, and imposed upon us by our incorporated bodies," the petitioners asked "that no incorporated body, or any individual or individuals, either private or associated, shall be allowed, except in case of emergency, to employ one set of hands more than ten hours per day."[48] In Worcester, the petitioners asked simply for a law establishing "Ten Hours per day as a days labor for all Adult Persons."[49]

The language of these petitions and the very act of signing them continued to be debated at the local level even as the petitions were circulated. Walter Sherrod, one of the leaders of the workingmen's movement in Lynn, found the language of the petition too submissive and inappropriate in view of the rights to which workingmen were entitled. Thus, at a December 7 meeting in Lynn, he criticized the petition that was presented, saying that "he was opposed to the sovereign people's presenting themselves as petitioners, where they had the right to demand that for which they petitioned." He then distinguished between what he considered the appropriate posture for artisans to take and the appropriate posture for factory workers, noting "that he was in favor of stating that he sympathized with the operatives at work in the various incorporated mills, and [the artisans should] demand of the Legislature, to grant them their request."[50] Despite Sherrod's reservations, the petition was submitted with the names of one hundred men, which were probably collected at one of the cordwainers' meetings. Of those signers who could be positively identified, 76 percent were cordwainers and another 8 percent were shoe manufacturers (see table 6.1). Male shoemakers who shared Sherrod's reservations about petitioning may have been reassured by the knowledge that their petition was clearly meant to benefit others.

In Fall River, petitioning was incorporated quickly into a political platform. The support for protective legislation for operatives represented a significant departure from the stand that mechanics had taken the previous spring, when they had attempted to rely only on their pledge and distanced their cause from that of the operatives. The strategy of petitioning would make the fates of mechanics and operatives more closely intertwined, for protective legislation would no doubt benefit men in the building trades as well as factory workers. But discussion among the Fall River mechanics quickly moved to "whether the ten hour men, as such, should make an exertion to send men to the Legislature who would vote for such a law." The group decided to enter the political arena by choosing candidates from all political parties and resolved to "recommend the support of those men only who will sign the petition that has been presented to this meeting, and who will pledge themselves, if elected, to do all in their power to have such a law passed as is prayed for in said petition."[51]

The fact that petitioning was becoming a political party issue may help to explain why there was such a broad occupational spread among petition signers in Fall River: 28 percent were from the building trades, but an additional 15 percent were skilled artisans from other traditional trades, and 21 percent were shopkeepers, merchants, and professionals. Only 12 percent were industrial workers in machine making and textiles. An additional 15 percent were unskilled workers, most of whom were designated as laborers in the census (table 6.1). Some of these men may have been factory workers also, since the term *laborer* was used instead of *operative* in Fall River. The political edge on petitioning in Fall River may be a further reason women did not sign the petition there.

Table 6.1. Occupations of Male Signers of 1845 Ten-Hour Petitions

| | Lowell[a] | | Lynn | | Fall River | | Andover | | Worcester | |
|---|---|---|---|---|---|---|---|---|---|---|
| Occupational Category | % | N | % | N | % | N | % | N | % | N |
| Traditional | | | | | | | | | | |
|   artisanal work | 14 | 8 | 76 | 45[b] | 15 | 24 | 28 | 29 | 13 | 8 |
| Building trades | 19 | 11 | 3 | 2 | 28 | 46 | 9 | 9 | 27 | 16 |
| Factory work | 21 | 12 | 0 | 0 | 12 | 19 | 29 | 30 | 53 | 32 |
|   Textile work | | [9] | | | | [10] | | [24] | | [0] |
|   Metal/machine work | | [3] | | | | [9] | | [5] | | [32] |
|   Other | | | | | | | | | | [1] |
| Unskilled work | 18 | 10 | 2 | 1 | 15 | 24 | 12 | 12 | 3 | 2 |
| Manufacturer | 9 | 5 | 8 | 5[b] | 0 | 1 | 7 | 7 | 0 | 0 |
| Clerical/professional work | 2 | 1 | 0 | 0 | 7 | 12 | 2 | 2 | 2 | 1 |
| Retail work | 9 | 5 | 7 | 4 | 14 | 23 | 2 | 2 | 2 | 1 |
| Agricultural work | 5 | 3 | 2 | 1 | 0 | 0 | 11 | 11 | 0 | 0 |
| Maritime work | 0 | 0 | 2 | 2 | 6 | 10 | 0 | 0 | 0 | 0 |
| Other | 4 | 2 | 0 | 0 | 2 | 3 | 0 | 0 | 0 | 0 |
|   Total | 101 | 57 | 100 | 59 | 99 | 162 | 100 | 102 | 100 | 60 |
|   % Traced | 33 | | 59 | | 35 | | 37 | | 53 | |

*Source:* Data from city directories of Worcester, Lowell, and Lynn in mid-1840s; marriage records in Massachusetts State Archives; vital statistics published by Essex Institute; 1850 Federal Census for Lowell, Lynn, Worcester, Andover, and Fall River.

[a] The figures for Lowell combine two petitions.

[b] All traditional artisans in Lynn were cordwainers, and all manufacturers in Lynn were shoe manufacturers.

In Andover there was also a broad spectrum of occupations among male petitioners, although in this case traditional artisans (many of whom were shoemakers), with 28 percent of the signers, and factory workers, with 29 percent, represented the largest groups, while unskilled laborers, with 12 percent, and farmers, with 11 percent, represented a significant minority. In the case of Andover, however, this broad occupational spread may have been due less to the movement's political character than to its family orientation. Whole families in Andover signed the petition, so that some of the male farmers and shoemakers who signed may have had children working in the factories.

This family orientation was also reflected in the language of the petition.

Table 6.2. Nativity of 1845 Ten-Hour Petition Signers

| | United States | | Foreign | | |
|---|---|---|---|---|---|
| | % | N | % | N | % traced |
| Lowell | | | | | |
| Women | 90 | 90 | 10 | 10 | 14 |
| Men | 67 | 21 | 33 | 10 | 18 |
| Andover | | | | | |
| Women | 88 | 44 | 12 | 6 | 29 |
| Men | 76 | 72 | 24 | 23 | 34 |
| Lynn | | | | | |
| Men | 100 | 53 | 0 | 0 | 53 |
| Fall River | | | | | |
| Men | 95 | 137 | 5 | 7 | 31 |
| Worcester | | | | | |
| Men | 94 | 32 | 6 | 2 | 30 |

Source: Marriage records, Massachusetts State Archives; vital Statistics of Lowell, Lynn, and Andover, published by the Essex Institute; 1850 Federal Census for Lowell, Lynn, Worcester, Andover, and Fall River.

While the introduction to the petition stated that it was from the inhabitants of the town, requesting a ten-hour day for all workers employed by corporations, a different meaning was given by the cover sheet that accompanied the petition. It claimed that the petition was from the citizens of Andover requesting that hours be limited for all women and minors employed in factories.[52] This suggested a different kind of document: one put forward by men (i.e., citizens) petitioning to protect women and children.

The strategy of men petitioning to protect women and children, though all would benefit from shorter hours, was at the time an approach far more common in British agitation than in the United States. Indeed, the different messages of cover sheet and petition may have been a product of the ethnic complexity of the movement in Andover. Although the male petitioners from Worcester, Lynn, and Fall River were almost exclusively native born, 24 percent of the male petitioners from Andover were foreign born (see table 6.2). Most of these foreign-born men were from England, Scotland, or Ireland, and most of them were factory workers.[53] They may have carried the ideology of the ten-hour movement in Great Britain with them, fusing it with the ten-hour agitation in the United States.

Table 6.3. Value of Real Property Belonging to Male Signers of 1845 Ten-Hour Petitions

| Assessed Value | Lowell | | Lynn | | Fall River | | Andover | | Worcester | |
|---|---|---|---|---|---|---|---|---|---|---|
| | % | N | % | N | % | N | % | N | % | N |
| $0 | 80 | 4 | 61 | 28 | 67 | 87 | 58 | 38 | 44 | 14 |
| $1–500 | 0 | 0 | 2 | 1 | 3 | 4 | 6 | 4 | 3 | 1 |
| $501–1,000 | 0 | 0 | 15 | 7 | 5 | 6 | 14 | 9 | 13 | 4 |
| $1,001–5,000 | 20 | 1 | 22 | 10 | 22 | 29 | 15 | 10 | 34 | 11 |
| $5,001+ | 0 | 0 | 0 | 0 | 3 | 4 | 6 | 4 | 6 | 2 |
| Total | 100 | 46 | 100 | 130 | 99 | 65 | 99 | 65 | 100 | 32 |
| % Traced | 3 | | 46 | | 28 | | 23 | | 28 | |

Source: 1850 Federal Census for Lowell, Lynn, Worcester, Andover, and Fall River

a The actual numbers from Lowell are too small to be meaningful.

As an occupational analysis of male petitioners makes clear, traditional artisans such as shoemakers and members of the building trades made common cause with factory workers in their petitioning campaigns. But as an analysis of their real property makes clear, this was not exclusively a movement of propertyless wage earners. The ten-hour petitions were signed by a significant minority of men whose wealth would have provided them with a comfortable independence (see table 6.3). In Lynn, 37 percent of the male signers had amassed real property worth between $501 and $5,000 by 1850. Most of these listed their occupation as cordwainer, and thus many of them might have been masters rather than journeymen. In Worcester, 53 percent of the signers, including six of the eight iron molders who signed the petition, had more than $500 in real property. In Fall River, 30 percent of the signers fit into this category, as did 35 percent in Andover. As a moral reform movement rather than a trade union movement, ten-hour agitation had clearly reached beyond wage earners in garnering support.

The movement also drew female support, though of different kinds. Women who signed petitions in Lowell and those who did so in Andover probably did so for very different reasons. Those in Lowell who signed were almost all single, wage-earning women, and virtually none of them were related to the men who signed the petitions. As might be expected, most (81%) of the female signers whose occupations could be determined were factory operatives.[54] The occupational homogeneity of the women who

Table 6.4. Median Ages of Signers of 1845 Ten-hour Petitions

| | Males | | | Females | | |
|---|---|---|---|---|---|---|
| | Age | N | % Traced | Age | N | % Traced |
| Lowell | 26 | 39 | 22 | 20 | 158 | 22 |
| Andover | 31 | 91 | 33 | 22 | 53 | 30 |
| Lynn | 33 | 52 | 52 | NA[a] | NA | NA |
| Fall River | 30 | 162 | 35 | NA | NA | NA |
| Worcester | 28 | 37 | 32 | NA | NA | NA |

Source: Marriage Records, Massachusetts State Archives; vital Statistics of Lynn, Lowell, and Andover, published by the Essex Institute; 1850 Federal Census for Lowell, Lynn, Worcester, Andover and Fall River.

[a] NA = not applicable.

signed stands in sharp contrast to the occupational diversity of the men from Lowell who signed.

In Andover, however, many of the women who signed were related to male petition signers. Thirty-six percent of the petition signers in Andover could be identified as women, and of that number, 25 percent could be identified as married when they signed. This in itself presents a very different profile from that of the women in Lowell who signed, almost all of whom were single. Even more striking, however, is the fact that 81 percent of the married women who signed the petition in Andover were married to men who also signed the petition. Marriage was a more significant factor for the women who signed in Andover than it was for the men. Thirty-three percent of the men who signed could be identified as married, but only 41 percent had wives who signed the petition. Among the unmarried petition signers were many of the children of these married couples.

It is difficult to know what to make of the women who signed the petition in Andover, since it is impossible to determine their occupational status and we have no other record of their participation in the New England Workingmen's Association. They do not appear to have formed their own organization, which may explain their absence from the workingmen's regional meetings. But when they signed the petition, they used their own first names rather than their husbands' names, an act of independence that reinforced their assertiveness in signing a petition to the government.

The most important similarity they shared with the women of Lowell was their age. Both groups of female signers were significantly younger than the men who signed. The median age of the women from Lowell who signed the ten-hour petition was 20 years, and the median age of the women from Andover was 22 (see table 6.4). The men were considerably older: in Lowell, the median age was 26; in Andover, 31; in Fall River, 30; and in Lynn, 33. The younger age of the women from Lowell is compatible with their status as factory workers. Men remained in artisanal and factory production for most of their working lives. Women labored in factories until they were married, after which their work centered on the household. The median age of the Andover women, then, suggests that the unmarried women who signed might have been engaged in factory work.

The fact that, both in Andover and in Fall River, female petition signers were younger than the men who were signing should remind us of an additional complication in the organizing activities of men and women, artisans and operatives, at this time. Further expectations of deference would be built into their relationship because of this age differential, particularly as the struggle for a ten-hour day assumed regional rather than local dimensions and young women from Lowell asserted their demands publicly along with men from towns such as Lynn and Fall River. These older male artisans might view their petitioning as a way of protecting the young women, while female operatives used the petitions as a way to assert themselves in the labor movement without threatening the men with whom they were forming an alliance.

The conflicts between male artisans and female wage earners has been well documented in recent years, making the activities and alliances of the New England Workingmen's Association all the more curious.[55] The organization did not unite all wage earners or all men and women in the struggle for a ten-hour day. But as the petitions reveal, it did unite many who had different social and economic experiences. Moreover, petitioning was one way these differences could be accommodated, though not eradicated. Indeed, the petitions would draw women into more active participation in the labor movement as they were called upon to justify themselves in the legislature. After this experience with public speaking these women moved on to positions of leadership in the New England Workingmens' Association, spearheading even more extensive petitioning campaigns in the next few years. Petitions did not bring about a legislative solution to long workdays, and when the petitions failed, so too did the coalition. But while petitioning flourished, it provided an important means for artisans and operatives to work together.

# 7

BRUCE LAURIE

# "Spavined Ministers, Lying Toothpullers, and Buggering Priests":
Third-Partyism and the Search for Security
in the Antebellum North

PRACTITIONERS OF the "new labor history" and the "new social history" are beginning to answer criticism that theirs is history without politics.[1] Recent work by Iver Bernstein, Amy Bridges, and John Brooke, among others, probes the outlook and social experience of ordinary people not as ends unto themselves but as context for understanding popular politics.[2] This essay is in that spirit. It explores third-party politics in the three decades before the Civil War, first by assessing the economic conditions of journeymen and small employers, or what in political terms may be called a popular bloc.[3] It then offers some tentative observations on the sources of insurgent politics. Its thesis is that the "second party system" was not as stable as received wisdom would have us believe. Insurgency in the form of third-partyism was a fact of political life, a systematic feature that reflected popular needs and interests. Third parties drew sometimes from different regions and often from divergent ethnic and religious groups, and put forth seemingly different programs. Yet third parties also rested on a similar social foundation formed by the popular bloc. In addition, they had common thematic threads, none of which proved stronger than the search for security. It is difficult to appreciate the question of security without understanding the conditions faced by small employers and skilled workers. We shall begin there.

The Problem of Economic Insecurity

It is no accident that mechanics figure prominently in virtually every discussion of class formation in the early industrial revolution.[4] After all, what the late Herbert Gutman called the "first American working class" derived not from the factories and peasant plots of Old Europe but from the fields and workshops of preindustrial America.[5] Historians used to believe that master mechanics carried their craft traditions pretty much intact into the nineteenth century. Now we know better. Only masters in small towns during the Jeffersonian period evoked their Revolutionary forbears; fellow tradesmen in big cities saw the craft system erode before their eyes. Between the Revolution and the turn of the new century wage-workers replaced bonded labor; the number of journeymen multiplied; and such trades as shoemaking and tailoring were already considered "dishonorable."[6]

Yet we should not overdo this "declension model." Masters in the first half of the nineteenth century actually followed one of three paths. Some— and from most accounts a minority—became entrepreneurs, bridging the world of craft production and mass output. Others, in such single-industry towns as Lynn, Massachusetts, where a classic two-class system emerged, led the Hobbesian existence of the declension model. According to Alan Dawley, they were "done in" by more efficient producers and slipped into the wage-earning class.[7] In big cities and smallish towns with mixed economies, some masters likewise tumbled into the working class. Still others—and clearly a substantial number—hung on and became part of an intermediate social class perched precariously between manual workers of various grades of skill, on the one hand, and an emergent middle class of bankers, merchants, manufacturers, and professionals, on the other. That class is the subject of much of what follows.

It has also become a bone of some historiographical contention. Thanks in part to what we might call the social analysis of occupations, which became the fashion during the 1970s, social historians have not only gained greater appreciation for this intermediate class but have also begun to think of it as a group apart, reversing the consensus historians' habit of sweeping just about everyone into a great middle class.[8] Debate has arisen over the composition and defining characteristics of this intermediate stratum, and over what to call it.[9] I favor the term *middling class,* partly because it passed into early-nineteenth-century usage and partly because the historian R. S. Neale has made a strong case for its use.[10] I differ from Neale, however, in one important respect. Neale argues for a political standard of class definition in place of more conventional economic criteria, and thus uses power and/or authority relations to distinguish one class from another. I prefer to use status and function (not simply relation to the means of production) to draw the class lines, and—more important to the task at hand— to separate the middling class from the middle class. By this dualist standard several social and occupational groups, usually described broadly as middle class, get demoted a social notch to the middling class of urban and rural America. The middling class embraced yeomen farmers and such lesser professionals as "quack" physicians and petty lawyers, as well as a wide array of small retailers, notably grocers and tavernkeepers. All of these groups, and the master mechanics especially, lacked the income, status, and staying power to be a part of the solid middle class. Even the wealthier, more secure masters found themselves snubbed by the resident bourgeoisie.[11]

Several things should be said of small employers straightaway. They were numerically significant in every urban place. They dominated the Main Streets of small-town America and remained prominent even in the most dynamic urban centers and in single-industry towns.[12] As late as midcentury, just over half the industrial establishments in Philadelphia—at least thirty-six hundred—had fewer than six employees.[13] Indianapolis had a much smaller industrial economy than the Quaker City at this time, but a similar configuration of workshops. Of slightly more than one hundred firms, roughly half consisted of a boss and a few employees.[14] These workplaces, moreover, were distributed unevenly across the craft spectrum. There were more of them in the old handicrafts than in metal refining, textiles, and other newer pursuits; even here, however, one must be careful. Small and smallish shops dominated such specialized sectors of the textile industry as rugs, stockings, and fancy thread.[15] Still, the small shop was synonymous with the crafts. It was the typical workplace throughout the antebellum period for most journeymen in food preparation, building construction, and the so-called luxury trades, and for good numbers of shoemakers, tailors, and cabinetmakers. It was one thing, however, to run a small jewelry firm, and quite another to be in charge of a shoemaker's shop. Master jewelers were independent producers who owned or rented their own shops and sold luxury goods displayed in elegant cases to wealthy customers.[16] The small shoemaker, by contrast, was likely to be a subcontractor lodged in a rented garret and forced to turn out cheap goods quickly, not for the casual shopper but for a demanding merchant capitalist.[17] In between these extremes stood such trades as printing, in which proprietors worked hard but had a claim to independence. Conditions and circumstances, in a word, varied widely at this level of production.[18]

Nonetheless, antebellum master craftsmen had much in common. They usually worked in their homes or in attached sheds, and resided in close proximity to their hands, sometimes forming communities of fellow tradesmen. They performed manual labor alongside their employees and, some observers believed, even dressed like sons of toil. "There is very little difference, if indeed any," wrote an English commentator, "in point of appearance, between the young men of most trades and their employer . . . or, in fact, the first tradesmen or merchants of the city."[19] Graphic evidence suggests that this picture of journeymen is only partly right. Daguerreotypes from the 1840s and 1850s capture merchants and professionals in vested gray suits and no headwear. Mechanics and workingmen rarely appear without an apron of heavy cloth or leather, or without a hat or cap of some sort which usually signified a given trade.[20]

Small employers also shared their workers' aspiration for what was called "competence" or "competency." This term meant different things at various points in time. It generally referred to an accumulation of income sufficient to support a family in modest comfort, get it through hard times, and provide an independent retirement for the head of the household. The textile producers of Philadelphia studied by Philip Scranton worked toward just such an aim. They had in mind a "determinate goal, a limit, a moment when one might . . . say 'Enough.'"[21] Not a few of Scranton's master mechanics realized the dream of retiring at middle age with a competence. Statistical evidence from Philadelphia and other cities suggests that they were exceptional. More typical was the master craftsman who had difficulty making ends meet. We get a sense of such individuals' living standard by comparing their earnings with those of members of other occupational groups and with what was considered a minimum budget for respectability. Historians agree that at midcentury it took from $500 to $600 a year for an urban family to live comfortably. At this time all workers averaged about $300 a year; skilled males in the honorable trades could expect $500 yearly, or just about what it took for respectability. Clerks did somewhat better, at $500 to $1,500, and retailers better still, at $2,000 to $5,000. If, as contemporary observers argued, solidly middle-class Americans earned $1,000 per year, master mechanics not only fell far short of that standard but didn't reach the minimum budget. In Philadelphia, employers with fewer than six employees in 1850 accumulated an average gross profit of only $480. If we subtract overhead and labor costs, such employers earned less than the best-paid skilled workmen and no more than the average worker.[22] Small wonder that few such employers gathered much income from their businesses. The New York cabinetmaker H. G. McGrath may have been unusually successful in this respect. Though described by Dun and Bradstreet investigators as "industrious, capable, and economical," McGrath had only $800 to show for twenty years in business.[23]

Master craftsmen not only earned less than skilled workers. They also had dim prospects for advancement. Studies of Boston and Philadelphia indicate that clerks were three to four times as likely as craftsmen to improve their occupational standing.[24] What these studies do not report is the failure rate for small businesses. Anecdotal evidence indicates that it was terribly high. The careers of two printers detailed in subsequent chapters in this book are instructive in this regard. The Baltimore and then Washington printer William Moore lost two shops before giving up on proprietorship and accepting a foreman's post.[25] His fellow tradesman Joseph T. Buckingham of Boston had an even bumpier ride. Between 1810 or so and the late 1820s, he founded but could not sustain several magazines, then established the *Courier*, a small but increasingly popular organ of National Republicanism and then *Whiggery*. But a decade later it, too, struggled, and Buckingham was fortunate indeed to retire in the late 1840s on the semblance of a competency.[26] The typical shopkeeper of the age didn't match Buckingham's achievement, according to the most systematic study we have. Master craftsmen and petty entrepreneurs, write Michael Katz and his collaborators about the town of Hamilton, Canada West, "failed in business with extraordinary frequency."[27] There and in American cities and towns it is likely that two-thirds to three-quarters of master mechanics went broke at least once; and like Buckingham, many experienced serial failures.

If the typical master couldn't expect to rise by his bootstraps, neither could he expect the independence traditionally associated with petty proprietorship. Indeed, quite the reverse was true. Men such as Buckingham found themselves in the ironic position of being dependent not simply on their social superiors, their children, or both, but also on their peers, and even on their employees. In 1817 a merchant guaranteed a note to help Buckingham set up on his own; fellow masters often lent him supplies and equipment; and at least once and possibly more often, his own journeymen came through with timely loans that kept their boss from debtor's prison.[28] Journeymen printers working for William Moore proved equally solicitous when several years later they took up a collection that spared the needy printer the indignity of imprisonment for debt.[29]

The humiliation of paltry income, dependence, and chronic business failure was not supposed to be. Such adversity ran counter to the official optimism that accompanied the acceleration of the market revolution in the North during the closing decades of the antebellum period. From press and pulpit came paeans to the self-made entrepreneur who rose from small beginnings.[30] Beginning in the 1850s, popular writers added their voice to this chorus by publishing weighty hagiographies of mechanics who made good.[31] None of these writers told of broken dreams or failure, but what was left unsaid was a universal concern. Nowhere was this clearer than in the statehouses of the North. Beginning in the 1820s, surging protest created the pressure for a flood of laws abolishing imprisonment for debt and providing for mechanics' liens. Both measures, which proved among the most popular of the period, derived directly from the insecurity of economic life for workers and small employers. This insecurity was also responsible for legislation that granted women limited property rights, or the privilege of "separate estates." The motivation behind such reforms in Virginia, writes Suzanne Lebsock, was not egalitarianism but the "desire to protect women's property from seizure when indebtedness was rampant and creditors impatient."[32]

Nor was failure very far from the thoughts of the antebellum authors who churned out voluminous literature on domestic economy and household management. Fear of falling was their great preoccupation. One of the first such tracts, Lydia Maria Child's *Frugal Housewife*, was an instant success that went through seven editions between 1829 and 1832, when it was renamed *The American Frugal Housewife* for the European edition.[33] For her part, Child had intimate experience with the fluctuating economic fortunes of middling Americans. She was the daughter of a successful small-town baker, one of the fortunate few of his social class to accumulate a competence and then some. David Convers Francis's famous "Medford Cracker" yielded a retirement income of fifty thousand dollars, but he didn't pass on his status to his daughter. She incurred his anger by marrying David Lee Child, a Harvard College graduate who prepared for the law but wound up distracted and financially strapped because of dubious reform projects, including one that involved employing free laborers to grow sugar beets to replace sugar cane produced by slaves. The young couple was hard pressed for money when in 1829, a year after marrying, they moved to Boston, where Child would write her classic. Written in a depression year by a young bride forced to make every penny count, *Frugal Housewife* exposed the angst of middling Americans. Child wrote for "people of moderate fortune" who practiced the virtues of hard work and economy. She had no use whatever for "extravagance," by which she meant conspicuous consumption and recreational travel, and even less for mechanics who emulated the rich by shunning manual labor or indulging the social pretensions of wives and daughters. She aimed to show how "money can be *saved,* not how it can be enjoyed."[34] With that in mind, Child laid out, in the same meticulous detail seen in craft manuals, how to do myriad domestic chores cheaply and efficiently. No one was exempt from housework, not even small children, who were encouraged to care for themselves so as not to keep mother from her labor, and to work at a variety of chores as well as such jobs as picking berries "from the meadow, to be carried to market."[35] Here was a household run like a workshop on Franklinesque principles.

The performance of manual labor, writes a recent historian of the middle class in the North during the nineteenth century, is precisely what separated workers and small employers from middle-class people, who did no manual work. It became the mark of bourgeois status to scorn manual work and distance oneself psychically and socially from those condemned to it.[36] The reverse of this bourgeois ethic is that manual labor provided both a means of identity and a common ground for master and journeyman. Some historians go a step further and argue that mutual respect for craftsmanship sealed a special bond between employer and worker.[37] It is perhaps more accurate to describe this relationship as an ambiguous one, both harmonious and troubled. On the one hand, even firebrand labor radicals considered small employers to be brothers in the fraternity of manual labor. As one of their number put it, as if to answer a critic with a more restrictive view of class, the "employer who superintends his own business (still more if he works with his own hands) is a working man."[38] The small employer was considered "one of the b'hoys," an appealing figure who mixed easily with his men and spent off-hours with them hunting, fishing, or hanging out on the corner or in the pub.[39] His workshop was not the remote, privatized factory of the entrepreneur, set off from society by a fence and sometimes patrolled by guards; it was quasi-public space that opened onto the colorful street culture of the antebellum city. All kinds of people—friends, relatives, and hawkers—came and went.[40]

Some small employers did favors for employees. They hired relatives of the hands in their employ and lent money to those in need. They rewarded workers with extra pay for special effort or work well done.[41] Some even supported as best they could the formal demands of wage earners. No issue, for instance, proved more galvanic for antebellum workers than the ten-hour day. The initial drive to shorten the workday in 1825–27 inspired the nation's first city central unions, which sponsored the first labor parties and in 1835 fueled the first general strikes.[42] In 1832 the maritime workers of Boston (for the second time in seven years) went on strike for a ten-hour day. Some master caulkers and shipbuilders seemed sympathetic until the real bosses stepped in. Merchant capitalists who owned the drydocks and contracted with the masters vigorously fought employer and worker alike. They issued what was derisively called a "ukase" asserting that they would hire no union man or "contract with any master mechanics" who did. The strike soon collapsed, as would yet a third strike for a ten-hour day three years later, in 1835.[43] The bearing of master mechanics in this third rehearsal is unknown. Perhaps they learned their lesson and thought better of testing the will of the city's powerful and cohesive merchant princes. In any event, the support shown by masters in the 1832 strike was not an isolated episode. The New York shipbuilder Henry Eckford, though his business was larger and considerably more entrepreneurial than that of the neighborhood master mechanic, actively worked with his employees for the ten-hour day.[44]

Workers in small shops had another reason to think well of their employers. They were paid better than their fellows on the rolls of larger workplaces and factories. Since this pattern was first revealed several years ago for Philadelphia, scholars have found confirming evidence for other cities.[45] A study of Indianapolis indicates that in 1850 workers in the smallest shops averaged $288 a year, while those in larger workplaces with and without steam power earned $253 and $266, respectively.[46] The reasons for this differential are unclear. Perhaps the workers in small shops were the most skilled; possibly they were better organized; maybe their employers, who coincidentally dealt directly with customers, enjoyed greater pricing flexibility and could easily pass on costs to consumers. For whatever reason, small employers paid a premium for labor, a premium that helped promote togetherness at the workplace.

It would be foolish to argue that harmony prevailed, however. As the ten-hour strike on the Boston docks in 1832 indicates, even friendly masters answered to merchant potentates who wielded the real power. Independent mechanics were free of meddlesome merchants but beholden to market forces that limited how far they were prepared to go. In addition, for every comradely employer there was an oppressive garret boss or imperious master worthy of Dickensian opprobrium. Garret bosses in the finishing trades were notoriously abusive and exploitative. The worst of them paid starvation wages and levied arbitrary fines for "faulty" or tardy work. Some even absconded with wages.[47] Such practices, however, do not vitiate the argument for the persistence of craft fraternalism. They simply remind us of the complexity of the social relations of production in the small shop.

The social identity of small proprietors proved equally complicated. Such employers were quintessentially men in the middle, suspended between two classes that were being etched into sharper relief. They belonged exclusively to neither the middle class nor the working class, but shared features of both. Like the ordinary workingman, they used their hands in manual labor, but unlike him they had at least a tenuous claim to ownership of the means of production. They further resembled solidly middle-class men because they managed their own shops, supervised their workers, and sold their own goods. The stigma of manual labor, however, thwarted acceptance into the middle class. If Lydia Maria Child and other commentators are any guide, not a few such employers tried to "pass" as bourgeois men, partly by avoiding manual work where possible and partly by emulating middle-class consumption.[48] Most seem to have carved out a separate identity as "mechanics," and more broadly as mainstays of the middling class.[49] The term *mechanic* was itself somewhat vague and flexible, perhaps deliberately so given the ambiguous status of such men. Mechanics practiced a skilled trade, which excluded unskilled laborers and factory hands, and they could be masters or journeymen. Usually they were both, for if it meant nothing else, *mechanic* meant a community of craftsmen. The mechanic celebrated the dignity and utility of manual labor. He thought of himself as an essential part of the community—provider of food, clothing, and shelter. He was a patriot and an eager participant in the parades and pageants on the "red letter days" of the early Republic.[50] He believed in sobriety, industriousness, and other pieties of evolving lower-middle-class respectability, but was no ascetic. By the 1840s respectable mechanics began to aspire to the better things in life—the material trappings of comfort, convenience, and status. They were no longer content to squeeze families of four or five into single rooms with barely enough space for the spartan furnishings— table, chairs, and straw mattress—of the plebeian household. Mechanics began to expect more spacious homes, properly furnished, with a parlor and perhaps a separate room or two for children, as well as running water and enough land for a garden.[51] Thus, the popular definition of competence had shifted by midcentury in accordance with the general improvement in living standards. The problem was that most antebellum mechanics—masters and journeymen—did not share in the prosperity. The acceleration of the transportation and industrial revolutions was unsettling enough. No less distressing in the late 1840s was the massive influx of European immigrants into northern cities and the seeming expansionist designs of an aggressive planter aristocracy, the infamous "Slave Power" that would subvert republican liberty and foul the safety valve of western land. The world of the master mechanic and the skilled worker, never particularly stable to begin with, looked rather more unsure and vulnerable. The question of security assumed new urgency.

## The Search for Security

The search for security took two basic forms. One was social, the other political. Neither can be treated with any degree of thoroughness in this short space. All we can achieve here is a general and somewhat speculative discussion of a neglected aspect of popular social life and politics before the Civil War. The social expression of the search for security can be summed up in the word *fraternalism*. As is now well known, the Masons and the Odd Fellows, the two most important fraternal orders before the 1840s, were European imports that found fertile soil on this side of the Atlantic. The Masons, the older of the two, never quite recovered—in the antebellum period, at least—from the scandalous murder of a disgruntled brother which triggered the Antimasonic movement in the late 1820s.[52] Odd Fellowship took off in the 1840s, following the formal break in 1845 with its English parent, and fraternalism itself became the craze of the common man. Fraternal lodges shot up everywhere, and proved more durable and more popular than any other social organizations except churches. Indeed, the late antebellum fraternity made the temperance society (itself a form of fraternalism) look brittle by comparison. Only the Washingtonians, the mass temperance crusade of the early 1840s, rivaled fraternalism, and even then, not for long.[53] By 1845 Washingtonianism was eclipsed by an astounding array of fraternities. No other organizations had such a hold on the popular imagination.

Fraternalism has been treated variously by modern historians. One interpretation draws a portrait of a mass organization popular with the middle and working classes, and with just about everyone in between. The lodge promoted social cohesion and passed on the dominant values of "self-discipline, temperance, and industriousness." It was a school for the hegemonic "habits . . . essential to an industrial work ethic."[54] Another position emphasizes the matter of gender, and maleness in particular, so that the lodge becomes a sanctuary for men in quiet rebellion against the dominant perception of woman as moral guardian. Here fraternalism promotes the male bonding integral to the craft tradition and assists the reclamation of moral authority.[55]

What these interpretations underestimate is the more practical appeal of the fraternal lodge for a membership that was heavily, and in some communities overwhelmingly, of the middling and working classes. The lodge offered a relatively comprehensive form of privatized welfare for people badly in need of some protection from the uncertainties of the market and unlikely to receive support from state governments, which in the mid-1820s drastically cut back relief programs and restricted eligibility. Fraternalism's benefits, to be sure, made for a flimsy cushion, but it was the only available one outside the charity of the church. For a small initiation fee and modest monthly payments, brothers drew sick benefits that kept penniless families from the bread line, and acquired a burial plot for a proper funeral. Some assistance was better than none.

My chief concern, however, is with the politics of insecurity as reflected in third parties. It is worth noting before we begin that until recently historians have not taken third-partyism seriously. Modern historiography draws attention to what a recent critic aptly calls "successive party systems separated by periodic critical elections."[56] *Party system* in this context almost invariably means dominant parties, not insurgent ones. Indeed, the notion that the American system was a two-party system has become so reified that modern scholars routinely use similar evaluative language. Such words as "stable," "durable," and "resilient" recur again and again. According to Michael Holt, author of a major national study, the two-party system showed "marvelous flexibility and resilience"; according to Ronald Formisano, one of the few recent scholars to examine the political margins, the two-party system in Massachusetts from 1836 to 1853 reached a "'stable' phase" of development.[57] Another study of nineteenth-century Massachusetts concludes that politics "was anything but fluid."[58] An otherwise perceptive analysis of New York City winds up in agreement with the broader framework of the two-party system, observing that political tensions, though chronic, "didn't move to center stage" until the breakup of the second party system in the mid-1850s.[59] A second feature of much, if by no means all, of this literature is the tendency to divorce politics from economics. Politics becomes a force unto itself, driven sometimes by ideas, sometimes by politicians, and occasionally by constituencies, but seldom by the economy. Holt thus argues that the crisis of the 1850s derived from broad values rather than sectional ideologies "based on fundamentally different economic and social structures," and that such values were "basically political, not social, moral, or economic."[60] This purely political perspective characterizes modern political history, and the "new political history" in particular.

Let me deal with each of these points in turn. There is a case to be made for the resiliency of the second party system only if one believes that it enjoyed a *relatively* long political life. This is doubtful. Twenty years was not especially long in light of the lifespans of the four or five party systems recognized by political historians. Of these systems, only the first had a shorter lifespan, and some historians question whether it was much of a system at all.[61] Even if we concede for the sake of argument that the second system was resilient, its stability remains in doubt. Whigs and Democrats gave the appearance of stability, but only that. Both suffered bolts and desertions that sometimes grew into third-party movements, and sometimes did not. In either instance, repeated challenge from the flanks and from below forced both major parties to adjust.[62] The defections varied in magnitude but proved recurrent enough to form a pattern worthy of our attention. Consider the following list of insurgent parties:

Antimasonry, 1827–33
Working Men's party, 1827–33
Nativism (first phase), c. 1834–35
Locofocism, c. 1836–40
Liberty party, 1840–47
Nativism (second phase), c. 1844–48
Free Soilism, 1848–52
Nativism (third phase), c. 1854–60
Republican party, 1854 and later

It should be stressed that this roster is incomplete. It excludes minor revolts that took place at the municipal level, such as the Equal Rights parties that flared up during the depression of 1837, and omits rural defections still unstudied. It also omits party factions with fairly discrete identities which were only loosely tied to mainstream parties. One immediately thinks of the radical Democrats in Philadelphia during the 1830s. In addition, as far as we know insurgency occurred more frequently in the North than in the South. To speak of stability and resiliency is to speak more accurately of the second party system in the South; the northern variant of the system was more dynamic. Finally, while the intensity of third-party activity mounted in time, insurgency had been there from the beginning, and it was stubborn. Third-party movements of all shapes and sizes occurred just about every three years in the larger, industrializing states. Regular parties had to respond. They did so by absorbing individual insurgents, selectively endorsing their programs, or using a little or a lot of both strategies depending on the context. Insurgency mattered and needs to be considered.

This gets to my second point, concerning the tendency to divorce politics from economics. As Sean Wilentz perceptively argues, if social historians can be faulted for ignoring politics, political historians can be faulted for ignoring social and economic forces.[63] It seems arbitrary at best to assume that industrialism, or any other nonpolitical force, stops at the polling booth. Economic factors cannot be ignored, not even in a nation such as the United States, in which regional affinity and ethnocultural identity have assumed special salience. Some recent studies of antebellum politics, nearly all of which deal with third parties, seek a more holistic analysis by integrating society and economy into politics. This otherwise encouraging trend has two shortcomings. In some cases the economy becomes backdrop, scenery for actors and institutions, rather than an agent that shapes group and class interest and helps define what is important.[64] Alternatively, some scholars who insist on the importance of doing the social history of politics wind up discussing labor and labor politics only when self-described workingmen's parties crop up, as if workers got behind only those parties that bore their name. The casualties of such an approach are the commonalities that characterized both the social base and the program of antebellum insurgency.

This is not to claim that all insurgencies shared an identical social composition, only that their social compositions were similar. It is hard to know precisely how similar, at this juncture, because of the lack of data. There is no systematic, comparative study of third-party leaders and followers, which forces us to rely on scattered work—studies of leaders, activists, and petitioners. These fragments form a pattern that features a close fit between middling folk, skilled labor, and third-partyism.

The Working Men's movement of the late 1820s, perhaps the best studied of all such movements, is a good place to start a social analysis of third-partyism. Systematic reassessment of the "Workeys" began in the late 1940s in response to Arthur Schlesinger's thesis that the labor movement was the cradle of Jacksonian democracy. For Schlesinger's critics, the question of the hour was, Did labor support Andrew Jackson? The answer was yes or no, depending on the place under investigation and the research method used. Scholars who delved into the backgrounds of nominees for public office concluded that the Working Men were impostors, members of the elite masquerading as plebeians. It was bad enough, wrote Edward Pessen about the Boston Working Men, that Whigs crowded the Working Men's election ticket; even worse, "many candidates . . . were among the wealthiest men in the community."[65] Others contested this conclusion by concentrating on voters and party activists. They found legitimate labor parties, run by workers for workers. Walter Hugins did the most thorough study of this kind, and his profile of more than five hundred Working Men's party activists is adapted in table 7.1. Like most such studies, this one does not differentiate masters from journeymen, and includes both occupational and sectoral designations.[66] Nonetheless, the table shows that the New York Working Men's party was not exclusively composed of workingmen. About 60 to 70 percent of its members were tradesmen, both masters and journeymen; the rest were small manufacturers, retailers, petty professionals, and the like. Far from being a labor party strictly conceived, the Working Men brought together working people and the lower middle class, or the middling class. We shall call this political formation a "popular bloc."[67]

Other insurgencies did not always copy this bloc. Studies of Antimasonry, for instance, show no consistent social configuration. Antimasonry in upstate New York united members of the elite with the middle class in prosperous small towns;[68] in Massachusetts it tended to be "widely based in the middle and lower middle classes."[69] In New England as a whole, Antimasonry was diverse. In the burgeoning shoe town of Lynn, Massachusetts, "Antimasonry's stronghold in Essex county," the movement drew in workers under the leadership of entrepreneurs, a rough approximation of what happened in Worcester County.[70] The most that can be said of Antimasonry is that it defies easy generalization. In some communities it looked like the popular bloc of "Workeyism," or what Whitney Cross once called a revolt of the lower middle class;[71] in others it had a more entrepreneurial cast. It is the one insurgency that seems to fall outside the pattern.

Still other movements conformed closely to the popular bloc. Edward Magdol's study of abolitionist petitioners and members of antislavery societies in seven northeastern towns during the 1830s discloses a social composition not unlike that described by Hugins (see table 7.2). About 10 percent of the signers were farmers, semiskilled workers, and casual laborers—occupational designations that do not appear on lists of Working Men's activists. Nevertheless, the core of abolitionism likewise came from skilled workers and small proprietors.[72] Magdol's abolitionists, of

Table 7.1. The New York Working Men's Party, 1829–30

| Occupational Category | Number | Percentage |
|---|---|---|
| Building trades | 103 | 20 |
| Food- and beverage-related work | 83 | 16 |
| Manufacture of house furnishings | 63 | 12 |
| Metal trades | 60 | 12 |
| Leather trades, shoemaking | 37 | 7 |
| Professional and clerical work | 25 | 5 |
| Clothing and dry goods work | 34 | 7 |
| Manufacturers/artisans | 31 | 6 |
| Printing and publishing | 17 | 3 |
| Marine trades | 23 | 5 |
| Merchants and tradesmen | 17 | 3 |
| Transportation | 18 | 4 |
| Public employees | 2 | 0 |
| Miscellaneous | 2 | 0 |
| | 515 | 100 |

*Source:* Adapted from Walter E. Hugins, *Jacksonian Democracy and the Working Class: A Study of the New York Working Men's Movement, 1829–37* (Stanford, 1960), 125, table 8.

course, did not have a separate party until 1840, when the politically inclined among them formed the Liberty party, which gave way to the Free Soilers in 1848. Occupational profiles for these parties do not exist. Impressionistic evidence from primary and secondary sources, however, is suggestive of the popular bloc. A recent study of Worcester County, a hotbed of antislavery sentiment, describes Liberty party supporters as a coalition of orthodox Protestants in rural areas and some textile workers in factory towns.[73] Another shows that the party galvanized "artisans and small businessmen," and that after 1845 it attracted millhands. By 1846 the Liberty party had effectively assembled a popular bloc of skilled workers and small proprietors which would form the foundation of Free Soilism in small towns and some industrial hamlets.[74]

Nativism, the last insurgency under analysis, went through three stages: a short outburst in the 1830s; a longer, more potent rebellion in major cities from 1844 to 1848; and a third stage, which produced a national party, the Know-Nothings, that stretched beyond urban America to the South. Southern nativism is still unstudied. Its northern counterpart is better known and still controversial. A contemporary critic mistakenly dismissed the Bay

Table 7.2. Occupations of Petitioners and Members of Antislavery Societies

| Occupational Group (N = 1530) | Petitioners in Seven Cities (%) | Society Members (%) |
|---|---|---|
| Unskilled and menial service workers | 4.0 | 1.1 |
| Semiskilled and service workers | 2.5 | 2.3 |
| Proprietors, managers, official | 22.5 | 18.4 |
| Skilled workers | 53.8 | 64.4 |
| Commerce and sales workers | 4.1 | 3.4 |
| Semiprofessional workers | 0.7 | 1.1 |
| Professional workers | 4.8 | 1.1 |
| Farmers | 6.3 | 4.6 |
| Miscellaneous | 1.5 | 3.4 |

*Source:* Adapted from Edward Magdol, *The Antislavery Rank and File: A Social Profile of the Abolitionists' Constituency* (Westport, Conn., 1986), 68, table 6-5.

State's powerful nativists as a group of "spavined ministers, lying tooth-pullers, and buggering priests."[75] Modern scholars are divided between those who see a vehicle for anti-Catholicism and those who see a populist movement with the kind of social base traditionally identified with that political expression. The latter have the stronger case. As Michael Holt argues, nativism was "overwhelmingly a movement of the poor and middle classes."[76] Others have used different terminology to make the same point. The most thorough scholar of Massachusetts nativism describes a movement of "Yankee mechanics, factory workers, common laborers, clerks, small jobbers, tradesmen, and struggling entrepreneurs in the cities and larger towns."[77] Except for the likelihood that in New York, Philadelphia, and other places nativism did not reach so deeply into the working class, that description fits the movement generally.[78] Nativism was a prototypical popular bloc.

This interpretation of third-partyism's social complexion differs from the interpretation found in a substantial body of scholarship.[79] Past and recent historians tend to emphasize distinctions between insurgencies, and with some reason. The Working Men's parties of the late 1820s, for instance, exerted a stronger pull on sweated tradesmen than on fellow craftsmen in honorable callings. Tailors, shoemakers, and woodworkers, among others, dominated "Workeyism's" leadership, and presumably its rank-and-file as well.[80] Such tradesmen supported the nativist movement of the 1840s, but not to the same extent as their more prestigious fellows in the building trades, printing, and the luxury crafts. A decade later, the last and final phase of nativism integrated these segments of the working class and reached below skilled labor to ordinary factory hands. This, at least, was the case in Massachusetts. Here "Sam," as the Know-Nothings were popularly known, swept the Bay State's shoe and textile towns as well as its big cities.[81] Know-Nothingism was not only the most successful third-party initiative before Republicanism; it was also the most plebeian.

Ethnic differences also set these movements apart. In some places Antimasonry was intertwined with evangelicalism; in others it was more religiously diverse.[82] Evangelicals probably avoided the Working Men, whose leading lights were closely identified with Universalism, deism, and other rationalistic religions antagonistic to mainstream churches.[83] Reform Protestants found the Liberty party in New York and New England more to their liking. They were its principal voice until the middle of the 1840s, when the party began to attract renegade Democrats who were not affiliated with evangelicalism but were troubled by their party's doughface leadership.[84] Regional differences were also salient. The Working Men and Know-Nothings did best in large port cities and industrial towns. Free Soilism favored the frontier, but not exclusively. Some manufacturing centers, though not big cities (other than Cleveland), returned strong Free Soil votes.[85]

Third parties also stood on different platforms and aired distinctive programs. Indeed, each group sought to exorcise its own demon. Working Men attacked "monopolists" and "speculators"; nativists vilified immigrants; and Free Soilers assailed southern planters in what proved to be a retreat from the racial idealism and sympathy for the slave which had been the hallmark of abolitionism and the signature of the Liberty party. Parties ventured beyond these major concerns to various degrees, campaigning on broad or narrow platforms. Working Men put forth the most comprehensive reform program. They coupled policies for financial restructuring and land reform with a host of proposals for improving conditions in working-class districts. Nearly all demanded free public schools, relief for debtors, and the abolition of lotteries and other taxes that fell most heavily on the poor. They also called on municipal government to clean the streets in poorer neighborhoods and provide such areas with hydrant water.[86] The agendas of succeeding insurgencies, preoccupied as they were with "popery" and the "Slave Power," seem to pale by comparison. This, at least, is the view of traditional political historians, who tend to focus on national politics and formal party platforms.[87] The platforms of the Liberty and Free Soil parties leave the impression that neither party stood for much on issues other than the slavery question, although they shared the antiparty animus common to all insurgencies. Liberty men included a vague reference to the need for general education and called for economy in government. The Free Soilers in 1848 were only slightly more expansive, echoing the Liberty demand for smaller government while supporting cheap postage and internal improvements.[88] The Know-Nothing platform of 1856 looks even more anemic. It, too, favored government retrenchment and little else other than its well-known program for curtailing the political rights of foreigners.[89]

Revisionist work on third parties at the state and local levels, however, presents a different picture. It indicates that it is a mistake to regard the third parties of the 1840s and 1850s as single-issue initiatives. The heated and sometimes hysterical attacks on immigrants and planters masked a broader reformist sensibility publicized in party organs and on campaign trails. In rarer cases, as in Massachusetts in the mid-1850s, the reformism of insurgency became law. The landslide victory of Bay State nativism in 1854 unleashed a reformist tide that crested a year later and did not subside until 1858. Know-Nothing lawmakers predictably restricted the rights and privileges of foreigners, though not as aggressively or thoroughly as one would have expected given the rhetorical extremism of party stumpers. Indeed, "Sam's" legislators invested more energy and imagination in tending to the economic and social interests of their followers. They failed to enact only two major reforms, a legally mandated ten-hour day and the secret ballot, both of which went down to narrow defeat.[90] However, they delivered relief to debtors by liberalizing an old homestead exemption law and abolishing imprisonment for debt. They strengthened a mechanics' lien law so that an unpaid worker could place a lien on his employer's land and buildings. They expanded public education by increasing funds for local schools and prohibiting factory owners from employing children who did not attend class for at least eleven weeks a year. Nativist reform reached farther still. Local communities were permitted to fund and build infrastructure, and state boards were set up to oversee certain businesses. The Board of Insurance Commissioners, for one, inspected the books of insurance companies to prevent fraud and abuse. Know-Nothings also blazed new trails with regard to women's rights, granting women limited property rights and easing restrictions on divorce.[91]

Not all such policies, of course, were invented by the Know-Nothings. Ever since the days of the Middling Interest, a group of Boston mechanics in the 1820s, activists had clamored for debtor relief and other reforms. The Know-Nothings pursued the traditional agenda of the popular bloc and significantly embellished it, largely by investing state and local government with new regulatory and administrative powers. Liberty men and Free Soilers seem to have picked up the torch of reform. We cannot know for certain at this juncture because the local activities of these groups remain cloudy. It may be significant, however, that in the mid-1840s dissidents within the Bay State Liberty party challenged the "one idea" strategy of the party leadership. This faction joined the group that met in 1847 at Macedon Lock, New York, to draft the "Nineteen Articles."[92] They then founded the Liberty League, a Liberty party splinter informed by a blend of abolitionism and the laissez-faire economic radicalism of Locofocoism. At least some Liberty Leaguers and Free Soilers, however, were general reformists who did not shy away from enlisting government on the side of the popular bloc and who may be seen as a link between the Working Men and the Know-Nothings.[93]

Elizur Wright was very much in this mold. Wright was the son of a Connecticut farmer and teacher who moved his family to the Ohio frontier in 1810 to start a farm and open an academy. He was a quirky man who rejected evangelicalism for atheism, and Garrisonianism for the Liberty party and then the Free Soilers. He had a Yale education, but before the Civil War never earned the income we would expect of one holding such a credential. He instead dedicated his life to reform, first in the 1830s as an antislavery organizer in New York, then in Boston during the 1840s as editor of the abolitionist *Chronotype*. Wright is best understood as a member of the middling class and a radical reformer with a special feel for the insecurities of ordinary people. He became a leading advocate for regulation of the fledgling insurance business, which led to his reputation as "the father of insurance."[94] But he was no more a single-issue reformer than numerous other Liberty men. Wright used the pages of the *Chronotype* to expand the base of the party by supporting the ten-hour day and other popular causes. According to a recent historian of the Liberty party in Massachusetts, Wright's agitation in the mid-1840s helped the party make headway in some textile towns.[95] When in 1848 Wright cast a reluctant ballot for the Free Soilers, he teamed up with activists who were distressed not only by slavery but also by the social costs of advancing industrialism and were determined to put government on the side of the weak and vulnerable. The problem, said a Free Soiler, was the combination of strong employers and limited government, which left working people increasingly dependent on wage labor and unable to protect themselves from what a party colleague called the "vast commercial interests."[96] "As wealth increases, and concentrates itself in fewer hands," intoned a leading Massachusetts Free Soiler, "the protection of the mass of working-men, who must be dependent in a very great degree upon the wealthy for employment, becomes doubly important."[97] This turned out to be the rationale for the secret ballot, a legal limitation on the hours of work, and other reforms supported by Bay State Free Soilers, Coalitionists, and Know-Nothings.

Contrary to most recent scholarship, although third-partyism differed in emphasis and in kind, it had an underlying continuity. The Working Men's abomination of financiers, the nativists' disdain of foreigners, the Free Soilers' hatred of planters—and slaves, for that matter—these may be interpreted as variations on the common theme of the search for security. Again and again polemicists for the Working Men assailed merchant capitalists, not only for skimming the rewards of manual labor but also for driving small proprietors to ruin. Speculation and competition, said a leading labor radical, turned the world of the mechanic upside down. Instead of being "an employment of the *first importance*, held in the highest estimation, and the surest means of a gradual and certain accumulation," petty proprietorship was demoted to "one of the meanest, most precarious, and most unprofitable modes of obtaining a subsistence."[98] Master craftsmen either lived on the edge of poverty, or went out of business and reverted to wage labor, which only increased the downward pressure on wages.[99] This dynamic rendered obsolete the old adage "Keep of thy shop and thy shop will keep thee."[100]

Labor radicals sought redress through both private activity and a blend of negative and positive government. Thomas Skidmore's followers, of course, preferred redistribution of land, but theirs was an extreme position, and one not widely shared. Cooperation and a more palatable version of land reform would continue to fire the imagination of the popular bloc, but the early 1840s saw a truce in the political war against merchant capital. It yielded, if only momentarily, to newly perceived threats embodied by immigrants and planters. That immigrants threatened the security of small employers and skilled workers needs no further commentary.[101] What needs to be explained is why in the mid-1850s nativists made a relatively easy transition from the politics of antiforeignism to the politics of antislavery. The ability of some Free Soil and Republican politicians to excite racist passion mattered. So did the rapid-fire national events—the Kansas-Nebraska Act, "Bleeding Kansas," and the Dred Scott decision—that riveted attention on the hated "Slave Power." Such alarming developments at the national level worked to the benefit of shrewd and wily politicians in the emergent Republican party, who could not succeed without blunting the thrust of Know-Nothingism and seducing nativist politicians with deals and bargains. The wheeling and dealing of such Republican operatives as Henry Wilson (as well as the naïveté of the nativists) continues to be seen by historians as a major cause of Republicanism's eclipse of nativism.[102] What such an interpretation fails to explain is why ordinary nativists went along. Many no doubt were impressed with the antisouthern animus of Republicanism. Many more may have been motivated by the same sense of vulnerability, intensified by the panic of 1857 and the secular trend toward the concentration of ownership in the crafts, that had arrayed them against bankers and then immigrants. This social aspect was the common denominator of insurgency and the helpmate of Republican politicians.

## Conclusions

Most of the evidence presented here pertains to the Northeast, and to Massachusetts especially. More work on insurgent politics within the region and in other areas—notably rural America—is needed before hard and fast conclusions are warranted. Nonetheless, several tentative observations are appropriate at this juncture. First, and perhaps most obvious, it is inaccurate to equate the nation's party system with a two-party system. Third-partyism was not abnormal, dysfunctional, or insignificant, but a recurrent, formative force that influenced the policies and conduct of conventional parties. It is axiomatic that the Working Men infused the Democrats with economic radicalism after 1828 and made them attentive to economic issues, that the evangelical moralism of Antimasonry flowed into Whiggery, and that the Liberty and Free Soil parties forced mainstream parties to reckon with slavery. Early third parties mobilized new voters and thereby contributed to the huge increase in turnout associated with the second party system.[103] They also anticipated the hoopla and pageantry of the 1840 presidential campaign.[104] Yet much remains to be done. We need a clearer understanding of how insurgency affected policy and politics at the state and local level, and how mainstream parties responded to their challenge. This necessitates asking different questions; that is, replacing the conventional query regarding why third parties failed with the more potentially fruitful question of what difference they made, not simply in electoral politics but also in public policy formation.

Second, to argue that third parties shared a similar social composition is not to argue that their social compositions were identical. There were palpable distinctions between such parties, but within the broader context of a popular bloc framed by the middling and working classes. The emphasis on the middling class is deliberate, partly because of its pervasive political presence and partly because I wish to stimulate dialogue about such an important group. The irony is that we continue to have only a vague impression of the middle class, and a dimmer one still of the middling class, in spite of the national creed that we are and have been a middle-class people. That middling men supplied much of the leadership for insurgencies that had working-class followings is easily understood. They did not reap their share of the bounty that was the commercial and industrial revolutions. For every master mechanic who became an entrepreneur there were several small proprietors whose businesses went under, not just once but often a few times, or who earned incomes that hovered at subsistence levels. Their standard of living was no better than that of their own workers and markedly inferior to that of the nonmanual middle class. This produced a tenuous social bond between small employer and employee which was reinforced by shared traditions of craft fraternalism, by the growing stigma attached to manual labor, and by mutual feelings of insecurity and vulnerability. Small proprietors, after all, were also workers who shared the wage earners' condition of dependence—not directly on a boss, as it turned out, but on merchants, financiers, and others who were in command of the credit, reputation, and other resources required for commercial success. Economic tensions between small proprietor and creditor sometimes carried over into politics, for the same men who controlled capital resources doubled as political leaders in regular parties. Economic forces helped propel middling men into insurgency, but neither the social relations of the market nor the insecurity these engendered were enough. They did not in and of themselves "cause" the political restlessness of insurgency, any more than hardship and exploitation alone "caused" labor unrest. The quality of local leadership figured in the equation, as did the conduct of politics. Regular parties that responded to political initiatives in some fashion from below and absorbed plebeian political talent seem to have escaped the challenge of insurgency. Conversely, in economically dynamic regions parties that resisted reform and limited access to their halls invited third-partyism. Massachusetts was one such closed place. Its Whiggish elite, conservative and clubby in the extreme, ran the Bay State without much opposition and without much regard for such popular causes as the secret ballot and the ten-hour day. Such indifference and arrogance eventually took its toll, for nearly every third party that emerged between 1825 and 1854 gained expression in the Bay State.

The ten-hour question directs us to another social facet of third partyism. Historians have been too quick to attribute a discrete social complexion to insurgency, characterizing third parties as "working class" or "middle class." This is unduly simplistic and is at odds with evidence indicating that no insurgency, not even the Working Men, represented a single social class or even the exclusive interest of one. It is more accurate to speak of an alliance, or what I have called a popular bloc, and to recognize the fact that the preponderance of the issues raised by insurgents—including debtor relief, banking reform, free soil, and the like—reflected the interests of this larger social formation. This also holds for the political stage (and possibly the earlier trade union stage) of the ten-hour movement. Workers were the strongest but by no means the only advocates of a shorter workday. Middling folk under certain circumstances joined their struggle. For some small employers the ten-hour day was a means of expressing opposition to the industrial elite. Others had more concrete grounds for support. In single-industry towns without alternative sources of employment, their children and sometimes their wives worked in the mills. Ten hours was no more of a class issue, strictly conceived, than was any other reform proposed by third parties.

Finally, if it can be said that political history would benefit from integrating economic history into its analysis, it can also be said that in the process it would do well to revisit the matter of social mobility. The mobility studies of the 1960s and 1970s put to rest the "rags-to-riches" myth but may have inadvertently left us with the myth of incremental improvement. It is doubtful that this relatively rosy formulation can be generalized to the middling class. One or two systematic studies, coupled with anecdotal evidence gleaned from underutilized autobiographies of mechanics and petty producers, indicates that failure was more likely than even modest success and that in any event fear of falling was common.[105] We need to assess the political ramifications of failure and the insecurity felt by ordinary people in nineteenth-century America. The industrial revolution, immigration, and southern expansionism seem to have enhanced such anxieties, which became the tinder of political insurgency.

# PART III

# BIOGRAPHICAL APPROACHES

# 8

GARY J. KORNBLITH

# Becoming Joseph T. Buckingham:
## The Struggle for Artisanal Independence
## in Early-Nineteenth-Century Boston

LIKE THE MYTH of agrarian self-sufficiency, the ideal of artisanal independence shimmers with nostalgic appeal in the postmodern age. By standard scholarly accounts, traditional craftsmen aspired to the proprietorship of their own small enterprises and to the achievement of moderate levels of material comfort, but not to the massive accumulation of wealth or capital for its own sake. The pursuit of artisanal independence was part of a system of social relations that was more egalitarian, more cooperative, and less exploitative than that associated with the rise of industrial capitalism.[1] Yet historians must be careful not to exaggerate the contrast between handicraft and capitalist modes of production and their corresponding social mentalities. There were, indeed, essential historical links between the struggle for artisanal independence and the emergence of modern bourgeois values such as self-reliance, self-interest, and self-aggrandizement. This essay explores these connections by examining the career and social thought of Joseph T. Buckingham, a printer, publisher, and editor in early-nineteenth-century Boston.

No case study can claim to be fully representative of a larger historical process, but for analytical purposes Buckingham may be regarded as a paradigmatic figure. While he does not stand out as one of history's "great men," his very lack of greatness suggests that his experiences were similar to those of many other artisans who labored mightily to survive and to succeed in early-nineteenth-century urban America. The analysis that follows is divided into three parts. The first traces Buckingham's uneven rise from rural poverty to urban respectability, thereby providing a biographical context for interpreting his social outlook. The second section focuses on how, as a newspaper editor and a spokesman for Boston's master mechanics in the 1820s and 1830s, Buckingham refashioned the ideal of artisanal independence to suit the demands of a developing market economy. The concluding section examines the difficulties he encountered in trying to realize this revised ideal in practice. Throughout his career, independence remained an alluring yet elusive goal.

## Buckingham's Rise to Respectability

Joseph T. Buckingham's early career reflected the persistence of customary craft patterns in post-Revolutionary New England. Born Joseph Buckingham Tinker in Windham, Connecticut, in 1779, he grew up in rural poverty and was indentured to a local farming family as a young boy. He took up printing at the age of sixteen, serving as an apprentice first in Walpole, New Hampshire, and then in Greenfield, Massachusetts. By the time he turned twenty, he was well skilled at both the press and the case, and he had taught himself the basics of English grammar. In 1800 he moved to Boston, where for the next few years he worked mainly as a journeyman for Thomas and Andrews, the city's largest printing establishment.[2] In 1804 he became superintendent of the firm's mechanical operations and signed a multi-year contract "as the Printer of Messrs. Thomas and Andrews' copyright and other publications."[3]

Although he was not yet the proprietor of his own enterprise—a prerequisite for independence as traditionally conceived—he was by the age of twenty-five his own boss, and he enjoyed a good deal of social autonomy. He marked his new status by changing his name and taking a wife. In 1804 he successfully petitioned the Massachusetts General Court for permission to transpose his middle and last names.[4] According to his memorial, he acted out of deference to the wishes of his mother's family, but he presumably also had another reason for making the switch: a desire for social respectability. With its aristocratic connotations, "Buckingham" was a considerably more distinguished surname than the plebeian "Tinker." So it was as Joseph T. Buckingham that he married Melinda Alvord in 1805. The next year she gave birth to the first of their thirteen children.[5]

Under his arrangement with Thomas and Andrews, Buckingham had complete charge of the day-to-day operations of the print shop, and he was paid according to a fixed price schedule for all work executed under his supervision. At the same time, he personally took part in the productive process. "Besides the general superintendence of the press, proof-reading, &c.," he later recalled, "I set the types of the Gloucester Grammar, all the Tables in Alden's Spelling-Book, the greater part (and all the difficult part) of Pike's Arithmetic, and generally, all that is technically called *table-work*." Almost invariably he spent "from twelve to sixteen hours a day in the office," usually staying "till all the workmen had left, and to see that fire and lights were all extinguished." Although, by his own account, "it was not fore-ordained that I should be rich," he did manage to rent a house and support his family in modest comfort.[6] "The prices allowed me but a small profit above the rate of a journeyman's wages," he explained in his *Personal Memoirs*, "but that small profit, added to the earnings of my labor *at the case*, enabled me . . . to gain a decent livelihood."[7]

While superintending Thomas and Andrews's shop, Buckingham launched his first two forays into the increasingly competitive world of Boston journalism. Neither survived for very long. The *Polyanthos*, a literary monthly, died after a year and a half; the *Ordeal: A Critical Journal of Politicks and Literature* lasted only six months.[8] Yet Buckingham did not despair. In 1810 he and a partner bought Thomas and Andrews's "whole printing apparatus" for forty-five hundred dollars, payable in installments. The partner soon opted out of the venture, but Buckingham went forward in the expectation that, as proprietor of his own enterprise, he would make "a better fortune" over the long term.[9] To signal his achievement of full-fledged master status and artisanal independence, he joined the Massachusetts Charitable Mechanic Association, which elected him its secretary in 1812.[10]

Buckingham's confidence in his prospects as a master printer proved misplaced, however. In 1815 he went bankrupt. To some extent, his financial woes can be traced to his journalistic ambitions. After experimenting for a short while with a weekly magazine titled the *Comet,* he revived the *Polyanthos* on a monthly basis in 1812.[11] It survived for two years but died a second death in the fall of 1814.

Compounding this failure was the deterioration of Buckingham's book-printing business. Control over the Boston book trade rested mainly with major booksellers, who doubled as publishers and contracted with printers for the production of specific works. Booksellers exchanged books among themselves to ensure an appropriate mix for retail purposes. As the Boston market expanded rapidly after the turn of the century, both booksellers and printers formed associations to regulate prices and maintain discipline within the trade. But the War of 1812 wreaked havoc on this guildlike system, and Buckingham, among others, suffered the consequence.[12] Lacking enough business "to employ so large an office" efficiently, he began to experiment with publishing books at his own risk.[13] Then he purchased "the stock of a small bookstore" and found himself saddled with an inventory of books that he could neither sell nor exchange with other booksellers. "Sales were insufficient to pay rent, interest, and current expenses," he later remembered. "Notes were protested. Attachments succeeded. Then a lawsuit. Then a sale at auction of every thing but what the law exempted from attachment."[14] At age thirty-five, with a wife and six children to support, he was left "entirely destitute of the means of prosecuting the business in which I was educated."[15]

Within two years, however, Buckingham regained master status. After teaching school temporarily to make ends meet, he returned to printing in 1817 "as a kind of overseer" for the firm of West and Richardson, booksellers and publishers.[16] While employed in this capacity, he issued a prospectus of the *New-England Galaxy and Masonic Magazine,* to be published weekly for the price of three dollars per year. The idea of including a special section on Masonic affairs came from Samuel L. Knapp, a recent acquaintance of Buckingham's who belonged to the fraternity. Though, like Buckingham, Knapp was recovering from bankruptcy, he volunteered to edit the Masonic department without compensation. He also helped with other editorial chores while Buckingham handled the manual tasks himself. Together they put out the inaugural issue of the *Galaxy* on October 10, 1817.[17]

Taking a major risk at a time when Boston's economy was in turmoil, Buckingham subsequently resigned his post with West and Richardson and set up his own shop for printing the *Galaxy* on a regular basis. That he managed to assemble the necessary equipment with little or no money in hand testifies to both his own resourcefulness and the survival of a cooperative ethos within the craft. He leased space above a dry goods store for an annual rent of $150, and he negotiated to buy a rusting press from a second-hand furniture dealer for the modest price of $95, payable (with interest) at the end of six months.[18] With his note guaranteed by a close friend, he purchased a font of used type for $165. He also drew on the generosity of his fellow printers. "Composing sticks, chases, and other articles . . . were lent by accommodating neighbors," and sometimes he "set certain portions of the paper . . . in smaller type" at other printing offices.[19] Buckingham's return to "independence," in short, depended heavily on the material assistance of others.

Unlike Buckingham's previous journalistic endeavors, the *Galaxy* soon developed into a profitable enterprise. With Freemasonry in its heyday in Boston, the magazine's Masonic focus attracted a respectable readership, and during the course of a year, circulation rose from two hundred to one thousand. In addition to subscriptions, advertisements yielded significant revenue. Although early on he had to turn to a friend for additional loans, over time Buckingham was able to retire his debts and achieve a modicum of financial security.[20]

As he grew more prosperous, he withdrew from direct engagement in the manual production of the magazine. At the start, with the help of an apprentice or two, he set the type as well as wrote much of the copy. Midway through the first year of publication, he appealed to readers for forbearance and sympathy. "Those who know [that] the weight of responsibility, both in the editorial and mechanical execution of this paper, rests upon an individual, we hope will look with softened severity upon its imperfections, and impute its faults to almost any other cause than indifference."[21] In 1820, however, he turned over management of the mechanical operation to Jefferson Clark, who was publicly identified as the magazine's printer. Having spent a quarter-century in the trade as a practical mechanic, Buckingham left manual labor behind so he could concentrate on the mental work of writing, editing, and publishing.

Once the *Galaxy* had achieved notoriety, Buckingham moved to drop the reference to Masonry from the magazine's title. Knapp had withdrawn from the enterprise in 1818, and by late 1820 the Masonic emphasis seemed a hindrance to further growth in readership. Thus for reasons of business, not religion, politics, or philosophy, the *Galaxy* forsook its Masonic identity several years before the rise of organized opposition to the fraternity.[22]

On national and state issues, the *Galaxy* (like the *Ordeal* before it) was staunchly Federalist. Buckingham bemoaned the decline in partisanship during the so-called Era of Good Feelings and sharply attacked advocates of cooperation with the Monroe administration. Yet on local matters, he struck a more radical pose. In 1820 he warned, "An order of nobility is growing up in the metropolis of New-England, which threatens to destroy every vestige of our boasted equality in society."[23] Two years later, he supported Boston's Middling Interest movement in its bid to wrest control of the municipal government from the local Federalist establishment. "Why should not the middling interest do every thing they can do," he asked rhetorically, "to overthrow the power, or at least, to neutralize the operations of a monied aristocracy, whose patriotism is nothing but selfishness and the love of power, and whose public spirit is deposited, *for safe-keeping,* in the vaults of the banks?"[24]

After six years of publishing the *Galaxy*, Buckingham in 1824 decided to expand his operations by launching a new daily newspaper, the *Boston Courier*. His startup of this paper differed considerably from his startup of the *Galaxy;* this time, he did not have to scrounge for supplies or settle for buying second-hand equipment on credit. With the financial backing of several local merchants and manufacturers—though evidently not from any of the so-called Boston Associates who invested in regional textile development—the *Courier* made its debut on March 1, 1824.[25] Fourteen months later, paid circulation approached one thousand.[26]

To lighten his multifarious burdens, Buckingham, like many master artisans before him, brought his eldest son into the business. In the fall of 1827, Joseph H. Buckingham officially became co-editor and co-publisher of the *Courier*.[27] When the younger Joseph withdrew to pursue a separate career the following year, Buckingham turned to his next oldest son, Edwin, for assistance. Edwin had quit high school at age thirteen "and entered the New-England Galaxy as an apprentice."[28] Once he had mastered the mechanical side of the business, he began to help out with the editorial side. In July 1828, Buckingham formally made Edwin, then eighteen years old, and another young man, Charles H. Locke, co-publishers (along with Buckingham himself) of the Galaxy.[29]

Only a few months later, however, Buckingham negotiated the sale of the Galaxy to two Boston lawyers, Theophilus Parsons and Willard Phillips.[30] This allowed Buckingham more time to devote not only to the Courier but also to government service. In May 1828 he was elected as a National Republican to the first of three terms he would serve in the Massachusetts House of Representatives.[31]

Yet in 1831, pressed by his son Edwin, who was "ardent, ambitious, active and panting for a pecuniary independence," he agreed to help launch a new monthly journal that would feature short fiction, poetry, reflective essays, literary criticism, and social commentary.[32] Together they "opened an entirely new, and extensive Printing Office at No. 22 Congress Street," from which they promptly issued the premier number of the New-England Magazine—complete with contributions by the Reverend Nathaniel L. Frothingham, Professor Henry Wadsworth Longfellow, Congressman Edward Everett, and Dr. Samuel Gridley Howe, among others.[33] The New-England Magazine rapidly attracted a wide audience, and it confirmed Buckingham's reputation as one of Boston's most influential editors and publishers in the early 1830s.

## Buckingham's Conception of Independence

In retrospect, one might interpret Buckingham's rise from apprenticeship to prominence as the story of an ambitious "man on the make" who deserted his craft for the lure of personal fame and fortune as an editor and entrepreneur. Yet Buckingham never forsook his identity as an artisan devoted to the trade in which he had enlisted as a youth, and he continued throughout his career to take an active part in the Massachusetts Charitable Mechanic Association, the foremost organization of master artisans in Boston. In 1830 he was elected the association's vice-president and gave the keynote address at its triennial festival. In 1832 he was elevated to president, a position he held for three years, the maximum allowed under the organization's by-laws.[34] Long after he had stopped setting type or working the press, he regarded himself—and was regarded by his contemporaries—as a master mechanic. This sense of identity, in turn, strongly informed his views on the social dynamics and political economy of Jacksonian America.[35]

Buckingham recognized that the traditional notion of artisanal independence had to be adapted to the new realities of a rapidly developing market society. No longer did the ownership of a shop or other enterprise ensure civic autonomy. No longer was public virtue, with its heroic connotations, a relevant social ethic. "Self-love," he believed, motivated persons of all ranks and occupations. Yet Buckingham did not despair of the materialism or individualism of Jacksonian society. Rather, he believed that self-love rightly understood (as Tocqueville might have termed it) could effectively sustain a republican social order if citizens agreed on what constituted fair behavior in an expanding marketplace. As both a social observer and a political partisan, Buckingham sought to formulate "new rules of the game" suitable to a democratic capitalist society.

"What is the chief end of Man?" Buckingham asked at the beginning of his speech to the Massachusetts Charitable Mechanics Association in 1830. "The answer," he said, "in a single word is HAPPINESS." But what was happiness? Personal enjoyment in conjunction with—not at the expense of—others. "No truth is more sacred or immutable than the oft-repeated maxim, 'Self love and social are the same,'" he declared. From this perspective, "Public Spirit" was little more than selfishness that, by accident or design, served the general welfare. "Every passion, which men have, is selfish to a greater or less degree," he insisted, citing *Cato's Letters* as an authority. "When, by the agency of these passions, individuals or the public are benefited, and the consequences of their operations are such as tend to the general good, they may properly be called *disinterested*, in the common acceptation of that word."[36]

Elaborating on this theme, Buckingham argued that persons in the "middling ranks of society" were especially well positioned to serve the public good by serving themselves. By "middling ranks" (or "middling class"—he used both terms), he meant "the farmers, the mechanics, the manufacturers, the traders, who carry on, professionally the ordinary operations of buying, selling, and exchanging merchandize, and most of the merchants." They were not particularly virtuous (in the classical republican sense of the term), but they were industrious. In contrast to both "the unproductive poor and the unprofitable rich," they relied for their livelihoods "on the active employment of their faculties, whether physical or intellectual." As a result, their "unextinguishable desire for more" gave "birth to invention, and impart[ed] vigor to enterprise," which in turn enhanced economic productivity and increased the wealth of society as a whole.[37]

In celebrating the acquisitive tendencies of the middling class, Buckingham did not embrace an ethic of unadulterated greed or reckless speculation. In traditional artisanal fashion, he prized work, and he disdained those "who are subjected to no necessity of manual labor, and who, for the most part are incapable of any mental exercise beyond that of calculating interest on notes and bonds." Selfishness and acquisitiveness only served the public good when tempered by "the science of self-government and self-control." "Let men," he advised, "be taught that independence—the only independence worth having—is an absolute and entire reliance on their own personal efforts. Let them be taught that their chief good is to be found in the enjoyment of subdued appetites, disciplined passions, temperate habits, moderate desires, well-informed minds."[38]

Here was an ideal of independence no longer contingent upon a particular material base—the ownership of a farm, a shop or other enterprise—but still tied to the cultural values of self-reliance, self-discipline, and industriousness. Possession of property, per se, mattered less than possession of character. In sum, independence, for Buckingham, was ultimately a state of mind: "It is wisdom and understanding that make the man independent. . . . Chains and fetters may be made of gold as well as of iron, but neither the one nor the other can keep down the energies of an intelligent, well-cultivated, independent mind."[39]

Underlying Buckingham's bourgeois reformulation of independence was his confidence in the dynamic potential of a market economy. In a society with a fixed amount of wealth, the pursuit of private advantage necessarily threatened the private interests of others and the public interest of the society as a whole. But in a society where the total amount of wealth was rapidly increasing, all could advance themselves at the same time—at least in theory. Significantly, although Buckingham celebrated personal ambition, he did not advocate cutthroat competition. On the contrary, he envisioned a rational (that is, fair, honest, and relatively stable) marketplace where commercial transactions were mutually beneficial to buyers and sellers alike. To create and sustain such a context, in turn, required the deliberate regulation of the general economy.

Like many other New Englanders of Federalist heritage, Buckingham in the late 1820s embraced the National Republican vision of an American System guided by the federal government and guarded by a protective tariff. He did so not from the perspective of a large-scale capitalist but from the vantage point of a master artisan and small entrepreneur interested in promoting the prosperity of the urban economy. When free-trade advocates claimed to speak for a majority of Bostonians, he retorted in the *Boston Courier*, "We cannot so libel the intelligence, sagacity, and good sense of the middling class,—which includes seven eighths of the whole population,—as to give currency to a supposition that they are ready to abandon the manufacturers of woollens and cottons . . . and those who are employed in almost every trade which furnishes articles necessary for comfort, convenience and luxury, to the mercy of Manchester and Birmingham agents."[40]

At issue, he argued, was nothing less than the question of independence, understood in both individual and collective terms: "We believe that all classes love independence too well, and know too well in what independence consists, to assent to, much less be active in producing, a state of things that must keep us forever poor and dependent."[41] For mechanics in particular, he suggested, independence was the paramount concern. He asked rhetorically, "Is it possible that the mechanics of this city, a bold enterprising, industrious race, who have made themselves independent by the labor of their hands under the protection of the government, will consent to give up the privilege of sustaining that independence and transmitting it to their children?"[42]

In the heat of the congressional contest between Nathan Appleton and Henry Lee in 1830, Buckingham took his argument a step further. "The people of this country want the freedom to pursue the occupations to which they have been educated," he wrote, and it was the duty of the government to protect them "in such pursuits, against the competition of foreign mechanics, manufacturers, and laborers." Free trade might enhance the wealth of a few shipowners, but it would destroy the livelihoods of many more farmers and mechanics. Both as productive individuals and as loyal citizens of a republic, middling folk deserved a better fate than an unregulated market would assign them. "The doctrine of free trade, in the unlimited extent contended for by its professed advocates," Buckingham concluded, "is opposed in principle and practice, to all kinds of *free labor.*"[43] And to underscore the artisanal heritage of his argument, he reprinted a pro-tariff circular issued more than four decades before by the Association of Tradesmen and Manufacturers of the Town of Boston.[44]

A similar concern for fairness and rationality in the marketplace informed Buckingham's attitude toward lotteries. Prompted by the suicide of a bookkeeper who had defrauded his employers of thousands of dollars to purchase lottery tickets, Buckingham in 1833 called for the active suppression of lotteries within Massachusetts. From his perspective, lotteries of all sorts were a form of gaming which rewarded speculation and vice rather than industry and virtue. "It is seeking property for which no equivalent is to be paid," he wrote on behalf of a committee of the Massachusetts House of Representatives, and thus violated the ethical principles of a market society. "Considered as a *means* to unfair and fraudulent dealing, lotteries are to be classed with those crimes, by which one man is cheated out of his property by another," he reasoned. "Considered in relation to *those who are thus operated upon* . . . and most especially those who may be defrauded by the operation, they are entitled to be protected against themselves, by removing the temptation to do wrong."[45] In other words, government was obliged to protect citizens against threats to their moral as well as their material independence.

This is not to say that Buckingham advocated a comprehensive restructuring of capitalist social relations. From National Republican ranks, he moved into the Whig party, not the Working Men's party. Indeed, he denounced the Working Men's campaign in 1834 as a "useless and absurd project," and he fiercely challenged the Working Men's claim "that there is nothing in the circumstances of this country, nor in its experience hitherto, which promises to the laboring class any ultimate exemption from the toil and penury and degradation, which have been, and now are, its invariable lot in older countries." "Does not every day's experience give the lie direct to this bold and reckless assertion?" he asked. So far as he could see, in New England, at least, "labor and prudence" were consistently and justly rewarded with "wealth and competence."[46]

Buckingham thus disputed those who portrayed society as sharply polarized between the rich and the poor, the few and the many. "One of the most foolish, as well as the most wicked tricks to which our American Tories resort," he wrote about the Democrats, "is that of exciting the poor against the rich, and pretending that the man who by honest industry has succeeded in attaining a competence, is an enemy to the working classes, and the oppressor of the poor."[47] He had no patience for economic levelers. Efforts to equalize wealth or income, he believed, would inevitably reward the lazy and vicious at the expense of the diligent and industrious. "How long could any community exist under the practical operation of such dogmas?" he wondered.[48] Common sense as well as justice dictated that property should belong to those who earned it. Otherwise the distinction between independence and idleness would be lost. Buckingham envisioned a self-regulated marketplace, not a risk-free economy or a radically egalitarian social order.

## Buckingham's Financial Crisis

Ironically, even as he argued publicly that in New England hard work produced prosperity, Buckingham privately confronted serious financial problems. In 1833, after a long illness, his son Edwin died, leaving him deeply distraught and burdened with "the double duty of conducting a monthly magazine and a daily newspaper" by himself.[49] Adding to his personal hardships was the economic turmoil generated by the Bank War. In a letter to Nathan Appleton dated April 17, 1834, Buckingham bemoaned the recent "embarrassments which have pervaded all sorts of business, and affected, more or less, all classes of men, and all trades and professions." "The utter impossibility of collecting the ordinary income of a newspaper (during the last eight months) with the necessary facility and in sufficient amount to meet the required expenditure," he explained, "has led to the necessity of *borrowing;* and now when a brighter day seems to be approaching . . . *our borrowed money*—borrowed not in very large sums but of many individuals, haunts the imagination, lies with the weight of a millstone upon all attempts to get free and depresses every thing like energy in the editorial department."[50]

To extricate himself from this predicament, Buckingham asked Appleton to arrange "among the friends of the American System and Domestic Industry the loan of five or six Thousand Dollars for the term of one year, the interest payable quarterly."[51] How Appleton responded to this request is not known, but Buckingham's fortunes took a brief turn for the better when in the fall of 1834 he sold the *New-England Galaxy* to Samuel Gridley Howe and John O. Sargent.[52] Soon thereafter he enlarged the dimensions of the *Courier* without raising the paper's price. As he explained his business strategy to his readers, he anticipated that the "increased expenditure for paper and labor" would be more than outweighed by "the augmentation of income from subscriptions and advertisements."[53]

Yet evidently he miscalculated. In the fall of 1836, lacking adequate resources to cover his outstanding debts, he sold a one-third interest in the *Courier* to Eben B. Foster, heretofore the principal clerk at a rival newspaper. This remedy proved inadequate, however. In the spring of 1837, Buckingham's "whole interest in the paper, with all my other personal estate, was placed in the hands of a trustee, to be appropriated to the benefit of creditors." Under the terms subsequently agreed upon, Buckingham was allowed to keep a half-interest in the paper, but he was forced to mortgage everything he owned and also to sacrifice some of his editorial authority.[54] At the age of fifty-seven, he found himself once again struggling to sustain his moral as well as his material independence.

Buckingham's experience reveals the precariousness of bourgeois status in early-nineteenth-century Boston. Contrary to popular myth, the self-made men of Jacksonian America—even those who voted Whig—were often insecure in their enjoyment of the private and public benefits of a developing market economy.[55] Within this unstable economic context, the pursuit of artisanal independence took on new meaning. Paradoxically, the more evident it became that faithful practice of bourgeois values did not guarantee the actual achievement of property or wealth, the more socially significant the inculcation of those values became. In an economy where property and wealth circulated beyond the collective control of a given community, material measures of personal worth could be highly deceptive. A dishonest speculator might succeed monetarily while a person of moral scruples failed. Consequently, notwithstanding its acquisitive orientation, bourgeois culture celebrated inner character more than outward accomplishments or the accumulation of possessions.[56] By redefining independence as adherence to an ethos of enterprise, rather than as the attainment of proprietorship per se, Buckingham illuminated the emergent social reality that he also exemplified.

# 9

WILLIAM S. PRETZER

## From Artisan to Alderman:
## The Career of William W. Moore, 1803–1886

WILLIAM W. MOORE was born into the family of a master artisan at the beginning of the nineteenth century. He was apprenticed to the artisanal trade of printing and worked nearly fifty years at that trade, many as the foreman of printing offices in Washington, D.C. He was twice ceremoniously fêted by journeymen who worked under his supervision. He was married to the same woman for sixty years and fathered twelve children, several of whom achieved local prominence in their own right. He was elected to the Washington City Board of Aldermen and to the Common Council, even serving two years as chairman of the council. When he died in 1886, one of the several newspaper obituaries that memorialized him bore the subtitle "A Sketch of His Useful and Honorable Career."[1] What artisan would have hoped for more?

This essay follows Moore's career as printer and foreman, family man, homeowner, church member, militia leader, member of fraternal organizations, and local politician. What earned him the "respect and esteem" of workingmen and employers alike? Moore's biography shows how one skilled man attempted to realign the artisanal ideals of respectability and mutualism to fit with an emergent economic individualism, while reconciling his own sense of personal independence with his economic dependency. Economic expansion and the division of labor in many antebellum trades limited artisans' opportunities for social mobility, preventing them from achieving entrepreneurial status. As journeymen were stripped of skill, status, and independence, it is not surprising that many sought new positions that seemed to provide those social qualities. In printing, although a few skilled craftsmen moved into the role of employer, many others moved into more modest positions as foremen or as owner-operators of small job shops, or into the roles of clerk, proofreader, or even editor. Moore's talents, ambitiousness, and respectability permitted him to live and work comfortably in the middle, between manual workers and employers. His biography suggests that his social status emanated more from personal character than from occupation. We will better understand the transition from a society of artisans and small producers to an entrepreneurial economy when we more fully recognize how Moore and others like him modified and exemplified ideals developed within the ranks of artisans.[2]

Driven by a notion of manly respectability and a sense of independence nurtured in the ranks of artisans, Moore engaged in a lifelong series of negotiations with both his subordinates and his superiors. These negotiations, which Bruce Laurie has termed "courting," took place in a series of reciprocal relationships existing at the workplace and in the community.[3] Because Moore was a "man in the middle," his support was routinely sought by both his inferiors and his superiors; he cultivated the approval of both groups and was, in turn, courted by them. His successes at mediating between labor and capital at work and in the community were mutually reinforcing.

## The Life of a Nineteenth-Century Printer

William Walker Moore was born on January 28, 1803, on the Manokin River, about twenty miles from Princess Anne, Somerset County, on Maryland's Eastern Shore. In 1807 his family moved to Baltimore, where his father became a successful housewright and contractor, and eventually held the position of governor-appointed inspector of lumber for some years.[4] Thus, Moore grew up as the son of a contractor and government functionary with conservative loyalties, in the politically charged atmosphere of an expanding and economically vibrant seaport where the "mechanic interest" was highly developed and influential. From that vantage point, he witnessed those crowd actions and local elections—pitting republican journeymen against the Federalist elite—that earned Baltimore the nickname "Mobtown."[5] Moore's early years in Baltimore provide the background to his conservative attitudes toward public propriety and social hierarchy; his reluctant acceptance of trade unions; and his promotion of the state's role in protecting property, fair dealing, and economic opportunity.

In 1819, just as Baltimore was slipping into an economic depression, Moore was apprenticed to Benjamin Edes, a Federalist job printer and the publisher of the *Federal Republican and Baltimore Telegraph*. Edes's office was a relatively large one, with four hand presses and perhaps as many as twelve workmen. Moore was talented, energetic, and well liked, so much so that Edes brought him to the family table rather than having him eat with the other apprentices. According to the reminiscences of Moore's daughter,

Moore was considered an older brother by the Edes children.[6]

Edes made Moore foreman of the office immediately upon the completion of his apprenticeship. If Moore was like other apprentices of the time, he probably served only until he turned twenty-one; thus his apprenticeship would have lasted five years. He became office foreman in 1824, just as the depression was passing. With work sporadic, journeymen printers often moved from office to office, even from town to town, creating a highly mobile work force. The foreman's job was salaried and relatively stable, however, and it was not unusual for a reliable young man, even one just out of his apprenticeship, to be named foreman. Making Moore foreman was Edes's way of offering his young protégé steady employment. For Moore, it meant that he did not have to face the trials of tramping for work, nor did he have to fear associating with those dissolute and disreputable journeymen printers who could not find and hold regular work.[7]

In 1829 Moore left Baltimore to take charge of a prominent printing office being enlarged in Washington, D.C., by Duff Green. The latter was an aggressive Missouri politician and editor who in 1826 had purchased the *United States Telegraph*, a Jacksonian-Democratic paper in Washington. Moore left Green's employ in 1834 and for more than a year ran his own commercial job office on Pennsylvania Avenue. In 1835 he gave up this office and went back to the *Telegraph* until Green sold the paper in 1837. A year later, Moore unsuccessfully tried to establish a weekly newspaper, the *Baltimore Merchant,* in collaboration with Green. When this paper failed, he returned to Washington to operate yet another job shop for a short time, and in 1839 he became foreman of the respected *National Intelligencer.* He held this post until January 1, 1865, when he retired from printing to became secretary-treasurer of an urban horse-drawn transit line. As will be seen, interpreting each of these occupational experiences as well as Moore's community activities provides insights into the infusion of artisanal values into lower-middle-class life.

Moore's career as a printer was checkered, but some signal events stand out. In January 1834, Duff Green announced plans to establish a "Manual Labor" school associated with the *Telegraph* which would train two hundred apprentice printers. The local journeymen's union, the Columbia Typographical Society, immediately opposed the plan because it would have flooded the labor market with half-trained compositors.[8] Simultaneously, Moore and Green were arguing over Moore's salary and the costs of operating the office. Their relationship grew steadily worse as conflict mounted over the plans to enlarge the office with apprentice labor. Echoing the rhetoric used by the journeymen's union, Moore responded to one of his employer's letters with an emphatic rebuff: "There are some sentences contained in it which, to me, are incomprehensible and require explanation.

Other passages might, *possibly*, be replied to by a *slave*, but I consider them unworthy the notice of a *freeman.*"[9] Facing a challenge to his personal independence equivalent to the threat to the journeymen's status, Moore quit and established his own job office.

Two days after writing the note just quoted, Moore received a letter signed by thirteen of his "Typographical Brethren" (as they called themselves), inviting him to a supper "as a testimonial of their respect and esteem." Behind this letter lay a petition that had circulated for days, accumulating the signatures of men in the book trades willing to pay one dollar each (more than half a day's wages) toward the testimonial dinner. The petition, which stretches more than four feet in length, contains 163 names, including those of nearly all the journeymen printers working in the city at that time. Moore attended the dinner, but evidently, nothing worthy of public notice came of it. Still, it is impossible to imagine that there were not toasts condemning Duff Green and speeches congratulating William Moore for his independent action and respectable character.[10]

Celebratory dinners were a well-established tradition in many artisanal trades, including printing. Drawing on the tradition of the English master printers' annual "wayz-goose," masters and journeymen in several eighteenth-century American cities gathered occasionally to celebrate a variety of events and anniversaries. In the nineteenth century, American journeymen transformed the tradition into an annual opportunity to entertain the printers who employed them, as well as local dignitaries; this was an assertion of the workers' own status within the trade and the community. In this particular instance, Washington's journeymen adapted the form for their immediate needs. They celebrated the character of William Moore in a traditional format. By offering their "respect and esteem," they offered the trade's affirmation of Moore's respectability and independence. This testimonial dinner represents a particularly obvious example of the "courting" that occurred between workers and supervisors.[11]

While Moore struggled to make a success of his job shop, Green in late 1834 abandoned the idea of a training school for apprentices after a series of strikes nearly crippled his business. But Green's problems continued: the journeymen hated the *Telegraph*'s new sub-foremen, the sub-foremen's attempts to institute new pay systems and work routines, and their use of "two-thirders"—young men who had not yet finished their apprenticeships but were paid as journeymen. In May 1835, the Columbia Typographical Society "ratted" the *Telegraph* office by publishing a list of the men working there, and advising journeymen not to accept work at the *Telegraph* and to shun those who did. This act threatened the *Telegraph* employees' ability to find future employment. With passions running high, a series of street fights broke out between *Telegraph* employees and union printers. Local authorities put a stop to the public battles by arresting several union men, including officers of the Columbia Typographical Society. The men were ultimately tried on assault and riot charges. With the union paying for their legal defense, some of the men were acquitted; those convicted had their sentences commuted by President Andrew Jackson.[12]

At about the time of the fights, Moore once again assumed the duties of general foreman of the *United States Telegraph* office. He gradually reinstituted acceptable work routines, discontinued the use of two-thirders, and maneuvered the dismissal of the offending sub-foremen. At times, he explicitly supported the union journeymen. When presenting Green with a petition the men had written to protest the actions of one sub-foreman, he wrote:

> If a reconciliation can be effected it will give me more pleasure than any other course that can be adopted. But on reading the memorial, and recollecting the nature of the circumstance, I am disposed to think the hands believe they have justice on their side, at least, and that they will not readily lay themselves liable to another insult. They were certainly wronged in the matter they complain of, and every allowance is to be made for the nature of their petition.[13]

Duff Green lost the subsequent election to choose the printer to the United States Senate, gave up editorial control of the *Telegraph* in October 1835, and finally sold his interest in the paper in 1837. Moore stayed as foreman until Green sold the office.

In the midst of the conflicts with Green, Moore had advised the strikers that their cause was just, recognizing that their objective was "to prevent the profession from becoming overburdened, and thus falling into disrepute." He suggested limiting the ratio of apprentices to journeymen in offices, a tactic finally agreed to by the Columbia Typographical Society some years later. He argued that the oversupply of compositors was exacerbated by the many boys who were introduced into offices as pressfeeders and then learned the skills of a compositor. Apparently feeling that women did not pose a similar threat, he suggested that they be hired as pressfeeders in order to stave off the entry of additional boys into the trade.[14] He offered his own opinions on other tactics that might prevent the use of boy labor but acknowledged that the major issue facing the journeymen was the rise of capitalism, the business control exercised by editors and publishers who cared much for profits but little for the customs of the trade.[15] He wrote letters in support of several journeymen's applications for admission into the union.[16] Given that Moore himself never joined the Columbia Typographical Society, his status among wage earners must have been due to the force of his moral character and the respect he gave to journeymen.

Moore's thorough knowledge of the trade—knowledge that came from experience and pride in his work—allowed him to make specific demands on and judgments of suppliers and workmen. Moore took full responsibility for the day-to-day operations of the printing offices. His Baltimore connections often stood him in good stead. Moore's letter book dating from the early 1830s is filled with directives to type founders, printing equipment suppliers, and papermakers regarding supplies and equipment. He demanded equipment made of specific materials; he insisted upon specific quantities; he rejected some items as overpriced or inferior in quality; he pressed suppliers for beneficial financial terms; he was adept at the accounting needed to run an office.[17] He was called to testify before congressional committees investigating government printing.[18] His taste and judgment were publicly recognized when he served as a judge for exhibits of the printer's and publisher's crafts at the 1853 industrial exhibition of the Metropolitan Mechanics' Institute.[19]

Although Duff Green has been credited with introducing steam-powered printing presses in Washington, Moore was, in fact, Green's active agent in this matter. The shift from hand presses to power presses, of either the bed-and-platen or the cylinder varieties, involved a major reorganization of the labor force and office routine.[20] He understood the implications of the new presses, acknowledging that power presses required the use of fewer workers and destroyed type more rapidly than did hand presses.[21] He knew just how dependent he was on the skills of his workers. Writing a letter of recommendation for a pressman, he said,

> I do not believe that the failure of the Cylinder Press is attributable to any want of execution on your part to make it useful. On the contrary, as far as I have had an opportunity of noticing your conduct, I think that you have done the utmost which you could have done towards improving and putting it into operation. . . . the Inking apparatus has been considerably improved by you; and I know that you have produced a better and fairer impression than has been brought off the press since it has been in this city.[22]

Originally, Moore was very skeptical of the new technology, saying at one point, "it is impossible to do good work upon a press constructed upon the principle of the cylinder press."[23] Within two years, however, he was selling the *Telegraph*'s hand presses and using a double-cylinder press and two bed-and-platen presses.[24] Moore's active role emphasizes the crucial role played by progressive overseers and skilled workers, in conjunction with inventors and entrepreneurs, in the introduction of innovative technologies.

Moore was forthright with employees and job applicants, casting his impressions of them in terms of their "moral worth."[25] He was not afraid to be critical of journeymen printers, but his criticisms reflected on the impact that the spread of the division of labor was having on urban trades. He expressed surprise that

> men possessing so much intelligence should have so little ambition to rise to the head of their profession, as to be satisfied with having obtained the reputation of being *either* a swift and clean compositor—or a good hand at rule & figure work—or an excellent workman at jobbing—or a good pressman— and thus be content with having acquired but part of their business.

Remarking that few qualified overseers came from the ranks of journeymen under these conditions, he noted that most journeymen were "totally destitute of that activity, energy and decision so indispensible to the good management of an office."[26] Still, he respected the independence asserted by the journeymen: "I have seen but few [journeymen] who were so stupid and contemptible as to endure even momentary insolance and oppression, whether inflicted by Foreman or Employer."[27] He exaggerated, of course, but his sentiments were genuine. Moore's ideal workman was a well-rounded craftsman; what Moore found available in the 1830s were men lacking the opportunity or ambition to become such workers.

Moore was more interested in maintaining the respectability of his trade than in supporting workers or the labor movement. For a time, his notoriety came from being the chief practical printer in the most notorious "rat" office in the nation. He willingly worked for Duff Green, a man who was attempting to destroy the workers' control over skill, wages, and the labor supply. Still, Moore asserted his own independence, disagreed with Green, castigated him, and occasionally persuaded him to appease the journeymen. He maintained his influence with both sides because they recognized his good character, his willingness to negotiate in good faith, and his ability to manage the work and the workers in mutually acceptable ways. And when the Duff Green affair was over, he was immediately and completely welcomed back into the fraternity.

The second signal event in Moore's printing career came thirty-one years later, with his 1865 retirement as foreman of the *National Intelligencer* office. Upon his retirement, he was presented with a gold-headed cane, inscribed "Presented to Wm. W. Moore, by his printer friends of the *National Intelligencer* office." A "large number of printers of the *Intelligencer* office" visited his home to present him with the cane as a "token of [the] esteem and regard" in which they held him after his nearly fifty years in the trade—the last twenty-five of which had been with the *Intelligencer* and had been free of major labor disputes. The presentation was made by James Crossfield, a thirty-five-year veteran compositor and proofreader and a twenty-three-year veteran of the Columbia Typographical Society. Clearly, Moore's career in the printing trade marked him as a man worthy of the "esteem" of those

who worked with him; and the term *esteem* in the nineteenth century con-
noted "the beginnings of affection."[28] Moore ended his printing career as he
had begun it with Benjamin Edes: he was once again considered nearly family by the printers who worked with him.

## William W. Moore, the Private and Public Man

Moore was anything but a downtrodden manual worker, but his quest
for a comfortable "competency" was a tortured one. His eventual material
success and social prominence were reversals of the earlier setbacks he had
suffered. For the simple fact is that during the 1830s he was unable to make
a success of himself as a master printer. After first leaving Green's employ in
1834 he operated a small job shop in Washington, but he gave it up to return to the *Telegraph,* as foreman. Upon closing down the *Telegraph* office in
May 1837 after Green sold the business, Moore took his family back to Baltimore to become overseer of the *Baltimore Merchant.* Four months later, he
was a desperate man, pleading with Green to arrange some aid, complain-
ing that he was in debt, and making only eight dollars a week. Unable to
pay creditors, he told Green that he was afraid to be seen in the streets lest
he be arrested for debt. He traveled to Washington on Saturday, September
16, partly to ask Green face-to-face for money and partly to avoid being arrested in Baltimore. Whether or not he served jail time for debt is unclear,
but it seems improbable.[29]

Moore experienced firsthand the feelings of desperation and economic
insecurity that abounded in the 1830s, and he made compromises that
would provide security. The *Merchant* ceased publication in November 1837,
and in January 1838 Moore was back in Washington again with the goal of
setting up his own office. He described his entrepreneurial ambitions both
as a rejection of wage labor and as an affirmation of his goals as a family
man:

> Being satisfied that I might become grey in laboring for the benefit of others
> without acquiring the means of properly educating my children and render-
> ing my family otherwise comfortable, I am resolved to make the best use of
> my experience and energetically exert my faculties in the prosecution of this
> enterprise.[30]

Moore's entrepreneurial aspirations were limited, in other words, to his desire for personal independence, an economic competency, and family respectability. His second shop failed as the first had done, however, and
within a year he accepted a salaried position as foreman of the *National Intelligencer.* He had failed to establish himself as a proprietor relying on his
own capital, and he resorted to the artisanal notion of "skill as capital" to

provide his family with the advantages of lower-middle-class status.[31]

As foreman he was not liable to "furloughs," or layoffs, and steady work at the high salary commanded by printers afforded him a rather secure and comfortable life. By the mid-1840s he was paying tuition for his adolescent daughters to attend private schools, and by the end of the decade he was contracting to build a house in Washington.[32] What he achieved, he accomplished as a salaried supervisor, not as an entrepreneur. Just as he had done twenty years earlier when Benjamin Edes first promoted him, Moore found stability, security, and status as a salaried overseer.

For men such as Moore, rebounding from disappointment and avoiding failure were as important as achieving success. Facing the growth of competitive individualism, these men did not look to promises of economic independence and of social mobility leading to bourgeois status. They found, instead, opportunity for economic and social respectability and moral independence in lower-middle-class occupations, which were as often salaried positions as petty proprietorships.[33]

Moore's standing within the community and his ability to function as mediator between entrepreneur and wage laborer were due to much more than simply his workplace demeanor. His outside activities reflected his occupational success, just as his respectable actions at work made him acceptable in other circumstances. In fact, the authority and affection Moore earned and maintained in the workplace were intensified by his activities outside the workplace. Most prominent among these activities were his home life and his participation in the Presbyterian church, the militia, the Independent Order of Odd Fellows, and local politics.

Evidence of Moore's independence and respectability can be seen in his activities as a church-going family man and homeowner. Moore had married Lucinda Ann Depass, three years his junior, in Baltimore on June 13, 1825. She bore twelve children, eight of whom lived to age twenty-one and six of whom still were alive when she died in August 1886, just four months before her husband's death. The Moores saw their oldest son become a minister, while the youngest became a journeyman printer; another rose from governmental clerk to be private secretary to the president of the United States, while yet another became a bank clerk; one daughter married a physician, another a lawyer. Intensely devoted to his family, Moore once paid one hundred dollars for portraits of Lucinda and himself.[34]

In the nineteenth century, the ability to own one's home and to maintain comfortable surroundings for one's family were indications of masculine success and economic independence.[35] In 1849, after working in Washington for most of the previous twenty years and renting houses for his growing family, Moore contracted to have a house built. He bought two lots just south of the house he had rented for some time, only three blocks away from the offices of the *National Intelligencer* and just north of an area near the city's downtown printing offices which was home to numerous journeymen. He did not move to the city's fringes or suburbs, as did many editors and publishers.[36] Moore lived between the working class and the middle class.

By the time Moore's family moved into the house at the corner of Sixth and F Streets on September 1, 1850, he had paid $3,400 for construction. By August 1855, when the construction was completed, he had paid an additional $700, making his total payment for two lots, a house, a privy, and a fenced yard more than $4,100. In 1852 his city taxes amounted to $31.88 based on two lots with a total value of $547, a house estimated at $3,400, and personal property totaling $550. Twenty years later, he was paying $144.22 in real estate tax based on land values totaling $4,837 and buildings valued at $4,000.[37] Such figures placed Moore far ahead of nearly all other wage earners in the city and nearly on a par with those printers who employed others. In the 1880s he embarked on an ambitious and costly plan to repair and renovate his house, paying for repairs to his chimney, cellar door, and gutters; hiring-out for the cleaning of gas burners and lamps; and buying new wallpaper, ingrain carpeting, a range, and an improved-style stove.[38] An elderly man, he evidently wanted to leave a respectable legacy for his children or for his wife, should he die before her.

Moore's homeownership and his employment of a servant were widely understood symbols of respectability. In 1830 Moore had employed a free black woman as a servant, and in 1840 the census counted a slave in his household. When he built his house, Moore's household consisted of his wife, seven of their children (four daughters and three sons) who were still at home, and Betsy Mahala, a free mulatto servant.[39] This shifting between free and slave labor on Moore's part appears logical in light of Washington's social composition, and Moore's finances and class aspirations. In 1830 Moore had a young family, was new to the city, and lacked resources; ten years later, he had accumulated sufficient capital and stability to afford an investment in household labor. In 1850, it made more sense to hire labor than to buy it.[40] Employing a servant was a indicator of respectability, and the availability of inexpensive black labor made hiring a servant an appropriate means of maintaining status in the eyes of his employers and his workers.

In the 1840s, the Moores identified themselves with the Fourth Presbyterian Church in Washington. The church had been established in 1828 after a disagreement over the replacement of the pastor at Washington's Central Presbyterian Church. One of the founding members of the Fourth was Jacob Gideon, proprietor of Gideon's Printing Office in Washington and one of the founding members of the Columbia Typographical Society. In 1840 Jacob Gideon had led the effort to construct a building for the Fourth on Ninth Street between G and H Streets, about four blocks from where Moore resided. Two of Moore's sons were especially active in the church, holding offices in missionary societies and teaching Sunday school. Moore remained a member of the church into the 1880s, when he was still paying $4.37 a month for the rent of pew 44.[41]

Moore's participation in the Fourth Presbyterian Church is yet another clue to his values, for the Fourth was a New School, pro-Union church. The Reverend John C. Smith served as pastor from 1839 until 1878, precisely the years of the Moore family's most active participation. Smith was a well-known moderate on racial issues (in Washington it would have been too much to advocate an outright antislavery position) and staunchly pro-Union. To the extent that Moore identified with the essential tenets of New School Presbyterianism—the centrality of God-ordained natural and moral law; the emphasis on individual freedom and responsibility; and the importance of the mission of American nationalism—his Presbyterianism reinforced attitudes associated with progressive, free-labor artisans.[42] He passed on his sense of moral responsibility and the importance of evangelical Protestantism and Americanism to his son, the Reverend Alexander D. Moore, who was pastor of the First Presbyterian Church of Bethlehem, Pennsylvania, at the time of his father's death.

Moore's militia career represented yet another source of his good reputation. When Baltimore came under attack by the British fleet on September 13–14, 1814, young William Moore had joined his father and thousands of other Baltimoreans in the defense of Fort McHenry. John Moore, William's father, was a member of the militia, and eleven-year-old William served as a fifer and powder boy during that famous engagement. Seven years later he was named ensign in a militia unit headed by none other than his master and mentor, the printer Benjamin Edes. Soon after, he became captain of the regiment, and subsequently he became commander of the Howard Volunteers of Baltimore.[43]

Thus, he had established his credentials as a patriot and a military leader while still a young man in Baltimore. His selection as captain of the Washington National Cadets soon after his arrival in the capital city probably came as a matter of course. The nearly thirty-year-old Moore surely was not surprised by the fact that his immediate commander was William Winston Seaton, the editor and publisher of the Washington *National Intelligencer* and for most of the 1820s president of the city's Board of Aldermen. Neither was Moore awed serving, as he did, under General of the Militia R. C. Weightman, previously a printer and editor, and mayor of Washington from 1824 to 1826. In Washington as in Baltimore, service in the militia brought Moore into contact with prominent merchants and master artisans. He came into the public eye, as when he led the National Cadets alongside the Friendship Literary Debating Society in a civic parade honoring General Lafayette in August 1834. When rumors of a "Negro insurrection" spread in 1832, he responded decisively to a potentially volatile situation, issuing arms to his men. With substantial responsibilities to both his superiors and those who served under him, Moore found that his militia service honed his ability to mediate between socially diverse individuals.[44]

Clearly, the ability to serve one's country in a military way was important to self-definition and public perception. Moore resigned from the National Cadets in 1834 but maintained his title and was referred to consistently as "Capt. Moore" throughout the rest of his life. He passed on his sense of civic duty and martial responsibility to his son, Colonel William G. Moore, who was commander of the Washington Light Infantry at the time of his father's death.

To the elder Moore, militia service was not only a sacred, patriotic duty but also an opportunity to demonstrate his leadership qualities and to successfully assert his ideas of masculine, martial responsibility. When his unit was presented with a flag sewn by local women, Moore delivered a spirited reply. He acknowledged the debt of his generation for the "rights and liberties bequeathed us by our venerated forefathers." He noted, using rhetoric familiar to artisanal festivals and trade societies, that the standard would serve as "a rallying point for the Sons of Freedom," who would defend it by sacrificing themselves "upon the sacred altar of Liberty."[45]

A similar sense of civic duty and personal responsibility were espoused by the Independent Order of Odd Fellows (IOOF), the fraternal organization to which Moore was devoted. The Odd Fellows had originated in eighteenth-century England and first appeared in the United States in 1819 at a meeting in a Baltimore tavern. A branch of the IOOF was established in Washington in 1828, and Moore joined in 1832. He moved rapidly through the ranks of the order and by 1846 was Past Grand Sire of the Columbian Encampment no. 1, of Washington. For the remaining forty years of his life he continually basked in the glow of his honored status among Washington's Odd Fellows. In later years Moore was considered the most important advocate of Odd Fellowship in Washington.[46]

Fraternal organizations were central elements in the making of nineteenth-century America, promoting moral and civic values in associational forms, and so providing voluntary sources of philanthropy, reform, recreation, and class accommodation. Recent analyses of nineteenth-century fraternalism have focused on its integrative functions, suggesting that its appeal lay in its embodiment of ritual, corporate idioms, and assertions of masculinity. According to Brian Greenberg, "the IOOF embodied the social values of the free labor order . . . an open-class, harmonious society in which all members acknowledged their obligations." The core obligations that Greenberg identifies, "diligence, sobriety, honesty, industriousness, and frugality—qualities essential to an industrial work ethic," were values that Moore had demonstrated before joining the order.[47] The IOOF was another venue for expressing his value system, not the source for a new moral code.

It seems unlikely that the order merely inculcated labor aristocrats and petty proprietors with acceptable industrial values. Rather, voluntary associations represented an arena in which skilled workers, petty proprietors, and professionals could participate together in social and benevolent activities. For members of the lower middle class, participation in fraternal organizations was one way of affiliating with social superiors in a community-focused manner. Mary Ann Clawson has suggested that fraternal organizations gained popularity specifically by promoting visions of social unity built around masculine brotherhood, ritual, proprietorship, and a corporate idiom. Focusing on these characteristics makes fraternal organizations seem less foreign to the aspirations and experiences of labor aristocrats and the middling sorts.[48]

As in the militia, moreover, Moore shared a common ethos with both strangers and acquaintances in the IOOF. Mirroring Washington's social composition, the IOOF's membership was made up primarily of master mechanics, shopkeepers, small merchants, professional men, and government clerks. The master printers William and John T. Towers were active members, along with proofreaders and foremen such as L. A. Gobright, Thomas Rich, John H. Thorn, George W. Cochran, W. R. McLean, and J. C. Franzoni, all of whom were also members of the Columbia Typographical Society. These were among the men who chose "Vis Unita Fortior" (Unity creates strength) as the motto of the Grand Encampment of the District of Columbia. It may be simple coincidence, but it is nonetheless indicative that in 1867, when it became a subordinate union of the International Typographical Union, the Columbia Typographical Society also chose "Vis Unita Fortior" as its motto. The role of the IOOF as a benevolent society and relief organization mirrored on a broader scale some of the functions of early trade societies. In fact, Moore's sense of mutualism found its most explicit expression in the Odd Fellows' commandments "to visit the sick, relieve the distressed, bury the dead, and educate the orphan."[49]

Involvement in the IOOF, and particularly the procedural and rhetorical duties attendant upon the Order's rituals, presented another venue for the demonstration of personal character and public ability. Moore presided over a number of civic functions in his capacity as Grand Sire; he regularly chaired combined meetings of Washington's several IOOF lodges; and he participated in public ceremonies as an exalted member of this important fraternal organization. No doubt one of the most satisfying events came in

1870, when a newly constructed Odd Fellows' Hall was dedicated. Moore had served as the chairman of the board of trustees of the building fund, and the Encampment commissioned a portrait of him in full Odd-Fellow regalia with his right hand upon the open pages of a Bible. The painting was to hang in the building's library as a sign of "affection and esteem."[50] Thus, for the third time in the public record, the word *esteem* is used in reference to William Moore; and *to esteem*, as the *Oxford English Dictionary* reminds us, means to regard with value, "chiefly with respect to moral characteristics."[51]

At the unveiling ceremonies, Moore provided clues to his own success by emphasizing his sensitivity to rhetoric and ritual. In noting his own "poverty of words" and commending the other speakers for their "words that burn and imagery that beautifies," Moore hinted at the importance of public speaking and once again demonstrated his own command of the language, a command that was part and parcel of the printer's upbringing and the experience of militia leadership.[52] His allegiance to the ritual of the Odd Fellows was implicit in his rapid rise through the orders and his long association with the organization. Moore was comfortable with rituals and formalities. As much as anything in the records about his political ideology or affiliation, it was Moore's attention to rhetoric and ritual that brought him political success.

Moore was among a group of printers who turned the holding of public office in Washington into a tradition of the printing fraternity. He was first elected to public office as a candidate of the Union (or Anti-Know-Nothing) party for alderman of the Fourth Ward in the city election of 1856. Subsequently he served six years as alderman, was out of office for two years (1862–63), and then served three years on the Common Council, four more years as alderman, and one year (1871) in the first legislative assembly of Washington's House of Delegates. Between 1802 and 1871, Washington, D.C., had twenty mayors; six of these, their terms totaling twenty-three years, were printers or editors. These included both of the proprietors of the *National Intelligencer:* Joseph Gales Jr. (1827–29), and William W. Seaton (1840–49). Another half-dozen men associated with the trade, including Jacob Gideon, James F. Haliday, John T. Towers, Charles P. Wannell, and Charles F. Lowrey, held other public offices. Haliday and Lowrey, it is worth noting, were active members of the Columbia Typographical Society and had played prominent parts in the campaign against Duff Green and the *Telegraph.*[53] Moore's political career was enhanced by the personal contacts he had made as church member, militiaman, Odd Fellow, and foreman of a prominent printing office.

Despite Moore's long tenure in office, and the fact that he served two years as president of the Common Council and was even acting mayor for a short time, his political career was nondescript. Or, at least, little evidence illustrative of his ideological or political values has been found. Moore had the usual round of committee assignments, serving on committees on improvements, wharves, and ways and means. He offered resolutions authorizing improvements to streets, gutters, sewers, and sidewalks in his ward. He often promoted special bills seeking rebates on taxes or relief benefits for his constituents. He was well versed in parliamentary procedure and often invoked technical rules during official proceedings.[54]

During the 1850s and 1860s, Washington's local politics were dominated by national issues. Moore's first term in office was marred by mid-term election riots involving the American, or Know-Nothing, party—including a group of "Plug Uglies" imported from Baltimore—and Washington's constabulary. Moore headed a committee to look into the affair and reported on the Know-Nothings' calculated measures to intimidate voters.[55] He also took the lead in drawing up opposition to high draft quotas during the Civil War. He, along with most of the city's other elected officials, argued that Washington's enrollments were faulty, making more men seem eligible for the draft than was the case. He did not oppose serving the Union, but he did oppose the unfair burden placed upon his constituents, arguing that the Fourth Ward was heavily overrepresented in the lists of eligible men.[56]

It was in local contests over city budget expenditures that Moore made what little reputation he acquired in politics. Washington was rife with corruption, and as the city expanded its physical infrastructure and services, the city coffers were opened to a variety of schemers and planners. Moore's support of the construction of an alms house and improvements to streets, sewers, and wharves illustrates his belief in governmental expenditures. However, he often voted against extravagant plans or urged amendments reducing expenditures if personal or partisan gain was implicit in the project. His 1868 opposition to the efforts of the Republican mayor Sayles Bowen to enrich his friends and himself by expanding the city's debt brought Moore the support of city Democrats. When voting irregularities postponed the naming of a mayor, Democratic members of the council elected Moore to serve as mayor pro tempore.[57] One obituary writer summed up Moore's political career by saying that he had "a reputation for staunch integrity as a legislator. He always insisted on the closest scrutiny of measures offered, and defeated, it is claimed, many measures that were designed to benefit not the public, but a few persons only."[58] Written some fifteen years after Moore had completed his public service, this lingering memory suggests the endurance of his image as a defender of the commonweal. This writer did not use the rhetoric of a corporate common-

A poster testifying to the political involvement of laboring men in 1872.
(Courtesy of Library of Congress)

wealth, but the implications of Moore's public record and his reputation show that he carried notions of fair dealing, equal opportunity, and independence into his political life.

Moore's initial terms as an elected official coincided with his final years as foreman of a printing office. His later years in politics coincided with his second career, as secretary-treasurer of the Metropolitan Railway Company, a position he held from 1865 until his death. Moore's operation of this commuter transit line provides one final, anecdotal glimpse at his character and reputation. Urban transit was one arena in which people of different classes were likely to meet one another in close quarters. The character of the Metropolitan, its routes, and its small cars operated by one man intensified the likelihood of contact. In November 1877 one of the drivers castigated a well-dressed gentleman for putting his feet on the cushions. The passenger, offended by the driver's manner, complained to Moore. Moore defended the policy of prohibiting everyone, including gentlemen, from putting their feet on the cushions, and represented it as a matter of courtesy to the entire community.[59]

Under the title "A Model Officer," his letter was reprinted in a local newspaper, with editorial comments lauding his effort to explain the rule's application to all classes, especially to the "gentlemen" who served as role models for the lower orders. The article referred to "Capt. W. W. Moore" as "a typo [typographer] of fifty years experience" who was "well and favorably known," and commented that his polite letter testified to the fact that his position had not led to any "insolence of office." And so, at age seventy-four, Moore was still self-consciously mediating between social orders and maintaining his reputation as a printer, a "model officer," a man known for the "grace of his composition," and one who had served the Fourth Ward "very creditably."[60]

Moore took ill in early December 1886 and died at his home on December 23, just weeks short of his eighty-fourth birthday. His Christmas-day funeral was presided over by the Reverend Joseph T. Kelly, pastor of the Fourth Presbyterian Church, and was attended by a large delegation of Odd Fellows. The printers George W. Pearson, Henry Polkinhorn, and Charles P. Wannell served as honorary pallbearers. Moore was buried in the family plot in Washington's Congressional Cemetery. As the inspiration for his sermon, Kelly chose a fitting proverb: "A good name is rather to be chosen than gold or silver."[61]

What Stuart Blumin has called the "nonmanual sector" was a fluid—and thus, to historians, confusing—amalgamation of people whose occupations and social advantages were created by the "progress" associated with capitalist development in the early nineteenth century. Therefore, they had reason to defend and support the *process* of change even while they clung to ideals that constricted the *pace* and *content* of change. Moore began life in a family of some competence, honed the skills of an artisan, and absorbed the artisanal values of independence, mutuality, and respectability. He built a reputation as a military leader and promoter of fraternal organizations. He maintained a respectable house, educated his children, and demonstrated a sense of civic responsibility. His career suggests that artisanal values found expression in a variety of arenas in which lower-middle-class men associated with their social superiors. In an earlier era, men of that class might have supported a moral community established on the bedrock of respectable trades, but in the nineteenth century they found a variety of venues for mingling their moral codes with those of their superiors. Moore's experiences illustrate how artisanal values—respectability, independence, and mutualism—fused with middle-class imperatives to form a new, lower-middle-class ethic.

This mingling became especially important as artisanal values increasingly came under attack at the workplace. Moore understood the ambiguity of his position as a salaried foreman: he was neither dependent nor independent. He was proud of the way in which he executed his responsibilities toward his employer and his men. As he wrote in 1830: "To discharge my duty faithfully toward my employer, and at the same time to conduct the business as to give satisfaction to those employed in the office, is the height of my ambition."[62] Men such as Moore ameliorated the impact of deteriorating conditions for wage earners by negotiating bearable, even acceptable, working conditions. They established their own respectability and independence relative to the more robust mutualism of labor radicals and the more aggressive individualism of entrepreneurs and capitalists. They served as a buffer that smoothed social relations in an increasingly contentious and competitive society. For this, Moore and others like him earned the "respect and esteem" of workers and the middle classes alike.

# PART IV

# ICONOGRAPHIC
# INTERPRETATIONS

# 10

HOWARD B. ROCK

# "All Her Sons Join as One Social Band": New York City's Artisanal Societies in the Early Republic

ARTISANAL SOCIETIES were an important element of the civic, fraternal, and economic lives of many craftsmen living in Jeffersonian America. They functioned as benevolent societies providing benefits to those who were in need because of illness, injury, death, or other misfortune, and as sources of fraternity where fellow mechanics could meet, dine, wine, and march with their comrades, celebrating the significance of their trade and the blessings of republican government. If organized by the masters, artisanal societies could look out for their trade in such areas as tariff protection and craft promotion, as well as respond to journeymen's demands. If organized by the journeymen, they could maintain wages, hours, and work traditions that would guarantee journeymen an adequately respectable status even if they were unable to attain master craftsman standing.[1]

## London Origins

The origins of American artisanal societies lay in England, principally in London, the center of the handicraft professions. Thus, it is helpful to examine the English trades prior to an analysis of New York's crafts. In the eleventh and twelfth centuries, English artisans organized religious fraternities centering around the patron saint of their craft. They would worship together on their saint's day and other holidays at a specific church. They also provided death benefits, and offered fraternal outlets through religious services and burials. By the sixteenth and seventeenth centuries the religious orientation had nearly disappeared, yet the associations continued to flourish. While maintaining their functions as sources of benevolence, and enhancing their comradely activities by erecting halls, some quite elaborate, they became significant economic institutions. Either through royal incor-

poration—the preferred and most prestigious route—or through municipal ordinance, the fraternities controlled both the quality of their product
and the prices and wages within their craft. Royal or municipal recognition
of a society meant that the organization's members received a monopoly
within their profession. No artisan who was not a freeman (member) of the
society could ply his trade in the marketplace except after payment of bur-
densome taxes. Generally only those who had served a seven-year apprenticeship were admitted to freemanship, and admission to apprenticeship in
the more prestigious crafts could be costly. The societies were allowed to
"search" the city's shops in their particular trades to ensure that the quality
of the products sold was up to their standards, and to prosecute those who
violated these standards or who used fraudulent weights and measures.[2]

The twelve most powerful companies were known as livery companies,
after the special attire that their leaders wore at ceremonial occasions. A
few of these societies, such as the society of grocers, were composed entirely of merchants; however, even in the more common craft associations,
the elite or liveried were more often of mercantile than of artisanal standing, operating largely as retailers and wholesalers rather than as handi-
craftsmen. Beneath them in the society were independent proprietors of
smaller shops, and the "yeomen," or journeymen, who could never reach
liveried status. At times the yeomen would organize independently within
the society because their interests were so clearly different from those of
the liveried.[3]

The craft societies, and especially the livery societies, played a major role
in the government of London. Assembling each Michaelmas Day (September 29) in Guildhall, they would nominate two aldermen, one of whom
would be chosen as lord mayor by the Court of Aldermen. The aldermen,
who as members of the Common Council governed the city, were elected
for life by the freemen of the respective wards. Individual companies were
governed by wardens and company courts of assistants, sometimes elected
by the membership at large and sometimes coopted by the company's
court.[4]

An examination of the iconography of the London guilds is instructive in
illustrating the goals and practices of the companies. Incorporation was a
major achievement, and when attained it was accompanied by an elaborate
charter spelling out the rights of the company. Each company claimed its
own coat of arms—an important symbol of both the organization and its
members. The lion of England stood conspicuously within the armorial
bearing of the Merchant Taylors Company. In the place occupied by the
lion, the holy lamb had originally stood. The lamb was moved to the crest,
where it replaced the Virgin and Child. The original symbols dated to the

MERCHANT TAILORS' COMPANY.

Armorial bearing of the London Merchant Taylors Company. This was a combination of ancient heraldry and a proud display of craftsmanship. William Herbert, *The History of the Twelve Great Livery Companies of London* (London, 1834, 1837; reprint, New York, 1968), 2:383.

company's founding as a fraternity of Saint John the Baptist. The lion symbolized loyalty to king and country; the camels and the ship represented the importance of trade; the shield and the scene at left displayed products of the tailors. The Latin motto "Concordia Parva Res Crescunt" (With harmony small things grow) may have been an attempt to elevate the standing of the tailor's craft above its traditional ignominy.[5]

The most important day of the year for these organizations, especially for the twelve great livery companies, was the Lord Mayor's Day. On that day the mayor elect, a member of one of the twelve companies, was escorted by the liverymen to present his credentials to the king or the king's representative. The pageant was sometimes on land and sometimes on water, and included choirs, poetry by the city's finest bards, and platforms bearing various scenes or pageants. Figures from English history, such as ancient knights, were common in the procession.[6] In speeches and in verse,

THE LORD MAYOR'S COACH

William Hogarth, the Lord Mayor's Day procession. Notice the mayor surrounded by the riotous crowd. (Ditchfield, *City Companies of London and Their Good Works*, 94).

orators extolled the glory of England, of London, of the deity, and of the various crafts. The livery company sponsoring the pageant, the livery company of the incoming mayor, had especially elaborate displays.

A number of companies held feasts and other occasions of revelry in halls that were quite elaborate in their construction. The societies also possessed furniture and regalia for their officers, such as special chairs for the masters, and crowns for both the masters and wardens. These were usually bedecked with symbols of the trade. The Carpenters Company, for example, had compasses and hammers woven into its headwear. The death of one of the societies' members was a somber event. For such occasions the societies had their own palls, bearing both religious and craft iconography, and issued death notices such as that of the Tin-Plate Workers, with its spooky motto.[7]

The English livery societies declined in the eighteenth century, and the Lord Mayor's Day procession lost most of its drama. British entrepreneurs (including many craftsmen), the leaders in consumer production and in-

Funeral invitation of the Tin-Plate Company. "Remember to Die" is an overly literal translation of the famous Latin quotation. (Unwin, *Gilds and Companies of London*)

vestment capital, had less and less patience with precapitalist traditions. In most of the wealthy livery companies, dominated by merchants, economic controls lapsed by the mid–eighteenth century; the exceptions were the companies of the goldsmiths and the fishmongers. The minor companies, whose membership included more working craftsmen, were in some instances able to keep their monopolies and privileges into the first quarter of the nineteenth century.[8]

## New York City Societies

In the United States, and specifically New York City, organized artisanal societies were rare before the birth of the Republic. After the ratification of the Constitution, however, members of many crafts formed their own societies, although, with the exception of the General Society of Mechanics and Tradesmen, they were unincorporated. The growth of the American market following independence, and the withdrawal of British mercantilism along with the development of sophisticated production techniques and ready access to commercial information and insurance, forced the more populous crafts to adopt workshop policies that saw the master and his employees, the journeymen, in increasingly separate and often adversarial roles. Both groups had common interests in the prosperity of their craft, but inside the workshop the two groups battled over wages, hours, and working conditions. Consequently, in New York City there were three distinct kinds of societies. The most common were the journeymen's associations. Masters' societies, for which we have considerable visual and very little written documentation, were also common. The third form of association was the "assistant" society, created for the express purpose of benevolence and fraternity. Open to all, societies of the last-named type likely contained more masters than journeymen.[9]

No visual record exists of the journeymen's societies of New York; the illustrations available for examination are those of the masters' societies. The masters' public outlook, as expressed in toasts and orations and recently termed "artisan republicanism," describes a perspective based upon long-standing republican traditions adapted to the new nation. To artisans, republicanism meant that society was best governed by those who were most critical to its well-being: the producers. They idealized, in the same manner as Jefferson idealized the independent yeoman, the small, independently owned craft shop. Artisans viewed the workshop as a place of harmony where masters and journeymen worked together providing the vital goods necessary for the economic welfare of the new nation. No employer-employee conflict need exist within the shop; journeyman standing was only a temporary stop on the road to full proprietorship. Furthermore, they believed that the cooperative spirit of the workshop should serve as the model for the entire Republic. Mechanics saw themselves as virtuous manufacturers—and hence the core of the commonwealth. They held politically suspect those who accumulated property without a productive trade, particularly mercantile speculators, bankers, and lawyers.[10] It is this credo that is most prominent in the artisanal societies' visual representations.

In a celebration somewhat similar to the Lord Mayor's Day Pageant—though there is no evidence that New York's mechanics were directly influenced by this dormant London tradition—the citizens of New York marched in procession in support of the ratification of the Constitution in July 1788. Each occupational subgroup paraded with its own displays and banners. In the published Order of Procession at the celebration, eight of the ten divisions were composed of members of mechanic professions.

Banner of the New York Pewterers Society, 1788. This was carried at a parade held to celebrate the U.S. Constitution and promote its ratification. (Courtesy of The New-York Historical Society, New York City)

Only one artisanal banner, that of the pewterers, is still extant from that parade. While English pewterers had adopted a religious motto with classical supporters (two seahorses), the New York banner carried the motto "Solid and Pure," and the ancient seahorses were replaced by two craftsmen. The shield bore a modern pewterer's instrument. Mainly, the banner celebrated republicanism, from the flag at the upper left to the verse over the scene of the pewterers' shop:

> The Federal Plan Most Solid & Secure
> Americans Their Freedom Will Ensure
> All Arts Shall Flourish in Columbia's Land
> And All Her Sons Join as One Social Band.

This clearly depicted a scene of national and craft harmony. All of the artisans in the shop worked together toward a common goal.[11]

The one exception to the lack of incorporation, as noted, was the General Society of Mechanics and Tradesmen, chartered by the State of New

York in 1785 after a legislative struggle that turned on the issue of whether or not the incorporation of artisanal associations would be financially harmful to society. The society of mechanics included representatives from the various trades in New York and acted not only as a fraternal and benevolent society but also as a promotional association that, for example, lobbied for protective tariffs. It was composed almost entirely of masters, although in its early years, when the gap between masters and journeymen was not as great as it would become in the next quarter century, a number of journeymen were admitted.[12]

To be admitted, a candidate had to be nominated by members and be voted upon, and then had to take part in secret rituals and oaths. The symbol of the society of mechanics, a symbol that would long denote American artisans, was a muscular arm hoisting a hammer and accompanied by the motto "By Hammer and Hand all Arts Do Stand." This was taken from the English Blacksmiths Company, whose armorial bearing had three hammers on the shield and a phoenix and sun at the crest.[13]

The representations on the certificate allow insight into the values of the society's members. The importance of benevolence was well displayed in the upper right corner: an emissary of the society bringing aid to the widow and children of a deceased society member. Most prominent among the rendered ideals was the centrality of the artisan trades to society. Represented were indoor craftsmen, portrayed through a turner and his assistant working on a piece of furniture, and outdoor craftsmen, depicted in an engraving of shipbuilding and land construction. The prominence of the classical column was surely intentional, considering the close connection Americans felt with the Roman republic. Also present at the center left was a blacksmith's shop, from which the motto and symbol of the society were borrowed. The third major theme was patriotism and the celebration of the American bounty. At the lower left was a portrayal of the American frontier: the virgin forest with baying wolf on the left; a peaceful stream, a fisherman, and a mill in the center; and the industrious ploughman, counterpart to the industrious mechanic, at work breaking the American soil. In the upper left was a depiction of American liberty in the form of the classically garbed woman at center, and behind her another woman holding a honeycomb, indicative of industry and peace; to the left is the American Indian as noble savage, representing the New World, free of European iniquities.

Thirty-four years later, the society was an elite fraternity of wealthy merchant artisans. Their 1825 bookplate reflected this: the single scene depicted is that of benevolence and education. The society at this time operated a fine school and library and had chartered a bank (though it no longer had financial control); and it had expanded its definition of *mechanic* to include

Membership certificate of the New York Mechanics Society, 1791. An elegant
engraving displaying nearly all of the values central to artisanal republicanism.
(Courtesy, The Henry Francis DuPont Winterthur Museum)

some whose businesses were in the mercantile sector. The dress of the society's representatives as they point the fatherless child toward their school
building reflected a change in the economy: the status of master craftsmen
now had little in common with that of journeymen. The belief in progress
and patriotism remained, however, as seen in the portrayal of the American eagle and the newly completed Erie Canal.[14]

The Society of Master Sail Makers, dating from the 1790s, designed a certificate with similar themes, though in this case restricted to a single craft.
The crest consisted of a ship, a lighthouse, and a motto. The latter, "Commerce Moves All," was in the same genre as "By Hammer and Hand, all
Arts Do Stand," and testified to the centrality of artisanal labor to the well-
being of mankind. Benevolence, too, was featured in the upper right corner, through an illustration of a bereaved widow, her house on fire, receiving succor from the sailmakers. Craft pride and significance again were
displayed in attractive figures of craft workshops and businesses. At center

Bookplate of the General Society of Mechanics and Tradesmen, 1825. The society was now an organization of wealthy tradesmen who were unlikely to work with their hands. (Eno Collection, Miriam and Ira D. Wallach Division of Art, Prints, and Photographs, New York Public Library, Astor, Lenox, and Tilden Foundations)

right was a depiction of shipwrights working on a large vessel, a finely dressed master craftsmen directing the journeymen. The lower right incorporated a carefully drawn scene within a sail loft, with the journeymen stitching under the master's watchful eye while the apprentice tended to the yarn. At lower left was a sailmaker at work on the loom, piecing sails together. The center left revealed the outside of the sailmaker's loft with its pulley and rolled sail being lowered, and the foreground contained a ship with sail partly furled and a master looking over the sail's installation. Assorted instruments of the sailing trade were scattered in the foreground. The upper left corner of the mechanics' society certificate, it will be remembered, illustrated American freedom with the classic "lady of liberty" and the American Indian. Significantly, the sailmakers, in the correspond-

Membership certificate of the Society of Master Sail Makers of the City of New York, 1793. The two most prominent values displayed are liberty and industry. (Courtesy of The New-York Historical Society, New York City)

ing corner of their certificate, chose to depict that lady bringing liberty to the black slave via a deed of "emancipation." Most artisans, while not free of racial prejudice, found slavery and competition with slave labor unacceptable. New York City, moreover, had more slaves than any other northern metropolis.[15]

The Union Society of Shipwrights and Caulkers was composed of independent craftsmen who worked for various contractors. Aside from its fraternal and benevolent aims, the association had specific economic goals: it sought to control the entry of unskilled workers into its craft and, in a constitutional provision requiring that members work only for qualified shipbuilders, it endeavored to control the quality of their employers. The certificate of the society revealed the artisanal themes of republican patriotism and craft pride. At the top was an American eagle with the motto "ORDER IS HEAVEN'S FIRST LAW" while at lower left the figure of liberty, holding an American flag, stood next to Neptune. At the lower right shipwrights worked.[16]

The Hatmakers' True Assistant Society, an association with strictly benevolent aims, devised its certificate of membership to display a journeyman on an equal plane with his master, shaking his master's hand and pointing to the American eagle, symbol of republicanism. The motto on the crest read, "We Cover," while the motto on what once could have been a shield spelled out, "So firm we bind as one were joind." Except for the hat on the crest, there was little resemblance to the earlier English society's certificate, which stressed religious fraternity. Republican and craft pride dominated the American certificate.[17]

The artisanal societies discussed above marched in the various Fourth of July processions such as the 1812 parade pictured in a painting by William Chappel. Members of the Tammany Society, a fraternal association allied with the Democratic-Republicans and including many craftsmen, led the parade, arrayed in Indian costumes. Following in the background were the various artisanal societies. On the side of the street near the park surrounding the new City Hall were booths and vendors, while other spectators stood on the balcony of the original Tammany Hall to observe the festivities. Following such marches, a speaker, often a prominent member of an artisanal society, delivered an oration; then the members of the various societies repaired to a tavern for an evening of dining, drinking, and toasting.[18]

In 1825 a spectacular parade, similar to that held in 1788 to commemorate the ratification of the Constitution, was sponsored by the city in celebration of the completion of the Erie Canal. Again the artisanal societies

Detail from a certificate of membership, Union Society of Shipwrights and Caulkers, New York, c. 1790. (Courtesy, Museum of The City of New York)

Membership certificate of the Hatmakers' True Assistant Society. Craft harmony combines with pride in the new nation. (Courtesy, The Henry Francis Dupont Winterthur Library Museum)

William Chappell, Fourth of July Parade, 1812. The republican order and deco-
rum contrasts markedly with the disorder of the London crowd on Lord Mayor's
Day. (Courtesy of The New-York Historical Society, New York City)

marched in ranks. The display of the Chair-Makers' Society at this parade
was typical. Leading the formation was a boy wearing a silk sash and carrying a blue silk banner with the motto "Support the Chair," which had a double meaning, as it referred also to the governor. The grand standard followed. On the front of the standard was a female figure with a cornucopia,
symbolic of peace and plenty; her left hand was on an ornate chair. In the
background was a chair manufactory, and beyond that Castle William of
New York Bay. The motto read, "By Industry We Thrive." On the reverse
side of the standard was the chairmakers' coat of arms, adorned only with
two chairs and a carpenter's tool on the crest and a simple utilitarian motto,
pointing again to the contribution of the artisan: "Rest for the Weary." Following the grand standard came the master chairmakers, wearing badges

Chairmakers' display at the Grand Canal Parade, 1825. The prominence of the ordinary chair in the epic of American commerce and industry is displayed in this illustration. (I. N. Phelps Stokes Collection, Miriam and Ira D. Wallach Division of Art, Prints, and Photographs, New York Public Library, Astor, Lenox, and Tilden Foundations)

of the society, and then eight boys hoisting a large gilt eagle grasping a miniature chair in its beak. The members of the Journeymen Chair Makers Society followed, wearing similar badges, then another eagle, and finally the apprentices, sporting the same badges and holding a banner emblazoned with the words "Liberty and Peace."[19]

The ropemakers' display included a stage with artisans both spinning yarn and winding rope. The display was summed up in a short stanza:

Our hemp is good, our cordage neat,
We will supply the American fleet.

The ropemakers' coat of arms was within a similar tradition. At the bottom was an engraving of the canal, cause of the celebration. The American flag, American eagle, and symbol of justice formed the center of the display, along with a ropemaker at work on a twisting wheel at the crest.

The supporters, both standing on coils of rope, were two ropemakers, one carrying the flag and the other the standard of the United States. At the bottom was a ropewalk over a canal bridge. The motto read, "Although We Go Backward Still We Advance." Again the artisan is depicted as central to the success of an egalitarian American republic.[20]

The Canal Parade also included at least two artisanal displays that generally copied their English forebears. The first was that of the House Painters Society. One hundred and thirty-nine tradesmen walked in the procession, bedecked in blue coats and white pantaloons; accompanying them was their president, similarly dressed, with the addition of a red velvet collar and a light blue sash. The banner, six feet by four feet, resembled that of the society's English counterpart. It depicted a shield in the center of two panthers. The panthers stood for color (via their spots). Both the English and American standards contained the Latin motto "Amor et Obedientia" (Love and obedience). On the reverse of the New York City banner were a golden pallet, pencils, a golden ribbon, and the motto "The useful and agreeable," which is similar to that of other American societies.[21]

Like the house painters, the members of the Bakers Society, 125 strong, wore blue coats and white pantaloons; in addition, they displayed white hats. They also brought along their own band of musicians. Their insignia displayed two deer surrounding a shield depicting sheaves of wheat and anchors and balances. The bucks stood for buckwheat, and the anchors were symbolic of Saint Clement, their patron saint, while the garb of wheat and the balances were the raw materials and the tools of the trade. This insignia is identical to that of the society's English counterpart, although the New York bakers added a phrase pointing out their ancient ancestry: "Incorporated by Edward the 2nd in 1307." The New York bakers were not incorporated under American laws.[22]

The insignia shown on the 1827 certificate of the New York Coopers Society differs from the standard that the members of similar societies carried at both the Constitutional Parade and at the Canal Parade. The standard was a six-foot-by-seven-foot banner emblazoned with a representation of the union at the top, the arms of New York State in the middle, and the traditional coopers' arms with the English motto "Love as Brethren" at bottom. This certificate ignored the British heritage and showed a more contemporary scene consisting of coopers working within a mercantile panorama. The rope was in the shape of a beehive; one member is giving alms to an indigent. The motto read, "With frugal care save whilst you can / Some aid for self and fellow man." The emphasis is on benevolence, industriousness, and the centrality of the craft. The corresponding English insignia was quite different, featuring camels (as symbols of trade), tools of the trade, and a demi-heathcock (a mythical bird).[23]

Ropemakers' arms, Grand Canal Parade, 1825. Rope binds master and journey-men in harmony to the American eagle, symbol of liberty. (I. N. Phelps Stokes Collection, Miriam and Ira D. Wallach Division of Art, Prints, and Photographs, New York Public Library, Astor, Lenox, and Tilden Foundations)

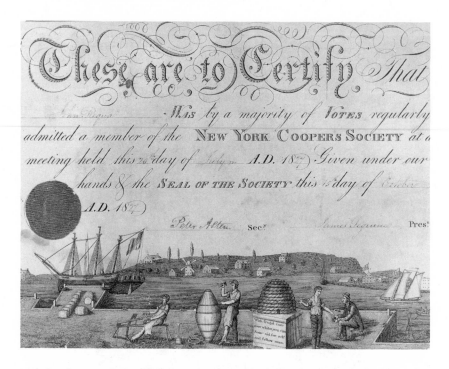

Membership certificate of the New York Coopers Society, 1827. The beehive-shaped rope stands for industry. (Courtesy of The New-York Historical Society, New York City)

## Iconography, Master Craftsmen, and Labor Conflict

What are we to make of these engravings? With only a few nostalgic exceptions, "artisan republicanism" has replaced the religious affiliation and loyalty to the crown common to the New York artisanal societies' English forebears. What is missing, however, is a second artisanal outlook which was also widespread, a perspective as prominent as the mechanics' republican commitment to the public good. The American Revolution had ignited a spirit of expectant capitalism within the ranks of Jeffersonian partisans, including many in the crafts community. Artisans, already in the colonial era men of singular ambition, expected to further expand their economic horizons now that the fetters of British mercantilism were lifted and a strong American government was in place. Indeed, much of their opposition to British measures had focused on the suppression of their right to fully participate in the market. The new Republic meant an open, accessible economy that would permit the meritorious—however humble their origins—to rise in the social order. American raw materials, combined with individual initiative and enterprise, offered individual hard-working farmers and artisans the opportunity to attain entrepreneurial independence and a better standard of living.[24] Republicanism and capitalism went hand in hand as the end of deference and aristocracy brought forth a truly open marketplace.[25]

Why, then, do the society certificates we have seen represent the classical republican artisanal viewpoint to the almost total exclusion of craftsmen's strong entrepreneurial aspirations and expectations? It was not because of the intellectual challenge of reconciling the two republican traditions, one based on the civic humanism of Machiavelli's Florence and the other on the individualism and contractual society of Locke. Craftsmen comprised both a highly ambitious and a deeply patriotic and public-spirited community. Rather, the answer may lie in the fact that the representations examined in this chapter are almost exclusively those of masters' associations, rather than journeymen's associations.

The burgeoning marketplace of the early Republic, oriented to national and international trade, allowed artisanal enterprises to extend well beyond the traditional family workshop. For successful masters this meant new avenues to wealth. For journeymen, however, the picture was less bright. Increased capital requirements made it more difficult for most of them to become masters, or to realistically contemplate becoming masters. It simply took too much money and too many business connections to become independent. How many, for example, could realistically envision owning an operation such as the workshop of Duncan Phyfe, which employed a hundred journeymen?

With the road to financial independence increasingly obstructed, the social and economic distances between master and journeymen widened. Masters bought fine carriages and elegant brick homes; journeymen had to crowd into rented wooden structures shared with several other families. Moreover, in their attempt to increase profits and compete in expanding marketplaces, masters cut wages and expanded the available labor pool by employing cheap and less highly skilled hands.[26] The ratio of journeymen to masters in Gotham's economy was growing constantly. In construction, shoemaking, chairmaking, and printing, a ratio of five to ten journeymen to a single master was not uncommon. Furthermore, masters were also intent on discipline and reliability, spelling out—in contradiction to preindustrial traditions—the hours that they expected their employees to be on the job.

These developments ran counter to the journeymen's sense of their place and role in society. How could the harmonious workshop of the independent artisan survive if fewer and fewer journeymen were able to attain the standing of independent proprietor? And how could the free market extinguish aristocracy and guarantee a genuinely republican society when the gap between the wealthy and the middling artisanal classes was growing and the influx of capital made economic independence less rather than more common? Out of journeymen's struggle against these barriers to the fulfillment of their Revolutionary inheritance came labor strife on a scale never before seen in New York. Determined to draw the line, these wage-earning craftsmen combined together to defend their wage, their job, and their standing.[27]

While the masters were tough entrepreneurs and hard-nosed employers, as a group they saw themselves as the protectors of all followers of their craft. As classical republican thought, with its emphasis on harmony and an organic society, reinforced this belief, they chose to represent themselves on their various insignia with symbols of cooperation and harmony within the workshop. Too, the masters' outlook provided a patriotic justification for their struggles against militant journeymen's societies. This ideology envisioned no place for such societies—they were seen as divisive and selfish. In their quest for ill-gotten gain they threatened social catastrophe.[28]

It has been argued that the journeymen were to some extent victims of artisanal republicanism. That is, they accepted the ideal of the harmonious workshop and of the unity of the trade after economic conditions had separated both the interests and the standing of masters and journeymen. Consequently, they were hindered in their attempts to successfully compete in the marketplace.[29] But for the most part journeymen were not at odds with the entrepreneurial ethos. Rather, they demanded the right to combine freely in negotiations. They did not reject capitalism; they wanted a fair opportunity to contend as organized labor. Rather, it was the masters, ambitious entrepreneurs when trading in the marketplace, who turned to an increasingly obsolete ideology in their attempts to thwart the journeymen. In this sense the visual representations might be seen as an outdated vision of the workshop, promulgated in the service of masters' pursuit of greater control over their employees.[30]

Masters, of course, had many motives in mind when forming their artisanal societies or approving designs for those societies' certificates and emblems. These organizations were also communal associations emphasizing benevolent spirit and action. Too, there were times when masters and journeymen made common cause in furthering the economic position of their professions with regard to credit and protective tariffs. Furthermore, at patriotic occasions such as Fourth of July celebrations, or at special events such as the parade in honor of the Erie Canal, they might join together in procession. Thus, to an extent, the insignia do portray common values. But there is no doubt that as early as the Age of Jefferson journeymen and masters had begun to go their own, independent ways. These visual representations are both more and less than what they seem to be: less, because the harmony they depict was less and less common; and more, because the masters in their struggles were attempting to invoke the past to control an unknown and precarious present.

HARRY R. RUBENSTEIN

# With Hammer in Hand
## Working-Class Occupational Portraits

IN THE PHOTOGRAPHIC COLLECTIONS of the Smithsonian Institution is a small tintype, dating from the 1860s, that shows a man in work clothes holding a hammer in one hand and a horseshoe in the other. No documentation concerning the image exists, and neither the man nor the photographer has been identified. Nonetheless, the photograph, along with similar portraits, offers a glimpse that few written documents provide into these workers' attitudes toward their occupations and their desired self-image.

The man in the photograph made a decision to have his portrait taken not in his more anonymous "Sunday clothes," but instead in a manner that would portray him as a farrier to all future viewers of the tintype. For him to have made this choice must have meant that he defined himself, in large part, by his trade. Through this image he acknowledged his occupational pride and his belief in the artisanal ideal of the productive citizen.

His decision was not unique. From the late 1700s through the 1880s many workers commissioned portraits that represented them as members of their craft. Posing with identifiable symbols of their trade, these workers made a statement about how they wanted to be viewed and remembered. Their portraits were personal declarations about their sense of self and the way in which they perceived their standing in their communities.

There is no way of knowing how much this farrier knew of the rich tradition of working-class occupational portraits on the day he decided to commission his portrait. Yet, a link between the few existing colonial portraits of artisans and the abundant photographic examples dating from the mid–nineteenth century seems evident. The relationship between these portraits is not merely one of trend or fashion. The individuals portrayed in them held common beliefs about the meaning of craft and work, beliefs

Tintype of farrier, c. 1870. This unidentified individual with a hammer in hand chose to have his likeness immortalized, as had so many others before him, with symbols of his trade. (Division of Photographic History, National Museum of American History, Washington, D.C.)

that perpetuated this genre in America for more than one hundred years.

In part, these workers were demonstrating, whether deliberately or unconsciously, their belief in the republican ideals of the productive citizen. In the rhetoric of the new nation, humanity was divided into productive and unproductive members. The laboring classes took pride in and found meaning in belonging to what they considered to be the useful segment of an interdependent society. They took to heart the motto used by New York's General Society of Mechanics and Tradesmen: "By Hammer and Hand, all Arts do Stand." They believed not only that work ennobled the individual but also that it was the true measure of the individual.

In the highly competitive world of industrial capitalism, however, artisanal republicanism began to lose much of its relevance. Slowly, traditional measures of status were superseded by new standards, and a decline in the number of occupational portraits followed. By the end of the 1880s few workers posed with tools for formal individual portraits, as personal status came to be gauged more by wealth than by occupation.

Before proceeding any further, let me state specifically how I have defined, in the context of this paper, working-class occupational portraits. They are pictorial images, either paintings or photographs, commissioned by the sitter, that through the use of symbolic accessories identify the subject as a member of a craft or working-class occupation. These portraits are very different from, and should not be confused with, images of work scenes or company photographs in which the subjects had little influence on the way in which they were shown. In personal portraits, although artists conformed to popular styles and conventions, the way in which they rendered the sitter was in most instances agreed upon by the subject. Additionally, successful portrait artists knew that they needed to please their clients and affirm their clients' self-images. It is for these reasons that commissioned portraits, unlike other works of art, can serve as important documents to illuminate the attitudes of the individuals they portray.

## Portraits of Artisan Republicans

Eighteenth-century and early-nineteenth-century portraiture in America drew on European, and largely English, traditions, which set conventions for future generations. In eighteenth-century England, portraits were the dominant subject of paintings; and examples of these works, in the form of prints, were widely available in the colonies. The often-stated goal of English portrait artists was to preserve the biography of the individual. By their selection of pose, setting, technique, and accessory objects, the artists sought to capture the essence of the sitter by combining accurate depiction and idealization.[1] The purpose of a portrait was to preserve the subject in the viewers' memory. The English artist Jonathan Richardson wrote in 1715, in *An Essay on the Theory of Painting:*

> The Picture of an absent Relation, or Friend, helps to keep up those Sentiments which frequently languish by Absence and may be instrumental to maintain, and sometimes to augment Friendship, and Paternal, Filial, and Conjugal Love, and Duty. Upon the sight of a Portrait, the Character, and Master-Strokes of the History of the Person it represents are apt to flow in upon the Mind, and to be the Subject of Conversation: So that to sit for one's Picture is to have an Abstract of one's Life written, and published, and ourselves thus consign'd over to Honour, or Infamy.[2]

Americans approached their portraiture by applying much the same techniques and goals. The majority of early American portraits were of members of the wealthier classes, and of certain professionals such as jurists, soldiers, and ministers. Through costume and accessories viewers could recognize the identity and class of the subject. An artist would paint a merchant with his ledgers, a soldier in uniform, and a landowner with a view of his estate.

Few artisans in the late eighteenth and early nineteenth centuries could afford the cost of a painted portrait. Most of those who could were among the most successful male members of their trade. By the time they were in a position to commission a portrait, many would have risen above the status of a mechanic and would in fact have been merchants or entrepreneurs.[3] When some of these successful craftsmen chose to be painted as gentlemen and others asked to be portrayed as artisans working at their craft, they were often making as much a political statement as a personal one. Those workers who requested that they be depicted with the tools or the products of their craft were identifying with a republican ideology that made the future of the nation dependent on a responsible citizenry of equals drawn from the producing classes of artisans, farmers, and manufacturers.

Artistic conventions did, however, contribute to the form of these paintings. Portraits were priced according to size, and it was customary to include fewer accessories in smaller works. Artistic conventions dictated that in smaller portraits, which would have been the most affordable for craftsmen, accessories served only to clutter the painting; thus, their inclusion was often discouraged. Therefore it is possible to say more about what is being projected in the typical small portrait of an artisan when symbols are present than when they are absent.[4]

One of the best-known and earliest artisanal portraits is John Singleton Copley's painting of Paul Revere (c. 1768–70). The painting has all the elements of this type of portrait. Revere is clearly depicted as a silversmith, dressed in his work clothes and surrounded by symbols of his craft. His pose is thoughtful and dignified.[5]

At the time the painting was produced, Copley and Revere were at the very least business acquaintances, if not friends. In the 1760s Revere had made several picture frames and miniature cases for Copley, and probably Revere had accepted the portrait in exchange for his work.[6] No letters or accounts exist which explain the arrangement between the two men or say who suggested the working-class theme. Copley had used this genre once before. In 1753 he had painted a portrait of his stepbrother, Peter Pelham, a print maker, in which he had depicted his subject with an assortment of engraver's tools to denote his occupation.[7] It seems likely that this earlier work served as a basis for Revere's portrait. Whatever the circumstances leading up to the painting, the approach undoubtedly would have been discussed and agreed upon by both men.

Many critics and historians have commented on the relationship between this egalitarian image of Revere and his activism throughout the Revolutionary era. The belief in the nobility and the rights of the common man underscores the manner in which the painter rendered his subject. Copley painted the portrait during a time when Revere was devoting less attention to his silver shop and was increasing his political involvement both in such organizations as the Sons of Liberty and in public opposition to the Townshend Acts.[8]

Yet the painting cannot be interpreted solely as a timely political statement. Also contributing to the creation of this image is a long tradition of occupational identification and pride which was thoroughly instilled in practitioners of the skilled crafts through apprenticeships, shop culture, and trade associations. The painting grows out of an amalgamation of traditional artisanal ideals that had existed for centuries and egalitarian principles regarding the rights of man that existed during the Revolutionary era. This blend of ideologies not only is evident in the Revere portrait but also characterizes later working-class occupational portraits in general. These ideologies found expression in public displays as well as in these more personal statements.

Several historians have noted that a form of artisanal republicanism was articulated in the urban parades and celebrations of the late eighteenth and early nineteenth centuries. In much the same manner that individuals surrounded themselves with symbols of their craft in portraits, artisans in public demonstrations found similar ways to convey their sense of artisanal identity. In the grand citywide celebrations such as those events supporting the ratification of the Constitution in 1788 and the completion of the Erie Canal in 1825, as well as in the small parades sponsored by local associations

John Singleton Copley, portrait of Paul Revere, c. 1768–70. This portrait of Revere, posed in his work clothes and holding a teapot, combined the egalitarianism of the American Revolutionary era with traditional values of craft. (Gift of Joseph W., William B., and Edward H. R. Revere. Courtesy, Museum of Fine Arts, Boston)

of mechanics, workers constructed elaborate displays that emphasized the history and contributions of their crafts.[9]

In Boston, fifteen hundred workmen marched in 1788 with tools, banners, and floats to celebrate Massachusetts's ratification of the Constitution. The procession included a model shipyard on a platform pulled by thirteen horses; on it, several boatbuilders constructed small ships. Masons carried trowels, ropemakers tied hemp around their waists, and carpenters marched "with the tools of every sort."[10]

Fifty-three years later, the local mechanics' association in Portland, Maine, concluded its 1841 fair with an hour-long parade. Coopers, printers, blacksmiths, and painters marched with representatives from each of the city's trades. Each group carried a banner that had been prepared for the occasion. The printers' banner was inscribed, "The Tyrant's Foe, The People's Friend." The hatters carried one that proclaimed, "We Crown the Sovereign People." Shipyard craftsmen declared, "We Lay the Foundations of Commercial Enterprise," and construction tradesmen asserted, "Our Labour & Skill are Indispensable for the Advancement of Civilization." A bit less lofty were the cordwainers, who marched behind the slogan "He that will not pay the Shoe-Maker is not worthy of a Sole."[11]

The artisanal community used these events to demonstrate its members' deep-seated craft pride and unity, and to emphasize to the larger society how essential was the role artisans played. One of the notable features of these demonstrations was the continued blending of English guild heraldry with republican symbolism and rhetoric. The emblems that appeared on trade societies' ribbons and banners had often been copied from the symbols of London guilds to demonstrate the craft's rich traditions.[12] These visual statements were combined with recognizable republican imagery of liberty and nationalism, infusing traditional craft imagery with a confirmation of adherence to the principles of independence, virtue, and citizenship. Although the elaborate artisanal celebrations of the nineteenth century declined in the 1830s and 1840s, much of the symbolism persisted into the Labor Day parades of the twentieth century.

The use of these occupational emblems and symbols of work both in public demonstrations and in portraits, which are essentially personal and private expressions, reveals not only a sharing of imagery between the public and private worlds but also a blending of these two worlds to construct a single persona.

In John Neagle's portrait of Patrick Lyon, painted in 1826–27, these same ideals were once again clearly set forth on the personal level. Neagle rendered Lyon as a proud, independent, and virtuous craftsman. This image did not develop by chance. In this instance, one of the few in which documentation was preserved, Lyon's intentions were straightforward.

John Neagle, portrait of Patrick Lyon, 1826–27. Lyon, who conceived the elements of his own portrait, sought to emphasize the ideals of artisanship which he believed he embodied. (Herman and Zoë Oliver Sherman Fund. Courtesy, Museum of Fine Arts, Boston)

At the time of his portrait, Lyon was a successful designer and manufacturer of fire engines. Nonetheless, when commissioning his portrait he wrote to Neagle with the now-famous instructions "I wish you, sir, to paint me at full length, the size of life, representing me at the smithery, with my bellows-blower, hammers and all the et-ceteras of the shop around me." He explained, "I wish you to understand clearly, Mr. Neagle, that I do not desire to be represented in the picture as a gentleman—to which character I have no pretention. I want you to paint me at work at my anvil with my sleeves rolled up and my apron on."[13]

The reason for Lyon's decision has often been tied to his wrongful arrest for a bank robbery when he was a young locksmith. Lyon maintained that his imprisonment had stemmed largely from the upper classes' distrust of mechanics. As a reminder and vindication of Lyon's false imprisonment, Neagle painted in the portrait's upper left corner a view of the Walnut Street Prison in Philadelphia, where Lyon had been confined. The portrait is, however, more than just a rejection of the upper classes: other approaches that were popular at the time could have been selected. Lyon chose to affirm his belief in the artisanal ideal and made clear his desire to be represented as an uncorrupted, independent producer.

The painting (which on several occasions was publicly displayed) struck a chord with like-minded artisans. The image of Lyon became an icon of artisanal republicanism and was adopted as a symbolic figure representing the virtues of all craftsmen. The critical acclaim with which the painting was received prompted Lyon to sell the portrait to the Boston Athenaeum in 1828, and he commissioned Neagle to produce a second version for his home. Images of the painting seem to have been widely distributed. By the 1830s prints of the painting had been published, and as early as 1837 a version of the portrait became a popular vignette for banknotes, municipal scrip, and bonds, in localities ranging from New York to Georgia.[14]

Occupational portraits were not limited to the work of such highly accomplished artists as Copley and Neagle. Less highly skilled painters and anonymous artists produced numerous portraits along very similar lines. The portrait of Evans Howell, a Philadelphia printer, painted in 1848 by Robert Street, in several respects echoes Lyon's portrait. Here again, the central underlying theme is a portrayal of the subject as a productive master craftsman. In this instance Howell's shop was large enough to employ several journeymen and apprentices, yet in commissioning this portrait Howell, too, wanted to be seen with his apron on and his sleeves rolled up.[15]

An image of an unknown watchmaker (c. 1840s) was characteristic in style of numerous portraits produced by several artists. The painter of the watchmaker's portrait repeated many of same devices used by Copley in the Revere portrait. In this instance, the figure posed with the product of

Georgia banknote printed around 1840 and issued in 1862. The portrait of Lyon had rapidly become the archetypal image of an artisan. (National Numismatic Collection, National Museum of American History, Washington, D.C.)

his labor, a watch, in one hand, and a sampling of his tools placed on a surface in front of him. One obvious difference in this work was the manner in which the subject dressed. Instead of being presented in his work clothes, this man selected a fine suit to wear for his sitting. His choice was not unusual, and in several occupational portraits the subjects are similarly clothed. This decision should not be interpreted as a denial that the subject

Robert Street, portrait of Howell Evens, 1848. The painting, though less skillfully executed, repeated in its composition the same basic elements of Lyon's portrait: a master craftsman at work in his shop. (Courtesy of Atwater Kent Museum, Philadelphia)

Unidentified watchmaker, c. 1840. The subject, dressed in formal clothing and posed with a few symbolic references to his occupation, was shown in a manner typical of how many portrait painters depicted their artisan clients. (Old Sturbridge Village, Sturbridge, Mass., photo by Henry E. Poeach, neg. no. B20811.

belonged to the artisanal class; rather, it was his way of emphasizing that he was a successful member of that group.

Whereas the portraits discussed above were commissioned for private purposes, occupational symbolism also found its way into material designed for public self-promotion. In the campaign broadside put out by Robert Smith while seeking election to New York's state legislature (c. 1842), the artist incorporates all the emblems of the artisan to promote the candidate.[16] Smith, a stonecutter from New York City, is employing the imagery of his craft not only to gain fellow workers' votes but also to stress his own ties to the ideals of the productive citizenry. The bust of George Washington was a not-so-subtle reminder of the Revolutionary tradition that he wanted voters to associate with his campaign.

The usefulness of these symbols was not lost on other politicians who could claim an artisanal past. On the national level, depictions of Abraham Lincoln as the Illinois rail splitter and Ulysses S. Grant as the Galena tanner became useful images for appealing to the labor vote.[17]

## Photographic Portraits

The availability of photography in the mid–nineteenth century made it possible for average workers to obtain portraits of themselves. While paintings would have been affordable only to successful master craftsmen, photographic likenesses were soon within the means of almost all members of the working class. Following the pattern of earlier occupational portraits, carpenters, blacksmiths, machine operators, and others—often dressed in their clean work clothes—brought their tools and other chosen items from their shops and factories into photographers' studios.

Samuel F. B. Morse introduced Daguerre's invention to America in 1839, declaring that the process was "Rembrandt perfected." The subsequent rapid spread of photography was a testament to the desire of Americans for personal images. Traveling photographers fanned out across the country competing for clients. Renting rooms or pulling wagon studios into empty lots, they stayed a few days and moved to the next town. By 1853 the New York *Daily Tribune* estimated that three million daguerreotypes were being produced annually.[18] The average cost of a daguerreotype in the 1840s ranged from two dollars to five dollars and represented a substantial, though feasible, investment for working people. However, by the 1850s competition among less expensive photographers drove the price down to as little as twenty-five cents. In the late 1850s the price dropped further with the introduction of paper photographs and tintypes. Images could be obtained for as little as five or ten cents at the cheaper studios.[19]

In the 1860s the itinerant photographers Papineau and Thomas, in their

*The Mechanic,*
ROBERT SMITH

Campaign broadside for Robert Smith, c. 1842. Smith, a New York City stonecutter, applied the style of the personal occupational portrait to the public arena of
campaign politics in his bid for an assemblyman's seat in the New York State legislature. (Division of Political History, National Museum of American History,
Washington, D.C.)

handbill, offered cabinet cards at fifty cents a dozen for the general trade: "We've come to suit all, both great and small, high and low, rich and poor, lame and lazy, married or single, apple women, scissors' grinders, tinkers, tailors, horse thieves, Assemblymen, Congressmen, You or Any Other Man."[20]

Daguerreotypes and the photographic processes and formats that quickly followed soon became part of the Victorian clutter of the mid–nineteenth century. Photographs mounted in small cases vied for space on whatnot shelves of bric-a-brac; and tintypes, *cartes de visites,* and cabinet cards filled the pages of albums. They were saved as mementos of one's life and given to loved ones as tokens of affection.

Photographers in the nineteenth century appealed to customers using much the same reasons and language that Richardson had used in 1715. The value of a portrait was that it preserved the memory of a relation or friend. "Since Daguerre first announced his wonderful discovery," a broadside from J. D. Wells's Daguerrian Gallery proclaimed in 1851, "it is now known wherever civilized man is found, and thousands there are who rejoice in the possession of the faithful miniature, which reveals the form, features and expression of some departed friend."[21] That one should be photographed so as to be remembered by others was a theme reiterated in many of the early advertisements. J. H. Hero and Company warned in 1847, "Delay not, then, as opportunity is now offered and while your children and friends are in the vigor of health, to secure one, two, three or six of these mementos of life, which under the trying circumstances of a final separation, no price can purchase."[22] More succinctly put was the motto printed on the handbill for Finch's Gallery, "Life is Uncertain."[23]

In the early days of photography, the manner in which one chose to be remembered was a decision taken with some thought and concern. Photographers displayed sample portraits in their waiting areas and on the street. These were intended to suggest proper attire and possible poses. Some studios published instructive guides on how best to have your portrait taken. Typically the instructions encouraged the sitter to come well groomed and in formal attire.[24] Many studios provided attendants to assist women with their hair and with the selection of jewelry.[25] Most of the existing documentation, however, is from established and expensive studios, which would not have catered to a working-class clientele.

The role of the photographer and the role of the subject in the creation of occupational portraits are difficult to determine. It soon became common practice for early photographers, like the portrait painters before them, to employ a host of props to embellish their subjects. Inventories of studios reveal that they were filled with furnishings, costumes, and oddities that were used to enliven the photographers' images. The photographic historian Brooks Johnson has argued that it seems reasonable for photographers, who were used to arranging and employing props in the creation of their portraits, to have suggested that craftsmen bring symbolic tools with them for their sittings.[26]

While this might have been the case, the use of props in general and the inclusion of tools as symbols in working-class occupational portraits are two very different things. As already noted, artisans have had a long tradition of employing tools as symbolic emblems in parades, paintings, and organizational insignia. At this point one can only speculate about how the use of such emblems in photographic imagery began. However, whether the photographer or the sitter was responsible for the image's composition is of secondary importance. More significant is the fact that it is unlikely that these portraits would have existed if customers had not felt that they were a true means of representing their self-image.

While origins are hard to know, sources that might have inspired these portraits are easier to identify. Certain of the earlier examples mentioned above, in particular the painting of Patrick Lyon, could have influenced photographers and sitters who looked to the fine arts for guidance in composing their images. Nineteenth-century prints would also have been likely contributing sources. Graphic representations of workers in encyclopedias on trades, political cartoons, labor association graphics, and campaign broadsides commonly included symbolic tools and machinery. Individuals who decided to represent themselves as idealized workers would have had many examples to use as models.[27] Once the practice of employing symbols of craft had been accepted in portraits, its spread and continuation would have depended on whether this type of image maintained its relevance and appeal.

In part, the appeal of such symbols for workers who had photographs made was not that different than it had been for those artisans who had commissioned paintings. As the photographs suggest, the desire to be seen as a productive member of a trade was widespread and significant. Workers' self-images were strongly tied to their occupations: to the status their occupations gave them, and the contributions that their work enabled them to make. Richard Oestreicher has stated: "The point of the occupational photograph was artisanship and status, not the work itself. The harnessmaker, the shoemaker, carpenters and blacksmiths who carried their tools to the local gallery lived within an artisan culture. They were citizen-craftsmen whose pride in their work was not only a pride in status and skill but an affirmation of republican values."[28]

Yet while the early paintings of artisans and these later photographs share a common approach and vocabulary, it is important to remember that the people depicted lived in very different worlds. By the 1840s the artisanal system of production was rapidly disappearing and was being replaced by a capitalist market economy. Whereas the subjects in the earlier paintings were independent producers, many, if not most, of the workers who had their portraits made in photographers' studios were wage employees. In this light, the photographic portraits also seem to be an expression of these workers' desire to be associated with a romantic artisanal past. By the mid–nineteenth century a sentimentalized vision of a disappearing class of independent artisans who were ennobled through manual labor had become popular in literature and art.

In their appearance there was nothing casual about most of the early occupational photographs. In part, the formality of the portraits results from the technological limitations of the equipment, which required long exposures, and from the unfamiliarity of the sitters with photography. It also stems from the serious and deliberate way in which the subjects approached their portraits. By selecting a few symbolic objects—a saw, a plane, or a wrench—they chose how they wished to be remembered.

Most of the occupational photographs represented skilled workers, such as a carpenter standing next to his tool chest, a plasterer holding his trowel and mortarboard, or a tailor sitting with the sewing machine he had brought into the studio. But portraits of people from what were considered semi-skilled and unskilled trades (e.g., teamsters, laborers, and millworkers) are not uncommon. Oestreicher, in a survey of occupational daguerreotypes from 1840 to 1865, estimated that skilled workers were represented in such portraits about twice as often as were semiskilled and unskilled workers.[29]

While numerous occupational portraits were produced of individual men, women in occupational portraits most often decided to be photographed in small groups. A similar pattern for women did not exist in nonoccupational images. There were no social taboos against women being photographed alone, and women often had individual portraits taken of themselves. Their tendency toward group portraits may possibly be explained by the close relationships they established while working and living together. Photographs of female textile mill operators, ceramic workers, and domestic servants testify to their wish to preserve the memory of their working friendships.[30] This desire was not exclusively felt by women, however, and many groups of men also faced the camera together.

All the portraits discussed above represented white sitters. Early portraits of African Americans are rare, and working-class occupational photographs of African Americans are even rarer. Although blacks would have been barred from certain studios, there were enough other photographers operating throughout the country that there would have been ample opportunity for portraits. The scarcity of such portraits can in part be explained as a

Ambrotype of woodworker proudly displaying selected tools, c. 1856–58.
(Division of Engineering and Industry, National Museum of American History,
Washington, D.C.)

result of basic economic factors. Photographs were a luxury item; many
African Americans simply needed to spend their money on more essential
things. It is also likely that the philosophical underpinnings of occupational
portraits, the belief that work was ennobling, would not have had the same
appeal to individuals who had recently experienced the degradation of
slavery.

Tintype of ceramic workers, c. 1860. In occupational portraits most women workers chose to be photographed in groups, rather than individually. The portraits were testaments to their occupational pride and their working friendships. (Division of Photographic History, National Museum of American History, Washington, D.C.)

## The Decline of Occupational Portraits

Toward the end of the nineteenth century, occupational portraits dramatically declined in popularity among workers of all types. Individual and family portraits containing no references to employment or occupation became the format of choice. Instead of being photographed with symbols of their trade, members of the working class went into the photographer's studio dressed in their "Sunday best."

Although it was not new for workers to have their photographs taken in formal attire, the apparent rejection of occupational portraits at the close of the nineteenth century raises important questions. The reason why occupational portraits lost favor is not clear or simple, but the change is certainly not merely attributable to stylistic fluctuations.

Interestingly, the decline in occupational portraits in the 1880s takes place during a period that labor historians have often described as being characterized by growing class consciousness, and coincides with the formation

Tintype of icemen, c. 1870s. Whereas portrait paintings were made exclusively of skilled artisans, inexpensive photographic portraits were commonly made of semiskilled and unskilled workers. (Division of Photographic History, National Museum of American History, Washington, D.C.)

Photograph of the carpenter Wilhelm Scheele and Minnie Scheele, c. 1892. By the end of the nineteenth century the popularity of working-class occupational portraits had declined. The formal family portrait was the image of choice. (Courtesy of Carl H. Scheele)

of the modern American labor movement. The coexistence of the weakening of personal occupational identification and the rise of organized labor and class consciousness may not be as contradictory as it seems. Both can be and have been explained as a response by workers to the turmoil and conflicts they experienced as industrialization challenged traditional work relationships and altered their position in the workplace and in society.

By the late nineteenth century, social standing was more often measured by income than by trade, and increasingly, status was demonstrated by one's ability to consume, instead of by what one produced. For many Americans, entrepreneurs and capitalists replaced yeoman farmers and artisans as the embodiment of the nation's values.

Longstanding prejudices against manual labor, which had been tempered by republican rhetoric about the respectable worker, were once again gaining ground. The gap in salaries and status between those who supposedly worked with their head and those who worked with their hands was increasing. Manual occupations that once had been viewed as elevating an individual's status in the community were by the late nineteenth century being associated with the lower segments of society. Reacting to these biases, labor journals were filled with stories that complained about how manual workers were being humiliated by the upper classes, and union leaders commonly called for the restoration of labor to its noble position as the producer of all wealth. The fact that so much attention was paid to labor's declining position indicates how widespread was this sense of a loss of status among the readers of the labor journals.[31]

In addition, labor increasingly was being viewed as a commodity rather than as a partner in the new industrial enterprises of the nation. The rapid expansion of large industry and the mechanization of production shifted control of the workplace from employees to their managers, lessening workers' sense of personal attachment to their trade. In many instances, employees no longer controlled either the pace of their work or the tools they had once so proudly displayed.

Confronted by a loss of status in both their communities and their workplaces, workers not surprisingly looked to aspects of their lives outside of their employment to define their self-image. While there was no sudden rejection of occupational portraits, it appears that they simply lost popularity and generally, with a few exceptions, disappeared from photographers' repertoire.

Although this change in portrait styles may indicate a dramatic shift in how workers saw themselves, it certainly does not mean that they abandoned all pride in or identification with their working life. Workers continued to seek personal ways to identify themselves with the products of their labor. Through the imagery and rhetoric of new labor organizations they continued to proudly proclaim their contributions to society. However, while the Labor Day parades of the twentieth century harkened back to artisanal festivals, and union leaders demanded a recognition of labor's role, workers' personal identification had been altered. American workers discarded the occupational portraits of the past, for these no longer expressed how they defined themselves or how they wished to be remembered.

# Notes

## Introduction: Identity and Independence

1. J. A. Leo Lemay and P. M. Zall, eds., *Benjamin Franklin's Autobiography: An Authoritative Text, Backgrounds, Criticism* (New York, 1986); David Freeman Hawke, *Franklin* (New York, 1976); Ormund Seavey, *Becoming Benjamin Franklin: The Autobiography and Life* (University Park, Pa., 1988); Esmond Wright, *Franklin of Philadelphia* (Cambridge, Mass., 1986).

2. Frederick Douglass, *Narrative of the Life of Frederick Douglass: An American Slave* (1845; reprint, New York, 1968); Nathan Irvin Huggins, *Slave and Citizen: The Life of Frederick Douglass* (Boston, 1980).

3. W. J. Rorabaugh, *The Craft Apprentice: From Franklin to the Machine Age in America* (New York, 1986).

4. Bruce Laurie, *Artisans into Workers: Labor in Nineteenth-Century America* (New York, 1989), 15–46.

5. Ronald Schultz, *The Republic of Labor: Philadelphia Artisans and the Politics of Class, 1720–1830* (New York, 1993), 6–7.

6. Carl Bridenbaugh, *The Colonial Craftsmen* (New York, 1950); Gary B. Nash, *The Urban Crucible: Social Change, Political Consciousness, and the Origins of the American Revolution* (Cambridge, Mass., 1979), 16–17, 58, 258–63.

7. *The Oxford English Dictionary* (London, 1961), 6:284; William Dwight Whitney, ed., *The Century Dictionary and Cyclopedia* (New York, 1889), 5:3678–79.

8. Nash, *Urban Crucible*, 35–37, 76–101, 129–57; Schultz, *Republic of Labor*, 3–35.

9. Lemay and Zall, eds., *Franklin's Autobiography*; Rorabaugh, *Craft Apprentice*, 3–15; Henry Steele Commager, *The Empire of Reason: How Europe Imagined and America Realized the Enlightenment* (Garden City, N.Y., 1977), 19–21; Wright, *Franklin of Philadelphia*, 1–13.

10. Many studies have been published on the contribution of artisans to the Revolution. See Carl Lotus Becker, *The History of Political Parties in the Province of New York, 1760–1776* (1909; reprint, Madison, Wis., 1968); Roger J. Champagne, "Liberty Boys and Mechanics of New York City, 1764–1774," *Labor History* 8 (1967): 115–35; Eric Foner, *Tom Paine and Revolutionary America* (New York, 1976); Dirk Hoerder, *Crowd Action in Revolutionary Massachusetts, 1765–1780* (New York, 1977); James H. Hutson, "An Investigation of the Inarticulate: Philadelphia's White Oaks," *William and Mary Quarterly*, 3d ser., 28 (1971): 3–25; Jesse Lemisch and John K. Alexander, "The White Oaks, Jack Tar, and the Concept of the Inarticulate: A Note on the Economic Position of Philadelphia's White Oaks," ibid., 29 (1972): 109–42; Staughton Lynd, "The Mechanic in New York Politics, 1774–1788," *Labor History* 5 (1964): 225–46; Pauline Maier, *From Resistance to Revolution: Colonial Radicals and the Development of American Opposition to Britain, 1765–1776* (New

York, 1972); Nash, *Urban Crucible;* Charles S. Olton, *Artisans for Independence: Philadelphia's Mechanics and the American Revolution* (Syracuse, N.Y., 1975); Stephen J. Rosswurm, *Arms, Country, and Class: The Philadelphia Militia and "Lower Sort" during the American Revolution, 1775–1783* (New Brunswick, N.J., 1987); Charles Steffen, *The Mechanics of Baltimore: Workers and Politics in the Age of Revolution, 1763–1812* (Urbana, Ill., 1984); Richard Walsh, *Charleston's Sons of Liberty: A Study of the Artisans, 1763–1789* (Columbia, S.C., 1959); Alfred F. Young, *The Democratic-Republicans of New York: The Origins, 1763–1797* (Chapel Hill, N.C., 1967); idem, "Revolutionary Mechanics," in *Working for Democracy: American Workers from the Revolution to the Present,* ed. Paul Buhle and Alan Dawley (Urbana, Ill., 1985), 1–9.

11. Alfred F. Young, "George Robert Twelves Hewes (1742–1840): A Boston Shoemaker and the Memory of the American Revolution," *William and Mary Quarterly,* 3d ser., 38 (1981): 561–623.

12. *New York Journal,* Nov. 26, 1767; ibid., Dec. 17, 1767.

13. Peter Force, *American Archives,* 4th ser. (Washington, D.C., 1837–43), 1:342–43, 6:895–98; *New York Journal,* June 6, 1776; Edward Countryman, *A People in Revolution: The American Revolution and Political Society in New York, 1760–1790* (Baltimore, 1981), 124–25, 138, 162–65.

14. Countryman, *People in Revolution,* 288–93; Alfred F. Young, "The Mechanics and the Jeffersonians: New York, 1789–1801," *Labor History* 5 (1964): 247–76; Howard B. Rock, *Artisans of the New Republic: The Tradesmen of New York City in the Age of Jefferson* (New York, 1979), 19–76; William Bruce Wheeler, "Urban Politics in Nature's Republic: The Development of Political Parties in the Seaport Cities in the Federalist Era" (Ph.D. diss., University of Virginia, 1967).

15. Gary J. Kornblith, "The Artisanal Response to Capitalist Transformation," *Journal of the Early Republic* 10 (1990): 315–21.

16. Many works deal with these developments. Among the most noted are Mary H. Blewett, *Men, Women, and Work: A Study of Class, Gender, and Protest in the Nineteenth-Century New England Shoe Industry, 1780–1910* (Urbana, Ill., 1988); Alan Dawley, *Class and Community: The Industrial Revolution in Lynn* (Cambridge, Mass., 1976); Thomas Dublin, *Women at Work: Transformation of Work and Community in Lowell, Massachusetts, 1826–1860* (New York, 1979); Paul G. Faler, *Mechanics and Manufacturers in the Early Industrial Revolution: Lynn, Massachusetts, 1760–1860* (Albany, N.Y., 1981); Paul A. Gilje, *The Road to Mobocracy: Popular Disorder in New York City, 1763–1834* (Chapel Hill, N.C., 1987); Paul A. Gilje and Howard B. Rock, eds., *Keepers of the Revolution: New Yorkers at Work in the Early Republic* (Ithaca, N.Y., 1992); Herbert G. Gutman, "Work, Culture, and Society in Industrializing America, 1815–1919," *American Historical Review* 78 (1973): 531–88; Susan E. Hirsch, *Roots of the American Working Class: The Industrialization of Crafts in Newark, 1800–1860* (Philadelphia, 1978); Graham Russell Hodges, *New York City Cartmen, 1667–1850* (New York, 1986); Paul E. Johnson, *A Shopkeeper's Millennium: Society and Revivals in Rochester, New York, 1815–1837* (New York, 1977); Judith A. McGaw, *Most Wonderful Machine: Mechanization and Social Change in Berkshire Papermaking, 1801–1885* (Princeton, 1987); Teresa Anne Murphy, *Ten Hours' Labor: Religion, Reform, and Gender in Early New England* (Ithaca, N.Y., 1992); Jonathan Prude, *The Coming of Industrial Order: Town and Factory Life in Rural Massachusetts, 1810–1860* (Cambridge, 1980); Howard B. Rock, ed.,

*The New York City Artisan, 1789–1825: A Documentary History* (Albany, N.Y., 1989); Rock, *Artisans;* Stephen J. Ross, *Workers on the Edge: Work, Leisure, and Politics in Industrializing Cincinnati, 1788–1890* (New York, 1985); Sharon V. Salinger, *"To Serve Well and Faithfully": Labor and Indentured Servants in Pennsylvania, 1682–1800* (Cambridge, 1987); Philip Scranton, *Proprietary Capitalism: The Textile Manufacture of Philadelphia, 1800–1885* (Cambridge, Mass., 1983); Cynthia Shelton, *The Mills of Manayunk: Industrialization and Social Conflict in the Philadelphia Region, 1787–1837* (Baltimore, 1986); Christine Stansell, *City of Women: Sex and Class in New York, 1789–1860* (New York, 1986); Schultz, *Republic of Labor;* Steffen, *Mechanics of Baltimore;* Richard B. Stott, *Workers in the Metropolis: Class, Ethnicity, and Youth in Antebellum New York City* (Ithaca, N.Y., 1990); Anthony F. C. Wallace, *Rockdale: The Growth of an American Village in the Early Industrial Revolution* (New York, 1978); Sean Wilentz, *Chants Democratic: New York City and the Rise of the American Working Class, 1788–1850* (New York, 1984).

17. John R. Commons, ed., *A Documentary History of American Industrial Society,* 10 vols. (Cleveland, 1909–11); John R. Commons et al., *History of Labour in the United States,* vol. 1 (New York, 1926). For a recent discussion of this work see Laurie, *Artisans into Workers,* 3–14.

18. The most influential of their work remains Gutman, "Work, Culture, and Society"; and E. P. Thompson, *The Making of the English Working Class* (New York, 1963).

19. Dawley, *Class and Community;* Faler, *Mechanics and Manufacturers.*

20. Bruce Laurie, *Working People of Philadelphia, 1800–1850* (Philadelphia, 1980); idem, "'Nothing on Compulsion': Life Styles of Philadelphia Artisans, 1820–1850," *Labor History* 15 (1974): 337–66.

21. Rock, *Artisans,* 205–63.          — *artisand rep*

22. Wilentz, *Chants Democratic,* 17.

23. Stuart M. Blumin, *The Emergence of the Middle Class: Social Experience in the American City, 1760–1900* (Cambridge, 1989), esp. 71. See also John S. Gilkeson Jr., *Middle-Class Providence, 1820–1940* (Princeton, 1986); Mary P. Ryan, *Cradle of the Middle Class: The Family in Oneida, New York, 1790–1865* (Cambridge, 1981).

24. Johnson, *Shopkeeper's Millennium.*

25. For a discussion of entrepreneurial planters see James Oakes, *The Ruling Race: A History of American Slaveholders* (New York, 1983); idem, *Slavery and Freedom: An Interpretation of the Old South* (New York, 1991).

26. Young, "George Robert Twelves Hewes," 561–623.

## Chapter 1 From Father to Son

1. Jacob Price has demonstrated this for mercantile families in *Perry of London: A Family and a Firm on the Seaborne Frontier, 1615–1753* (Cambridge, Mass., 1992), vii, 2.

2. Carl Bridenbaugh, *The Colonial Craftsman* (1950; reprint, Chicago, 1961), 44; W. J. Rorabaugh, *The Craft Apprentice: From Franklin to the Machine Age in America* (New York, 1986), 157–58. Robert Blair St. George argues that craft dynasties were important in families involved in the elaborate woodworking trades in "Fathers, Sons, and Identity: Woodworking Artisans in Southeastern New England, 1620–1700," in *The Craftsman in Early America,* ed. Ian Quimby (New York, 1984), 97–119.

3. Stephanie Grauman Wolf, *Urban Village: Population, Community and Family Structure in Germantown, Pennsylvania, 1683–1800* (Princeton, 1976), 307–10; Rorabaugh, *Craft Apprentice*, 16–24.

4. Historians have not generally used orphans' apprenticeship indentures, available for virtually every colony, arguing that orphans were not representative of apprentices as a group. They have assumed instead that apprenticeship was an unchanging institution and have used indentures from the early national period as a source of data on apprentices during the colonial period. See, e.g., Rorabaugh, *Craft Apprentice*, 3–4, 91–98, 120–28. Orphan's Court indentures are not a perfect source for the study of apprenticeship. Orphans rarely participated in capital-intensive crafts such as silversmithing or coachmaking. They did, however, resemble privately bound craft apprentices in virtually all other ways. By contrast, apprentices in the early national period bore little resemblance to colonial apprentices. Christine Daniels, "Alternative Workers in a Slave Economy: Kent County, Maryland, 1675–1810" (Ph.D. diss., Johns Hopkins University, 1990), 164–72.

5. Paul Clemens, *The Atlantic Economy and Colonial Maryland's Eastern Shore: From Tobacco to Grain* (Ithaca, N.Y., 1980); David Klingaman, "The Significance of Grain in the Development of the Tobacco Colonies," *Journal of Economic History* 29 (1969): 268–78; Carville Earle and Ronald Hoffman, "Staple Crops and Urban Development in the Eighteenth Century South," *Perspectives in American History* 10 (1976): 7–76; John J. McCusker and Russell Menard, *The Economy of British America, 1607–1789* (Chapel Hill, N.C., 1985), 129–31; Daniels, "Alternative Workers," 12–57.

6. Earle and Hoffman, "Staple Crops and Urban Development," 11, 26–41; Daniels, "Alternative Workers," 58–113.

7. The data on Chestertown are from Kent County Court Proceedings (hereafter cited as "Proceedings"), 1767–68, 267. All manuscript sources cited in this chapter are located at the Maryland Hall of Records, Annapolis, Md., unless otherwise noted. Information on Kent County's economic development and the growth of Chestertown is from Daniels, "Alternative Workers," 11–153. Population was estimated using a nontaxable-to-taxable ratio of 1:1.94. To obtain the ratio, the total Kent County population of 1755, enumerated as 9,443 persons in "An Account of the Number of Souls in the Province of Maryland," *Gentleman's Magazine* 34 (1764), reprinted in Edward C. Papenfuse and Joseph N. Coales III, *The Harmon-Harwood House Atlas of Historical Maps of Maryland* (Baltimore, 1982), was compared with the levy list made that year, which included 3,213 taxables. The tax list of 1749 lists each hundred separately; by 1749, Chestertown Hundred had separated from adjoining Chester Hundred, and included 437 taxables.

8. This description of where artisans worked is based on Kent County Tax List, 1749. Part of the list is missing. The list for the entire county includes 1,610 names, or 56.5 percent of the 2,852 taxable individuals listed in the Kent County Levy Book, 1749.

9. This discussion is indebted to the work of Jean Russo, *Free Workers in a Plantation Economy: Talbot County, Maryland, 1690–1759* (New York, 1989), 211–311.

10. Billy G. Smith, "The Vicissitudes of Fortune: The Careers of Laboring Men in Philadelphia, 1750 to 1800," in *Work and Labor in Early America*, ed. Stephen Innes (Chapel Hill, N.C., 1988), 39–240.

11. Daniels, "Alternative Workers," 58–153, 242–86.

12. Ibid., 86–92.

13. John Gresham paid shoemakers between 1s. 3d. and 2s. per pair. He paid 2s. during the War of the Austrian Succession, when imported shoes were unavailable. Account Book, 1716–50, 113, 134, Jane Sprinkle Collection. At the same time, Richard Tilghman generally paid shoemakers 2s. per pair, except for "Tom Casson the Shoemaker," who received 2s. 6d. per pair. Ledger A, 1716–41, 21–22, 51, and Ledger B, 1725–65, 62, Tilghman Family Papers, Manuscript Collection, Georgetown University Library, Washington, D.C. Tilghman did not increase wages during the war.

14. These figures certainly underestimate the number of boys bound to craft dynasties, as some kin connections undoubtedly remain elusive. However, this factor should not affect any craft disproportionately.

15. Daniels, "Alternative Workers," 72; Russo, *Free Workers,* 240.

16. The miller James Tibbet specified in 1728 that his mill was to have "new millstones and irons" sent from Europe. Kent County Wills (hereafter cited as "Kent Wills"), 1709–34, 250.

17. Kent County Bonds and Indentures (hereafter cited as "Bonds and Indentures"), 1772–82, 105; Prerogative Court Wills (hereafter cited as "Wills"), 38:182.

18. Bonds and Indentures, 1743–46, 146; Bonds and Indentures, 1754–58, 62, 117; Wills, 38:182; Kent Wills, 1735–46, 93.

19. Account Book, 1716–50, 89, Sprinkle Collection; Proceedings, 1734–35, 60; Kent County Original Inventories, box 19, folder 37; Kent County Original Inventories, box 29, folder 42; Russo, *Free Workers,* 255; Daniels, "Alternative Workers," 272–73.

20. Kent Wills, Transcript, 1669–1710, 157; Kent Wills, 1735–46, 9; Kent County Original Wills (hereafter cited as "Original Wills"), no. 100; Kent Wills, 1735–46, 222–23; Original Wills, no. 130.

21. Daniels, "Alternative Workers," 126–32. Before 1783, sharpening plows and shoeing horses made up about 40 percent of the work done by local smiths. After 1783, about 90 percent of their work consisted of those two tasks.

22. Before the Revolution, thirteen of seventeen blacksmith's apprentices (76.5%) had identifiable relatives in the trade. After the Revolution, four of thirteen (30.1%) did.

23. Kent Wills, 1709–34, 250–51; Kent Wills, 1756–69, 269.

24. Daniels, "Alternative Workers," 136–45. See also Prerogative Court Inventories (hereafter cited as "Inventories"), 89:246; Inventories, 105:292; Inventories, 106:212; and Wills, 34:66, which contain listings of the estates of pre-Revolutionary tanners. Kent County Inventories (hereafter cited as "Kent Inventories"), 10:287, 433, 528; and Kent Inventories, 11:198, contain such listings for post-Revolutionary tanners.

25. For descriptions of leatherworkers in early-nineteenth-century cities, see, for example, Sean Wilentz, *Chants Democratic: New York City and the Rise of the American Working Class, 1788–1850* (New York, 1984); Alan Dawley, *Class and Community: The Industrial Revolution in Lynn* (Cambridge, Mass., 1976); Paul Faler, *Mechanics and Manufacturers in the Early Industrial Revolution: Lynn, Massachusetts, 1760–1860* (Albany, N.Y., 1981); and Charles Steffen, *The Mechanics of Baltimore: Workers and Politics in the Age of Revolution, 1763–1812* (Urbana, Ill., 1984).

26. Before the Revolution, 37.5 percent of boys apprenticed to tanners had identifiable relatives in the trade. After the Revolution, 60 percent did.

27. Wills, 20:755; Wills, 38:137; Inventories, 22:110; Kent Wills, 1735–46, 154–55; Kent Wills, Transcript, 1669–1710, 49; Russo, *Free Workers*, 216–19.

28. Kent Wills, 1746–56, 313; Kent Wills, 1770–76, 2; Kent Wills, 1781–98, 107.

29. The description of trades is from R[ichard] Campbell, *The London Tradesman* (London, 1747; reprint, London, 1969), 160–61, 243.

30. Wills, 20:755; Inventories, 22:110; Bonds and Indentures, 1720–26, 47–48, 96–99.

31. Campbell, *London Tradesman*, 243.

32. Inventories, 45:70; Kent County Tax List, 1749; Proceedings, 1755–56, 427; Bonds and Indentures, 1772–82, 185.

33. Tennant worked as a boatwright as early as 1746. Proceedings, 1752–53, 341–42; Kent Wills, 1756–69, 237–38; Kent Wills, 1770–76, 111. The first Alford apprenticed as a shipwright was bound in 1714. Bonds and Indentures, 1707–15, 65.

34. Russo, *Free Workers*, 266–98. The quotations are from Kent Wills, 1735–46, 26; Kent Wills, 1756–69, 218; Kent Wills, 1770–76, 45, 229.

35. Before 1783, 51 out of 117 boys (43.6%) bound to capital-intensive crafts were members of craft dynasties; after 1783, 30 out of 52 (57.7%) were.

36. Rorabaugh, *Craft Apprentice*, esp. 17–31.

37. This group of ninety-three wills includes one written by a craftsman's widow, who had inherited her husband's estate and who made provisions for their son in her own will. I use the word *fathers* here for ease of reading.

38. Kent Wills, 1735–46, 259, 27; Kent County Wills, 9:8; Kent Wills, 1746–56, 46, 235.

39. Kent Wills, 1756–69, 121, 329.

40. Kent Wills, 1709–34, 332; Kent Wills, 1735–46, 13; Kent Wills, 1746–56, 357; Kent Wills, 1735–46, 119.

41. Minutes of the Cecil Monthly Meeting (hereafter cited as "Monthly Minutes"), 1698–1779, 54–55, Friends Historical Library, Swarthmore, Pa.

42. Kent Wills, 1709–34, 252; Monthly Minutes, 1768–79, 68; Monthly Minutes, 111.

43. Quotation from Kent Wills, 1756–69, 53. Also see Kent Wills, 1735–46, 97, 269; and Kent Wills, 1770–76, 180–81.

44. Quotation from Kent Wills, Transcript, 1669–1710, 122. Also see Kent Wills, Transcript, 1669–1710, 81–82; Kent Wills, 1735–46, 119; Kent Wills, 1756–69, 23.

45. Kent Wills, 1709–34, 181, 263–64, 241–42; Kent Wills, 1735–46, 250–51; Kent Wills, 1709–34, 250–51; Kent Wills, 1735–46, 223; Kent Wills, 1770–76, 111.

46. Kent County Wills, 9:8.

47. Quotation from Wills, 20:755. Also see Inventories, 22:110; Inventories, 45:70.

## Chapter 2 Freemen, Servants, and Slaves

1. Two recent exceptions to this generalization are Sharon V. Salinger, *"To Serve Well and Faithfully": Labor and Indentured Servants in Pennsylvania, 1682–1800* (New York, 1987), which provides important evidence on those who worked in craft shops in Philadelphia; and Billy G. Smith, *The "Lower Sort": Philadelphia's Laboring People, 1750–1800* (Ithaca, N.Y., 1990), which provides a detailed analysis of the standard of living of cordwainers and tailors. For a debate over the shortcomings of recent studies of eighteenth-century artisans, see Hermann Wellenreuther, "Labor in the Era of the American Revolution: A Discussion of Recent Concepts and Theories," *Labor History* 22 (1981): 573–600; Gary B.

Nash, Billy G. Smith, and Dirk Hoerder, "Laboring Americans and the American Revolution," ibid., 24 (1983): 414–39; and Hermann Wellenreuther, "Rejoinder," ibid., 24 (1983): 440–54.

2. For the centrality of independence and dependence to eighteenth-century life, see Gordon S. Wood, *The Radicalism of the American Revolution* (New York, 1992), 43–77.

3. For a brief overview of Baltimore's early development, see Sherry H. Olson, *Baltimore: The Building of an American City* (Baltimore, 1980), chaps. 1, 2. The wheat and flour statistics are from Geoffrey N. Gilbert, "Baltimore's Flour Trade to the Caribbean, 1750–1815" (Ph.D. dissertation, Johns Hopkins University, 1975), app. D, 185.

4. Carville Earle and Ronald Hoffman, "Staple Crops and Urban Development in the Eighteenth-Century South," *Perspectives in American History* 10 (1976): 28–29, 34–36; William Ottey to John Cook, 18 May 1761, Cook Family Papers, MS. 2202, Maryland Historical Society (hereafter cited as "MdHS"), Baltimore. "Linkage network" is a key concept employed in the staple theory of colonial economic development, for which see John J. McCusker and Russell Menard, *The Economy of British America, 1607–1789* (Chapel Hill, N.C., 1985), 23–26.

5. Clarence Gould, *Money and Transportation in Maryland, 1720–1765* (Baltimore, 1915), 160–61. For the dominance of English- and Philadelphia-made silver in Maryland during the colonial period, see Jennifer F. Goldsborough, "Silver in Maryland," in *Silver in Maryland*, ed. Jennifer F. Goldsborough (Baltimore, 1983), 2. For the dominance of English- and New England-made furniture in Maryland during the colonial period, see Gregory R. Weidman, *Furniture in Maryland, 1740–1940: The Collection of the Maryland Historical Society* (Baltimore, 1984), 43–44.

6. Arthur Pierce Middleton, *Tobacco Coast: A Maritime History of Chesapeake Bay in the Colonial Era* (Newport News, Va., 1953), 259–60.

7. The account book of the prominent town tailor James Cox reveals the importance of clothing for children, servants, and slaves to his business. See Cox Account Book, MS. 262, MdHS. For local consumption of craft goods, see also William Russell Account Book, MS. 1989, MdHS; Weidman, *Furniture in Maryland*, 44–45; John N. Pearce, "The Early Baltimore Potters and Their Wares, 1763–1850" (M.A. thesis, University of Delaware, 1959), 18; and Goldsborough, "Silver in Maryland," 2. For the colonies as a whole, see McCusker and Menard, *Economy of British America*, 277–94.

8. *Maryland Gazette* (Annapolis), Apr. 9, 1767; *Dunlap's Maryland Gazette* (Baltimore), May 2, 1767; ibid., Nov. 23, 1775; *Maryland Journal and Baltimore Advertiser* (hereafter cited as *Maryland Journal*), Feb. 2, 1779; ibid., Aug. 28, 1773. One study of early Baltimore cabinetmakers concluded: "The manufacture of household furniture was by no means the sole activity of the cabinet and chairmakers of Baltimore. In order to survive in the competitive environment which had in part been created by the merchant importers, it was necessary for local furniture craftsmen to perform a wide variety of services for their patrons." John H. Hill, "The Furniture Craftsman in Baltimore, 1783–1823" (M.A. thesis, University of Delaware, 1967), 218.

9. *Dunlap's Maryland Gazette*, Oct. 24, 1775; *Maryland Journal* Dec. 4, 1781; *Dunlap's Maryland Gazette*, May 23, 1775; *Maryland Journal*, Oct. 27, 1778; *Maryland Gazette* (Annapolis), Aug. 17, 1769.

10. See the advertisements of the tailor Cornelius Garretson, *Maryland Journal*, May 29, 1781; of the tailor Henry Speck, ibid., Feb. 4, 1783; and of the cloth dyer Jacob Hen-

ninger, ibid., Dec. 10, 1782. See also Nancy Baker, "Silversmiths in Colonial Annapolis," in Goldsborough, ed., *Silver in Maryland,* 18–19.

11. *Dunlap's Maryland Gazette,* Jan. 19, 1775; ibid., July 25, 1775; *Maryland Journal,* May 18, 1784.

12. *Maryland Gazette* (Baltimore), Sept. 24, 1784; *Maryland Journal,* May 23, 1780.

13. *Maryland Journal,* June 22, 1784. For other artisans selling imported and ready-made goods, see the advertisements of the saddler Matthew Patton, *Maryland Gazette* (Baltimore), July 25, 1783; the brassfounders Causten and Weir, *Maryland Journal,* Sept. 24, 1784; the ship chandler, oil and colourman Richard Jones, *Maryland Gazette* (Baltimore), Apr. 2, 1784; the currier Robert Hutton, *Maryland Journal,* June 11, 1784; and the cabinetmakers John Bankson and Richard Lawson, ibid., Sept. 6, 1791. Writing on the condition of American manufactures in 1785, "A Plain But Real Friend to America" complained that too many craftsmen were becoming merchants because they could not make a living by their trade. Without encouragement to manufacturing, he warned, "in half an age, perhaps, there may not be a sufficient number found to carry on some of the most useful branches." *Maryland Journal,* Oct. 11, 1785; ibid., Aug. 16, 1785.

14. For the involvement of merchants in these industries in Baltimore, see Tina H. Sheller, "Artisans and the Evolution of Baltimore Town, 1765–1790" (Ph.D. dissertation, University of Maryland, 1990), 42, 45–50, 147–48, 162–63, 218–20; and Charles G. Steffen, "The Pre-Industrial Iron Worker: Northampton Iron Works, 1780–1820," *Labor History* 20 (1979): 89–99.

15. *Maryland Gazette* (Annapolis), Jan. 1, 1767; ibid., Aug. 9, 1764.

16. Henry Johnson to Hewes and Anthony, Nov. 14, 1783, Johnson, Johonnot, and Company Letter Book, 1783–85, MS. 498, MdHS.

17. *Maryland Journal,* Oct. 30, 1773; ibid., Nov. 6, 1773; *Maryland Gazette* (Annapolis), Apr. 25, 1771.

18. See, for example, the advertisement of Edward Preston in *Maryland Gazette* (Annapolis), Oct. 1, 1767; and the advertisement of John Wolfe in ibid., May 7, 1767.

19. See, for example, the advertisements of Walter Osburn and of Knapp and Whetcroft, *Maryland Gazette,* Feb. 21, 1771; ibid., Dec. 3, 1767.

20. See the advertisements of Richard Thompson, *Maryland Gazette,* Aug. 10, 1769; George Parker, *Maryland Journal,* Oct. 9–16, 1773; and Robert Riddle, ibid., July 3, 1776. For the out-of-town work of the cabinetmaker Gerrard Hopkins, see Weidman, *Furniture in Maryland,* 46. For Cox's connection to the merchant Jonathan Hudson, see Cox Account Book, MdHS, s.v. John Howard, Dec. 1769; William Smith, "Doctor up the Bay," Nov. 1770; and Capt. Joseph Henderson and Mate, Jan. 1770. See also "The Estate of Jacob Giles in A/C Currt. with Saml. & Robt. Purviance," 1766–68, Baltimore Customs House Papers, MS. 806, MdHS.

21. Joseph Goldenberg, "With Saw and Axe and Auger: Three Centuries of American Shipbuilding," in *Material Culture in the Wooden Age,* ed. Brooke Hindle (Tarrytown, N.Y., 1981), 105–6; Sheller, "Artisans and the Evolution of Baltimore Town," 45–50.

22. Account of James Cox with Richard Lemmon, Mar. 23, 1773–Oct. 6, 1777, Cox Papers, MS. 1909, MdHS. See also the numerous accounts of artisans held by the merchant William Russell in Russell Account Book, MS. 1989, MdHS, especially those of John Dalrymple, a carpenter (accounts for 1774–77), John Wells, a bricklayer (accounts for 1774–77), and Jeremiah Norwood, a house carpenter (accounts for 1776–78).

23. Paul K. Walker, "The Baltimore Community and the American Revolution: A Study in Urban Development" (Ph.D. diss., University of North Carolina, 1973), 46; John Cannon to Mark Alexander, Aug. 1788, Vertical File, MdHS; Account of James Cox with Richard Lemmon, Mar. 23, 1773–Oct. 6, 1777, Cox Papers.

24. For Scotch-Irish Presbyterians, see "First Presbyterian Church Membership, 1766–1783," *Maryland Historical Magazine* 35 (1940): 256–61; and First Presbyterian Church Records, microfilm, Church Records, MdHS. For brief accounts of the beginning of the Society of Friends, Methodist, and German Lutheran and Reformed congregations in Baltimore, see J. Thomas Scharf, *The Chronicles of Baltimore* (Baltimore, 1874), 192, 76–77, 41–46. For the Baptists, see *History of the Baptist Churches in Maryland* (Baltimore, 1885), 31. For the overlapping nature of ethnic and business ties in Philadelphia, see Thomas Doerflinger, *A Vigorous Spirit of Enterprise: Merchants and Economic Development in Revolutionary Philadelphia* (Chapel Hill, N.C., 1986), 59.

25. George W. McCreary, *The Ancient and Honorable Mechanical Company of Baltimore* (Baltimore, 1901), 14–19; Ronald Hoffman, *A Spirit of Dissension: Economics, Politics, and the Revolution in Maryland* (Baltimore, 1973), 38–41. For the merchant-mechanic coalitions in the Committee of Observation and the Whig Club, see Sheller, "Artisans and the Evolution of Baltimore Town," 65–67, 85–86.

26. McCreary, *Ancient and Honorable Mechanical Company,* 13–18, 21–22; Daybook, Mechanical Fire Company Papers, MS. 584, MdHS.

27. See the numerous accounts that James Cox maintained with other tradesmen in Cox Account Book, MdHS; Cox correspondence in Corner Collection, MS. 1242, MdHS; and Richard Britton to Mary Cox, Mar. 11, 1778, Vertical File, MdHS. The sharing of shop space is evident in artisans' advertisements. See, for example, the advertisement of Jonathan Jones, saddle-tree maker ("at the House of Gerard Hopkins, Cabinetmaker"), *Maryland Gazette* (Annapolis), Oct. 18, 1770; the advertisement of James Ormsby French, watch- and clock-maker from Dublin (who "has moved to the House now occupied by Mr. Gabriel Lewyn, Goldsmith and Jeweller"), ibid., May 23, 1771; the advertisement of William Askew, cabinetmaker and chairmaker, (who "hath removed his shop from Mr. Gerard Hopkins's over to his own house"), *Maryland Journal,* Feb. 22, 1780.

28. This theme is developed in Sheller, "Artisans and the Evolution of Baltimore Town," chaps. 2, 5.

29. Kenneth Morgan, "The Organization of the Convict Trade to Maryland: Stevenson, Rondolph, and Cheston, 1768–1775," *William and Mary Quarterly,* 3d ser., 42 (1985): 215–23; David Galenson, *White Servitude in Colonial America: An Economic Analysis* (New York, 1981), 137–40, 160.

30. Abbot E. Smith, *Colonists in Bondage: White Servitude and Convict Labor in America, 1607–1776* (Chapel Hill, N.C., 1947), appendix, 325.

31. George Woolsey to James Forde, n.d. [c. Dec. 8, 1774], Woolsey and Salmon Letter Book, 1774–84, Peter Force Papers, ser. VIIID, Library of Congress, Washington, D.C.

32. One advertisement did not specify the port of origin of the servants. The reliability of advertisements of servants is questionable considering the great demand for skilled workers and the higher prices such workers could command. Nevertheless, other evidence indicates that many skilled servants were indeed aboard these ships. For the importance of skilled bondsmen in the servant trade, see Morgan, "Organization of the Convict Trade to Maryland," 215–16, 222–26.

33. Bernard Bailyn, *Voyagers to the West: A Passage in the Peopling of America on the Eve of the Revolution* (New York, 1986), 243, 208–9, 211, 213.

34. George Salmon to George Moore, Feb. 4, 1784, Woolsey and Salmon Letter Book; Aubrey C. Land, ed., *Letters from America: William Eddis* (Cambridge, Mass., 1969), letter 6, 36, 40; Bailyn, *Voyagers to the West*, 256–59.

35. *Maryland Journal*, Aug. 28, 1773.

36. Moore's ad was in the *Pennsylvania Packet*, Dec. 19, 1774, as cited in Henry Berkley, "A Register of the Cabinet Makers and Allied Trades in Maryland, as Shown by the Newspapers and Directories, 1746–1820," *Maryland Historical Magazine* 25 (1930): 12; the Davidson and Collins quotations are from *Maryland Journal*, Oct. 30, 1776; and ibid., Sept. 7, 1779, respectively. See also *Maryland Gazette* (Annapolis), Apr. 13, 1769; *Dunlap's Maryland Gazette* (Baltimore), Jan. 2, 1776; ibid., Apr. 7, 1778; *Maryland Journal*, Oct. 2, 1781. The data on the purchase of convict servants are from Record of Convicts, 1770–74, Baltimore County Court Records, Maryland State Archives, 366, 367, 368, 369–70.

37. Census of Deptford Hundred, 1776, Revolutionary War Collection, MS. 1814, MdHS.

38. *Maryland Journal*, Apr. 3, 1781; ibid., Feb. 27, 1871; ibid., Jan. 22, 1782. Two of the advertisements (Worthington's advertisement, and the advertisement for the sale of the smith's shop) appeared in the same issue, that of Apr. 3, 1781.

39. Sharpe to Board of Trade, Dec. 9, 1766, *Archives of Maryland*, ed. William H. Browne et al. (Baltimore, 1883–1970), 14:359–60; Adams quoted in Olson, *Baltimore*, 15.

40. Gary B. Nash, "Artisans and Politics in Eighteenth-Century Philadelphia," in *Race, Class, and Politics: Essays on American Colonial and Revolutionary Society* (Urbana, Ill., 1986), 248.

41. Servants, however, unlike slaves, possessed personal rights to life, and contractual rights to a minimal standard of living, and they could bring suit to enforce these rights. Linda Grant DePauw, "Land of the Unfree: Legal Limitations on Liberty in Pre-Revolutionary America," *Maryland Historical Magazine* 68 (1973): 359–60.

42. In her study of indentured servants in Pennsylvania, Sharon Salinger found that by the mid-eighteenth century, indentured servants "labored under extremely harsh conditions. They were commodities in a business enterprise, and the level of social conflict as measured by runaways rose dramatically." Salinger, *"To Serve Well and Faithfully,"* 133.

43. Richard S. Dunn, "Servants and Slaves: The Recruitment and Employment of Labor," in *Colonial British America: Essays in the New History of the Early Modern Era*, ed. Jack P. Greene and J. R. Pole (Baltimore, 1984), 183.

44. Richard Walsh, *Charleston's Sons of Liberty: A Study of the Artisans, 1763–1789* (Columbia, S.C., 1959), 17.

45. With regard to convict servants, William Eddis observed: "Those who survive the term of servitude seldom establish their residence in this country: the stamp of infamy is too strong upon them to be easily erased; they either return to Europe and renew their former practices; or if they have fortunately imbibed habits of honesty and industry, they remove to a distant situation, where they may hope to remain unknown." Land, ed., *Letters from America*, 36–37. See also Lois Green Carr and Russell Menard, "Immigration and Opportunity: The Freedman in Early Colonial Maryland," in *The Chesapeake in the Seventeenth Century: Essays on Anglo-American Society*, ed. Thad Tate and David Ammerman (Chapel Hill, N.C., 1979), 235; Salinger, *"To Serve Well and Faithfully,"* 115;

Bailyn, *Voyagers to the West*, 266–67; Sheller, "Artisans and the Evolution of Baltimore Town," 185–87.

46. Census of Deptford Hundred, 1776, MS. 1814, MdHS; Maryland Tax List, 1783, microfilm, MdHS.

47. *Heads of Families at the First Census of the United States Taken in the Year 1790: Maryland* (Washington, D.C., 1907), 17–22.

48. Sheller, "Artisans and the Evolution of Baltimore Town," 244–45.

49. *Heads of Families at the First Census*, 17–22. By the end of the century, slaves were also an important part of the labor force in brickmaking and tanning. See Lee Nelson, "Brickmaking in Baltimore, 1798," *Journal of the Society of Architectural Historians* 18 (Mar. 1959): 34; and "Hints on Tanning," *Baltimore American and Daily Commercial Advertiser,* Jan. 20, 1808. For the continuation of this pattern of labor recruitment into the early national era, see Charles G. Steffen, *The Mechanics of Baltimore: Workers and Politics in the Age of Revolution, 1763–1812* (Urbana, Ill., 1984), chap. 2.

50. Sheller, "Artisans and the Evolution of Baltimore Town," 151–61.

51. For the expansion of these crafts during the 1780s, see ibid., 213–43.

52. Joseph A. Goldenberg, *Shipbuilding in Colonial America* (Charlottesville, Va., 1976), 61–68.

53. Galenson, *White Servitude in Colonial America*, 159–60; Walsh, *Charleston's Sons of Liberty,* 124–25.

54. Salinger, *"To Serve Well and Faithfully,"* 137–52.

55. For one attempt to create a structure for a highly competitive craft, see *Constitution of the Carpenters' Society of Baltimore* (Baltimore, 1791), esp. 8. For another argument challenging the "declension model" of eighteenth-century artisanal experience, see Gary J. Kornblith, "The Artisanal Response to Capitalist Transformation," *Journal of the Early Republic* 10 (1990): 315–21.

## Chapter 3 Planters in the Making

1. Carl Bridenbaugh, *The Colonial Craftsman* (New York, 1950), 15–16.

2. Artisans are herein defined as "those engaged in the direct production of commodities, masters as well as journeymen, but not apprentices." Sean Wilentz, *Chants Democratic: New York City and the Rise of the American Working Class, 1780–1850* (New York, 1984), 27 n.

3. On the distinctiveness of the slaveholding economy, see Allan Kulikoff, "The Transition to Capitalism in America," *William and Mary Quarterly*, 3d ser., 46 (1989): 120–44.

4. This phrase is borrowed from James Oakes, *The Ruling Race: A History of American Slaveholders* (New York, 1982). See also Steven Hahn, *The Roots of Southern Populism: Yeoman Farmers and the Transformation of the Georgia Upcountry, 1850–1890* (New York, 1983), esp. pt. 1.

5. William J. Cooper Jr., *The South and the Politics of Slavery, 1828–1856* (Baton Rouge, La., 1978); This conception also borrows from George Frederickson's "Herrenvolk democracy" idea in *The Black Image in the White Mind: The Debate on Afro-American Character and Destiny, 1817–1914* (New York, 1971), although this author is not convinced that the white southern belief in the democratic nature of society among the "master race" originated in the Jacksonian period. See Frederickson, *Black Image*, 59, 61, 66–68.

6. James C. Bonner, *A History of Georgia Agriculture, 1732–1860* (Athens, Ga., 1964); Kenneth Coleman, ed., *A History of Georgia,* 2d ed. (Athens, Ga., 1991).

7. Donald B. Dodd and Wynelle S. Dodd, *Historical Statistics of the United States, 1790–1970* (Tuscaloosa, Ala., 1973), 18–21.

8. Rachel N. Klein, *Unification of a Slave State: The Rise of the Planter Class in the South Carolina Backcountry, 1760–1808* (Chapel Hill, S.C., 1990); Allan Kulikoff, "Uprooted Peoples: Black Migrants in the Age of the American Revolution, 1790–1820," in *Slavery and Freedom in the Age of the American Revolution,* ed. Ira Berlin and Ronald Hoffman (Charlottesville, Va., 1983), 143–71.

9. Bruce Laurie, *Artisans into Workers: Labor in Nineteenth-Century America* (New York, 1989), 18–21. Information available on 18 of 34 Savannah furniture makers identified in local newspapers during this period indicates that all 18 came from places outside the state: Ireland (2), England (4), France (2), Massachusetts (2), Rhode Island (1), New York (3), Pennsylvania (1), and South Carolina (3). The nativities of forty-six Savannah silversmiths and watchmakers during the same period tell a similar story: England (9), Scotland (1), Ireland (1), Germany (2), Switzerland (2), France (3), Massachusetts (1), Connecticut (10), New York (6), Pennsylvania (2), Maryland (2), and the Carolinas (4). Only 3 of these 44 craftsmen were native Georgians. Will M. Theus, *Savannah Furniture, 1735–1825* (n.p., 1967), 43–69; George Barton Cutten, *The Silversmiths of Georgia* (Atlanta, 1958).

10. Advertisements from the *Augusta Chronicle* (hereafter cited as *"AC"*), Sept. 3, 1792; ibid., Feb. 16, 1793; *Georgia State Gazette,* Jan. 24, 1789; ibid., Oct. 4, 1805; ibid., May 3, 1800.

11. Advertisements from the *Columbian Museum and Savannah Advertiser* (hereafter cited as *"CMSA"*), Mar. 21, 1800; ibid., June 16, 1797; ibid., May 13, 1796.

12. *AC,* Oct. 19, 1799.

13. Mrs. Paschal M. Strong Jr., "Glimpses of Savannah, 1780–1825," *Georgia Historical Quarterly* 33 (1949): 28.

14. Virginia Steele Wood and Ralph Van Wood, eds., *Collections of the Georgia Historical Society,* vol. 15, *The Reuben King Journal, 1800–1806* (Savannah, Ga., 1971), 1–22.

15. Joseph A. Ernst and H. Roy Merrens, "'Camden's Turrets Pierce the Skies!': The Urban Process in the Southern Colonies during the Eighteenth Century," *William and Mary Quarterly,* 3d ser., 30 (1973): 549–74; Carville A. Earle and Ronald Hoffman, "Staple Crops and Urban Development in the Eighteenth-Century South," *Perspectives in American History* 10 (1976): 7–78; Jacob M. Price, "Economic Function and the Growth of American Port Towns in the Eighteenth Century," ibid., 8 (1974): 123–86.

16. In 1800 Charleston's population stood at 20,473, whereas Savannah's was 5,166. Richard C. Wade, *Slavery in the Cities: The South, 1820–1860* (New York, 1964), 325–27.

17. Newspaper advertisements placed by Savannah artisans in the construction and forging trades increased by 7 percent between the decades 1791–1800 and 1811–20; advertisements placed by cabinetmakers, chairmakers, and upholstery makers increased 40 percent over the same period; and advertisements placed by silversmiths and watchmakers increased 54 percent. Calculated from the Museum of Early Southern Decorative Arts Research Files, Index of Early Southern Artists and Artisans (hereafter cited as "MESDA Index"), Chatham County, Georgia, microfiche, Georgia Department of Archives and History (hereafter cited as "GDAH"), Atlanta, Ga.

18. Edward J. Cashin, *The Story of Augusta* (Augusta, 1980); Charles C. Jones Jr., *Memorial History of Augusta, Georgia: From Its Settlement in 1735 to the Close of the Eighteenth Century* (Syracuse, N.Y., 1890).

19. The number of master craftsmen advertising furniture and carriages increased 63 percent between the decade of the 1790s and the decade of the 1810s, a change explained by the growing wealth of upcountry cotton planters. MESDA Index, Richmond County.

20. *CMSA,* June 21, 1796.

21. Theus, *Savannah Furniture,* 45–46.

22. *Georgia Gazette,* Aug. 18, 1796.

23. Ibid.

24. Wood and Wood, eds., *Reuben King Journal,* 54.

25. Ibid.

26. Chatham County General Tax Return, 1799, GDAH.

27. Robert Saunders, "Modernization and the Free Peoples of Richmond: The 1780s and the 1850s," *Southern Studies* 24 (1985): 244–45.

28. For examples of newly arrived artisans in diverse trades who placed advertisements seeking apprentices see *CMSA,* May 13, 1796; ibid., Aug. 2, 1796; and *AC,* May 13, 1797; ibid., Dec. 16, 1797; ibid., May 8, 1801; ibid., Aug. 27, 1803; ibid., May 14, 1808; ibid., May 23, 1817; ibid., Feb. 8, 1821.

29. *CMSA,* May 19, 1797.

30. *AC,* May 2, 1797; Chatham County Tax Digest, 1806, GDAH; *AC,* July 27, 1799.

31. See *AC,* Sept. 13, 1811; *Georgia Express,* Aug. 27, 1808; *AC,* Oct. 4, 1817; ibid., Mar. 7, 1820; ibid., Sept. 21, 1825.

32. U. B. Phillips, "The Economic Cost of Slaveholding in the Cotton Belt," *Political Science Quarterly* 20 (1905): 257–75. For example, slaveownership best characterized the resources of a handful of elite master craftsmen who transformed themselves into planters and politicians in the early nineteenth century. See Michele Gillespie, "Artisans and Mechanics in the Political Economy of Georgia, 1790–1860" (Ph.D. diss., Princeton University, 1990), chap. 2.

33. Cutten, *Silversmiths of Georgia,* 96.

34. Ibid., 100–101.

35. Records of the 1820 Census of Manufactures, Schedules for North Carolina, South Carolina, and Georgia, roll 19, Chatham County, microfilm, GDAH.

36. Examples include *Georgia Gazette,* Apr. 16, 1789; ibid., Apr. 23, 1789; ibid., Dec. 3, 1789; ibid., July 8, 1790; ibid., July 15, 1790; ibid., Aug. 26, 1790; ibid., Mar. 20, 1800; *AC,* July 11, 1789; ibid., Oct. 23, 1790; *CMSA,* Feb. 7, 1797.

37. On skilled runaways in a lowcountry economy similar to Georgia's see Phillip D. Morgan, "Black Society in the Lowcountry, 1760–1810," in Berlin and Hoffman, eds., *Slavery and Freedom,* 100, 140–41.

38. Robert William Fogel, *Without Consent or Contract: The Rise and Fall of American Slavery* (New York, 1989), chap. 2; *Aggregate Amount of Persons within the U.S. in the Year 1810* (Washington, D.C., 1811), 80.

39. *AC,* Mar. 9, 1794; and ibid., Aug. 30, 1794. Between 1790 and 1800, advertisements seeking skilled slaves appeared in the *AC* only on July 17, 1790, Dec. 10, 1791, May 13, 1794, and Dec. 30, 1797.

40. *AC,* Apr. 4, 1789; ibid., Mar. 25, 1793; ibid., July 7, 1805.

41. Kulikoff, "Uprooted Peoples," 143–71.

42. *Second Census of the United States* (Washington, D.C., 1801), 2N, 4N; *Aggregate Amount of Persons within the United States in the Year 1810,* 80.

43. Chatham County Court of the Ordinary, Register of Free Persons of Color, 1817, microfilm, GDAH; Richmond County Court of the Ordinary, Register of Free Persons of Color, 1819, *AC,* Mar. 31, 1819.

44. *AC,* Jan. 18, 1800.

45. MESDA Index, Richmond County; Richmond County Tax Digest, 1807, GDAH.

46. U.S. Bureau of the Census, Manuscript Returns, Chatham County, Georgia, 1820, microfilm, GDAH.

47. Richmond County Tax Digests, 1794–97; Chatham County Tax Digests, 1802–5; and Richmond County Tax Digests, 1809—all in GDAH.

48. Richmond County Tax Digest, 1809; and Chatham County Inventories and Appraisements, 1805–23, Ansley Inventory, Mar. 25, 1823—both in GDAH.

49. Richmond County Tax Digests, 1794–97, 1818, GDAH; Ruth Blair, *Some Early Tax Digests of Georgia* (1926; reprint, Easley, S.C., 1971), 56.

50. Richmond County Tax Digests, 1808, 1818, GDAH.

51. Ibid.; Blair, *Early Tax Digests,* 54; MESDA Index, Chatham County.

52. Richmond County Tax Digest, 1809, GDAH; MESDA Index, Richmond County.

53. William Allen, Will, Oct. 7, 1795, Richmond County Wills, 1798–1839, microfilm, GDAH; *AC,* Mar. 6, 1790; *Index to the Headright and Bounty Grants of Georgia, 1756–1909* (Vidalia, Ga., 1970), 8.

54. *AC,* Aug. 8, 1801.

55. Richmond County Tax Digest, 1818, GDAH.

56. MESDA Index, Richmond County; Richmond County Tax Digests, 1809, 1818; U.S. Bureau of the Census, Manuscript Returns, Richmond County, 1830, microfilm, GDAH.

57. MESDA Index, Richmond County; Richmond County Tax Digests, 1818; U.S. Bureau of the Census, Manuscript Returns, Richmond County, 1830, GDAH.

58. *Georgia State Gazette,* July 19, 1788; U.S. Bureau of the Census, Manuscript Returns, Richmond County, 1820, microfilm, GDAH.

59. *CMSA,* June 14, 1796; *Index to Headright and Bounty Grants,* 703.

60. MESDA Index, Richmond County, Chatham County; Blair, *Early Tax Digests,* 307, 137, 115, 112, 131, 280, 308, 210.

61. MESDA Index, Richmond County; Richmond County Tax Digest, 1809; *Index to Headright and Bounty Grants,* 416.

62. William Harris Garland, letter to his wife, May 4, 1841, William Harris Garland Papers, Southern Historical Collection, University of North Carolina, Chapel Hill, N.C.; William Price Talmage, diary, 2–14, Hargrett Library, University of Georgia, Athens, Ga.

## Chapter 4 Slave Artisans in Richmond

1. Allan Kulikoff, *Tobacco and Slaves: The Development of Southern Cultures in the Chesapeake, 1680–1800* (Chapel Hill, N.C., 1986), 382–87, 396–401.

2. There are important exceptions, but they remain exceptions. For a slave artisan who acquired freedom and slaves in South Carolina, see Michael P. Johnson and James L. Roark, *Black Masters: A Free Family of Color in the Old South* (New York, 1984).

3. This assumption has dominated slave historiography since Kenneth M. Stampp, *The Peculiar Institution: Slavery in the Ante-Bellum South* (New York, 1956). For explicit developments of this theme see John W. Blassingame, *The Slave Community: Plantation Life in the Antebellum South*, rev. ed. (New York, 1979); and Eugene D. Genovese, *Roll, Jordan, Roll: The World the Slaves Made* (New York, 1972). See also Mechal Sobel, *The World They Made Together: Black and White Values in Eighteenth-Century Virginia* (Princeton, 1988), which is not based on this assumption.

4. Gerald W. Mullin, *Flight and Rebellion: Slave Resistance in Eighteenth-Century Virginia* (New York, 1972), 116–23. For an expansion of this argument see Michael Mullin, *Africa in America: Slave Acculturation and Resistance in the American South and the British Caribbean, 1736–1831* (Urbana, Ill., 1992), esp. pt. 3. See also Kulikoff, *Tobacco and Slaves*, 382–87, 396–401.

5. Richard C. Wade, *Slavery in the Cities: The South 1820–1860* (New York, 1964), 3. See Barbara Jeanne Fields, *Slavery and Freedom on the Middle Ground: Maryland during the Nineteenth Century* (New Haven, 1985), chap. 3, for a theoretically sophisticated discussion of the history and historiography of urban slavery.

6. The most notable exception is Philip D. Morgan, "Black Life in Eighteenth-Century Charleston," *Perspectives in American History,* n.s., 1 (1984): 187–233, which does not deal with Virginia.

7. These figures are from the United States, Third Census, 1810, as are all other population figures in this chapter unless otherwise noted. By comparison, in Maryland, Baltimore alone had 46,555 residents in 1810, but only 4,672 slaves compared to 5,671 free blacks. Fields, *Slavery and Freedom,* 62.

8. Rodney D. Green, "Industrial Transition in the Land of Chattel Slavery: Richmond, Virginia, 1820–60," *International Journal of Urban and Regional Research* 8 (1984): 239; see Charles B. Dew, "David Ross and the Oxford Iron Works: A Study of Industrial Slavery in the Early Nineteenth-Century South," *William and Mary Quarterly,* 3d ser., 31 (1974): 189–224, for a discussion of an iron-working enterprise near early Richmond.

9. The best single work on slave life in eighteenth-century Virginia towns remains Thad W. Tate, *The Negro in Eighteenth-Century Williamsburg* (Williamsburg, 1965). See also Mullin, *Flight and Rebellion,* chaps. 3, 5; Kulikoff, *Tobacco and Slaves,* chap. 10, esp. 413–16; and Douglas R. Egerton, "Gabriel's Conspiracy and the Election of 1800," *Journal of Southern History* 56 (1990): 194–200, for black urban life in eighteenth-century Virginia. The best work on black urban life in a British North American slave society is Morgan, "Black Life in Eighteenth-Century Charleston." For black artisans in northern seaports see Shane White, *Somewhat More Independent: The End of Slavery in New York City, 1770–1810* (Athens, Georgia, 1991), esp. chaps. 1, 7; and Gary B. Nash, "Forging Freedom: The Emancipation Experience in the Northern Seaport Cities, 1775–1820," in *Slavery and Freedom in the Age of the American Revolution,* ed. Ira Berlin and Ronald Hoffman (Charlottesville, Va., 1983), esp. 4–8, 16–18. See also Wade, *Slavery in the Cities,* chap. 2 (esp. 33–36 for Richmond), for slave occupations and slave hiring in antebellum cities; and James E. Newton and Ronald L. Lewis, eds., *The Other Slaves: Mechanics, Artisans and Craftsmen* (Boston, 1978), for a convenient anthology of essays.

10. The 1784 Richmond city census is in the Richmond City Common Hall Council Minute Book, microfilm, Virginia State Library (hereafter cited as "VSL"), Richmond, Va. I have considered anyone sixteen years or older an adult. I wish to thank Michael Lee Nicholls for sharing a data base that he compiled from the 1784 census. These occupation figures are minimums: the census takers sometimes failed to record free men's occupations; some of those men may have been artisans, but I have assumed that they were not. Three women were listed as skilled workers in 1784: a mantua maker, a seamstress, and a saddler.

11. *Virginia Argus,* Jan. 3, 1806. Many Richmond professionals owned and kept more slaves in the city than would seem necessary for purely domestic service: in 1800 Dr. James Cringan paid taxes on five adult slaves; Dr. William Foushee, on eight; the lawyer Charles Copland, on five; the merchant John Hopkins, on ten; and the merchant James Brown, on fifteen. Richmond City Personal Property Tax Book, 1800, microfilm, VSL. Some of these slaves may have been craftsmen whose masters hired them out in the city on a daily or monthly basis. I wish to thank Michael Lee Nicholls for sharing a print-out of the Richmond City Personal Property Tax Book, 1800.

12. In 1784 25 percent of adult male slaves—or roughly 8 percent of all slaves—living in Richmond would have been artisans. Had the age profile of the town's slave population remained stable and the proportion of slaves with skills remained the same, then Richmond would have been home to approximately 118 slave artisans in 1790, 183 in 1800, and 300 in 1810. These are crude and tentative estimates. The number of slave artisans in the town fluctuated with economic development and in response to large construction projects (such as the capitol building, the state penitentiary, and the James River Canal). Also, following the rapid growth of the town's free black population during the 1780s and 1790s free blacks probably displaced some slave artisans. The important point is that skilled slaves provided much of the town's labor supply.

13. Richmond City Personal Property Tax Book, 1800. This tax book does not distinguish between male and female slaves, and it includes no listing of slaves under twelve years old. I refer to all slaves listed in the personal property lists as adults.

14. John Pearman (eighteen years old) and Thomas Lennox (seventeen) were listed as apprentices. Fourteen-year-old Robert Martin's occupation was left blank by the census taker, but he too may have been an apprentice.

15. These households are reconstructed from the 1784 Richmond City census. For an elaboration of these arguments and a discussion of the distribution of different kinds of artisanal households in the eastern and western ends of Richmond, see James Sidbury, "Gabriel's World: Race Relations in Richmond, Virginia, 1750–1810" (Ph.D. diss., Johns Hopkins University, 1991), chap. 2.

16. This total is compiled from runaway, hiring, and sale advertisements found in the *Virginia Gazette or Weekly Advertiser* from the period 1782–1800 and in the *Virginia Argus* from the period 1793–1810 (this paper changed names twice during that period; I call it the *Argus* throughout to avoid confusion); and from Richmond City Hustings Court records, VSL. I found evidence of male slaves characterized by occupation as follows: 3 bakers, 5 barbers, 13 blacksmiths, 3 brickmakers, 2 brick masons, 2 butchers, 22 carpenters, 1 carriage painter, 1 caulker, 1 coachmaker, 2 coal miners, 1 cook, 29 coopers, 3 ditchers, 9 draymen or wagoners, 5 gardeners, 1 hatter, 2 hostlers, 5 house carpenters, 2 nailors, 2 plasterers, 1 planer, 2 postillions, 1 racehorse keeper, 2 ropemakers, 1 sail-

maker, 23 sailors (or boatmen), 14 sawyers, 3 ship carpenters, 11 shoemakers, 3 spinners, 1 stonemason and paver, 2 tailors, and 5 tanners. Slaves' occupations found their way into the court records serendipitously, and many trades practiced by only a few Richmond slaves surely escaped the records. This list does not include all of the slaves who practiced crafts in early Richmond, but it probably includes most of the crafts commonly practiced by slaves and provides a rough indication of the distribution of slaves among crafts. The list excludes female slaves. For a preliminary discussion of slave and free black women's work in early Richmond see Sidbury, "Gabriel's World," 137–41.

17. For example, a "yellow man named Ned" who ran away from James Semple had been "working in Richmond as a carpenter" but was also "acquainted with shoe-making"; the runaway Major Jackson's master described him as "a tolerable barber, understands the management of horses, drives a carriage well, and is capable of making an excellent house servant." *Virginia Gazette,* Feb. 11, 1795; ibid., Mar. 11, 1795.

18. Free people who hired slaves for a year paid taxes on them, so Bates may not have owned all of the 29 adult slaves on whom he paid taxes. (Bates definitely used slaves at his construction projects, as shown by his 1799 petition seeking relief from cost overruns incurred in building the state armory when "a valuable . . . slave" was crushed beneath "an immense mass of . . . earth." Richmond City Legislative Petitions, box 5, VSL.) The James River Company hired many slaves (see Sidbury, "Gabriel's World," 78–79) and almost certainly did not own all of the 33 slaves it paid taxes on. Gallego owned a large merchant mill and hired slave coopers; several of the adult slaves listed in 1800 probably made barrels for Gallego's flour. I have not systematically analyzed the personal property lists to determine the distribution of slaves among different occupational groups, because I cannot determine the occupations of most property owners in Richmond in 1800. Richmond's 406 property owners paid taxes on 1,309 slaves, for an average of 3.22 productive slaves per property owner. Three hundred seventy-nine people listed at least one slave, meaning that 93 percent of Richmond's personal property owners paid taxes on slaves. The city taxed slaves, wheels, horses, and mules. Many free residents of Richmond were not listed in the property tax lists.

19. Mayo's Bridge connected Richmond with Manchester, the small town across the James River. The information on rebuilding the bridge can be found in John Mayo Cash Book, 1800–1801, Valentine Museum Archives, Richmond. See Sidbury, "Gabriel's World," 146–50, for a fuller account of this building project.

20. Barrett's account of work performed for the Facklers was submitted as evidence in a debt suit and can be found in *Barrett v. Facklers,* Richmond Suit Papers (hereafter RSP), box 30, Nov.–Dec. 1802 bundle, VSL.

21. *Gordon v. Means,* RSP, box 38, Nov. 1805 bundle. Solomon was black, or Gordon would have listed him with a last name. He may have been free or a slave. The white workers included Peter, Tom, and George Seldon.

22. See, for example, John Mayo's Cash Book, 1800–1801, in which he records buying "casks of whiskey . . . for the laborers on the bridge" and an account for "Sheeting the Capitol" which includes a charge for "Geting the Lead on the Roof, Rum, etc.," in *Enery v. Austin,* RSP, box 15, Mar. 1793 bundle. One white man and three black men received wages for sheeting the capitol.

23. Sidbury, "Gabriel's World," 73–77, 143–45.

24. Morgan, "Black Life in Eighteenth Century Charleston," 204.

25. See *Harrison v. Mountcastle et al. [the Journeymen Cordwainers]*, RSP, box 32, Nov. 1803 bundle, for the origins of the Journeymen Cordwainers of the City of Richmond, *Virginia Argus*, Apr. 2, 1802.

26. *Virginia Argus*, Apr. 2, 1802.

27. *Virginia Argus*, Nov. 27, 1798. This case should serve as a warning against romanticizing these integrated workshops. Blacks and whites worked together for Grantland, but he was not a humane employer even by his contemporaries' standards. Several years after he placed this advertisement he denied medical care to a slave apprentice with a gangrenous leg because the care would have limited the boy's labor. See Sidbury, "Gabriel's World," 131–35.

28. Alan Dawley, *Class and Community: The Industrial Revolution in Lynn* (Cambridge, Mass., 1976), 16. Dawley says that "the coming triumph of market manufacturing over custom shoemaking was clearly signaled by 1800." Dawley, *Class and Community*, 16.

29. *Harrison v. Mountcastle et al.*

30. The argument for artisanal republicanism is most fully elaborated in Sean Wilentz, *Chants Democratic: New York City and the Rise of the American Working Class, 1788–1850* (New York, 1984). For an argument that black and white Richmond-area artisans shared this ideology, see Egerton, "Gabriel's Conspiracy and the Election of 1800." As will be clear below, I disagree with Egerton on this point. For Baltimore artisans see Charles G. Steffen, *The Mechanics of Baltimore: Workers and Politics in the Age of Revolution, 1763–1812* (Urbana, Ill., 1984).

31. *Harrison v. Mountcastle et. al.* As noted above, the proto-union's charter also prohibited working for employers who "had negro workmen in [their] employ."

32. The information on Dick is from *Virginia Gazette*, May 7, 1794. See also the story of the slave blacksmith named Davy, below.

33. Mullin, *Flight and Rebellion*, 142 n. 10. Even Ditcher's case is ambiguous: he was often called Jack Bowler or "Jack Bowler alias Ditcher."

34. For an analysis of the growth of a small urban area (Chestertown, Maryland), its displacement by a larger urban area (Baltimore), and the movement of artisanal activity that accompanied those processes, see Christine Daniels, "Alternative Workers in a Slave Economy: Kent County, Maryland, 1675–1810" (Ph.D. diss., Johns Hopkins University, 1990), chaps. 2 (for the rise of Chestertown) and 3 (for the effects of the rise of Baltimore). Richmond's rise affected rural hamlets such as Hanover Town, Virginia, just as Baltimore's rise affected Chestertown. More important, it drew many plantation craftsmen into the city.

35. Slave hiring is discussed in more detail below. The Richmond slave-hiring market is analyzed in Sidbury, "Gabriel's World," chap. 3. For one former slave's perceptions of self-hiring, see Frederick Douglass, "Narrative of the Life of Frederick Douglass, an American Slave," in *The Classic Slave Narratives*, ed. Henry Louis Gates Jr. (New York, 1987), 315–19.

36. Richmond Hustings Court Order Book 4:438 (for order that Bob be sold), 444 (for his discharge); *Commonwealth v. Bob*, RSP, box 25, June–July 1800 bundle. All of the Richmond Hustings Court Order Books (hereafter cited as "RHCOB") are on microfilm at the VSL.

37. Presumably all slaves who hired their own time sought, or at least welcomed, that privilege. That practice was common in Richmond despite the laws prohibiting it;

evidence of fifty-two slaves hiring their own time between 1782 and 1810 has survived in the Richmond Court records—a figure that represents the tip of an iceberg. For a discussion of self-hire in Richmond see Sidbury, "Gabriel's World," 123–25. Some rural slaves legally hired into the city also sought that privilege (as the discussion below illustrates), but there is no way to know how many.

38. The Richmond Hustings Court called grand juries quarterly after 1788. Complaints about disorderly houses, tippling houses, and gambling houses can be found in many presentments. For specific examples other than those listed in the text see RHCOB 3:52, 105, 159, 183, 261, 295–96. For the "toleration" of "evils" and the "negro dances" see RHCOB 3:315–16. For "great disorders" see RHCOB 4:16. For "numerous collections" and "dancing at night" see RHCOB 4:273.

39. Governor James Monroe to the Speakers of the General Assembly, 5 Dec. 1800, Executive Letter Book 1800–1803, 35, microfilm, VSL.

40. Most historians agree that daily life in the quarters remained relatively free from white intervention. For a historian who stresses the almost complete autonomy of the quarters see Thomas L. Webber, *Deep Like the Rivers: Education in the Slave Quarter Community, 1831–1865* (New York, 1978); for a far less sanguine view see Peter Kolchin, *Unfree Labor: American Slavery and Russian Serfdom* (Cambridge, Mass., 1987). For an important recent evaluation of this argument see William W. Freehling, *Road to Disunion: Secessionists at Bay* (New York, 1989), chap. 5.

41. Ira Berlin and Philip D. Morgan, "Introduction," in *The Slaves' Economy: Independent Production by Slaves in the Americas,* ed. Ira Berlin and Philip D. Morgan (London, 1991), 1–27.

42. See Armistead Russell's advertisement in the *Virginia Argus,* Jan. 27, 1807.

43. *Virginia Argus,* Feb. 26, 1808. Armistead Russell reported that his slave was "called by the Negroes John Russell," rather than simply John, only in this second advertisement. By then John had lived away from Armistead for three years and had demonstrated his willingness to defy his master. John's decision to take his master's name did not reflect any identification with his master; rather, it may have represented an attempt to establish a recognizable link to the plantation on which he was raised.

44. This interpretation fits Suzanne Lebsock's finding that free black women in nearby Petersburg, Virginia, often raised families without marrying. Towns such as Petersburg and Richmond were full of slave artisans. Had the women Lebsock studies been married to such men, they would have been listed as unmarried in legal records. Lebsock's emphasis on free black women's determination to protect their property works quite well with a simultaneous and complementary desire on the part of enslaved craftsmen to father free children. See Suzanne Lebsock, *The Free Women of Petersburg: Status and Culture in a Southern Town, 1784–1860* (New York, 1984), 103–10.

45. Manumission was never impossible in Virginia, but before 1782 and after 1806 it was difficult. See Ira Berlin, *Slaves without Masters: The Free Negro in the Antebellum South* (New York, 1974), 29–50. For a discussion of free blacks throughout Virginia buying slaves with the "object . . . [of] manumission," see Philip J. Schwarz, "Emancipators, Protectors, and Anomalies: Free Black Slaveowners in Virginia," *Virginia Magazine of History and Biography* 95 (1987): 321.

46. The deed of emancipation is in RSP, Box 56, Dec. 1810–Feb. 1811 bundle.

47. Henrico County Deed Book no. 3, 588 (Kennedy); Henrico County Deed Book

no. 4, 715 (Gibson); and that on Hawkins from Henrico County Deed Book no. 6, 78–79 (Hawkins). For a description of Hawkins's practice as a dentist see Samuel Mordecai, *Richmond in By-Gone Days* (Richmond, 1856), 205–6. For other examples of manumissions by free blacks see Henrico County Deed Book no. 3, 158; Henrico County Deed Book no. 4, 465, 500, 692; Henrico County Deed Book no. 5, 383, 686; and Henrico County Deed Book no. 7, 205. This is not a complete list of emancipations by free blacks; it includes only cases in which I am almost certain the emancipator was a black artisan.

48. *Virginia Argus*, Oct. 25, 1808.

49. *Virginia Argus*, Jan. 9, 1801. Ransom's master listed four different places his slave's father might have lived.

50. *Virginia Argus*, July 19, 1799.

51. *Virginia Argus*, June 10, 1793.

52. *Virginia Argus*, Oct. 12, 1798.

53. *Virginia Argus*, Dec. 25, 1807.

54. *Virginia Argus*, Aug. 13, 1806. Logan was one of the newly risen master shoemakers of whom the journeymen complained in 1802 (see n. 25 above). By 1806 he was obviously using black labor in his shop.

55. Davy's master believed that his slave would be very careful about whom he would work for: "I cannot think the fellow would agree to be sold to any one without a trial." *Virginia Argus*, Dec. 22, 1804.

56. See Mullin, *Flight and Rebellion*, esp. chap. 3; and Philip D. Morgan and Michael Lee Nicholls, "Runaway Slaves in Eighteenth-Century Virginia" (paper presented at meeting of the Organization of American Historians, Washington, D.C., 1990), for the goals of Virginia runaways. I wish to thank Morgan and Nicholls for giving me a copy of their unpublished paper. I counted sixty-five runaways advertised in the *Virginia Gazette*, 1785–1800, and the *Virginia Argus*, 1793–1810, who were specifically listed as artisans with some tie to Richmond. About 10 percent of these advertisements contained no guess about the slaves' intent. The descriptions of the presumed intentions of most of the rest of the slaves concentrated on a few motives: running to a town, attempting to escape Virginia, and visiting family or friends. Often masters mentioned combinations of these possibilities. For example, James Scott, a "very good waterman," was believed to be "lurking" near the home of a former master in Hanover County, but the advertisement also warned that he might "aim for Norfolk, Williamsburg, York, Fredericksburg, or Alexandria," and that he aimed "to get a free pass . . . and go out of the state and work as a ship carpenter." *Virginia Gazette*, Oct. 3, 1807. I have found attempts to categorize advertisements such as this one to be so subjective as to be arbitrary and have chosen instead to discuss the range of choices artisanal slaves made.

57. Sidbury, "Gabriel's World," chap. 4. My argument that religion played a key role in Gabriel's Conspiracy runs counter to Gerald Mullin, *Flight and Rebellion*, chap. 5; and Egerton, "Gabriel's Conspiracy and the Election of 1800." My views are more congenial to the interpretation of black resistance to slavery in Sylvia R. Frey, *Water from the Rock: Black Resistance in a Revolutionary Age* (Princeton, 1991). Frey argues that "what is most distinctive about Gabriel's Revolt" and other contemporary slave conspiracies is the "combination of both evangelical and traditional religious elements." Frey, *Water from the Rock*, 320.

58. *Virginia Gazette*, Feb. 26, 1794.

59. *Virginia Argus*, Dec. 22, 1804.

60. See J. Carroll Moody and Alice Kessler-Harris, eds., *Perspectives on American Labor History: The Problems of Synthesis* (DeKalb, Ill., 1989) for discussions of this trend. See Sean Wilentz, "The Rise of the American Working Class, 1776–1877: A Survey," in Moody and Kessler-Harris, eds., *Perspectives on American Labor History*, for the best attempt to synthesize these various stories into a coherent single analysis. Especially see pp. 100–106 for a rare and interesting example of the inclusion of slave labor in the history of American labor. Wilentz does not deal in any detail with slave artisans, but that largely reflects their absence in the literature he is synthesizing.

61. Claudia Dale Goldin, *Urban Slavery in the American South, 1820–1860: A Quantitative History* (Chicago, 1976).

62. See Michael Tadman, *Speculators and Slaves: Masters, Traders, and Slaves in the Old South* (Madison, Wis., 1989), 47–64, 217–21, for the scale of the interstate slave trade and its effects on slaves from the Upper South.

63. Historians of slaves must also pay closer attention to the labor process. For two recent overlapping collections that accept this challenge see Ira Berlin and Philip D. Morgan, eds., *Cultivation and Culture: Labor and the Shaping of Slave Life in the Americas* (Charlottesville, Va., 1993), Berlin and Morgan, eds., *Slaves' Economy*.

## Chapter 5 Alternative Communities

1. For a fuller discussion of the small-producer tradition, see Ronald Schultz, "The Small Producer Tradition and the Moral Origins of Artisan Radicalism in Philadelphia, 1720–1810," *Past and Present* 127 (1990): 84–116; and idem, *The Republic of Labor: Philadelphia Artisans and the Politics of Class, 1720–1830* (New York, 1993), chap. 1.

2. On the early use of the value of labor to justify guild formation, see Antony Black, *Guilds and Civil Society in European Political Thought from the Twelfth Century to the Present*, chaps. 1, 2; Lauro Martines, *Power and Imagination: City-States in Renaissance Italy* (New York, 1980), 180–83; and Mack Walker, *German Home Towns: Community, State, and General Estate, 1648–1871* (Ithaca, N.Y., 1971), chaps. 2–4.

3. E. P. Thompson, *The Making of the English Working Class* (New York, 1963). The radical and democratic ideas of artisans in civil war England are analyzed in Christopher Hill, *The World Turned Upside Down: Radical Ideas during the English Revolution* (New York, 1972); and Brian Manning, *The English People and the English Revolution, 1640–1649* (London, 1976).

4. On artisanal suffrage struggles of the late eighteenth and early nineteenth centuries see, for New York City, Sean Wilentz, *Chants Democratic: New York City and the Rise of the American Working Class, 1788–1850* (New York, 1984); and Howard B. Rock, *Artisans of the New Republic: The Tradesmen of New York City in the Age of Jefferson* (New York, 1979); for Baltimore, Charles G. Steffen, *The Mechanics of Baltimore: Workers and Politics in the Age of Revolution, 1763–1812* (Urbana, Ill., 1984); and for Philadelphia, Eric Foner, *Tom Paine and Revolutionary America* (New York, 1976); and Steven Rosswurm, *Arms, Country, and Class: The Philadelphia Militia and "Lower Sort" during the American Revolution* (New Brunswick, N.J., 1987).

5. Claire Cross, *Church and People, 1450–1660: The Triumph of the Laity in the English*

*Church* (Atlantic Highlands, N.J., 1976), chaps. 1, 2; Anne Hudson, *The Premature Reformation: Wycliffite Texts and Lollard History* (New York, 1988); Euan Cameron, *The European Reformation* (New York, 1991), chaps. 1, 5.

6. Cross, *Church and People*, chaps. 6, 7; A. G. Dickens, *Lollards and Protestants in the Diocese of York, 1509–1558* (Oxford, 1959); J. F. Davis, "Lollard Survival and the Textile Industry in the South-East of England," in *Studies in Church History*, vol. 3, ed. G. J. Cuming (Leiden, 1966), 191–201.

7. J. F. McGregor, "The Baptists: Fount of All Heresy," in *Radical Religion in the English Revolution*, ed. J. F. McGregor and B. Reay (Oxford, 1984), quotation on 26.

8. The transference of English dissenting traditions to seventeenth-century America is discussed in Philip F. Gura, *A Glimpse of Sion's Glory: Puritan Radicalism in New England, 1620–1660* (Middletown, Conn., 1984); Carla Gardina Pestana, *Quakers and Baptists in Colonial Massachusetts* (New York, 1991); and Barbara Ritter Dailey, "Root and Branch: New England's Religious Radicals and Their Transatlantic Community, 1600–1660" (Ph.D. diss., Boston University, 1984).

9. Much of this evidence is collected in Patricia U. Bonomi, *Under the Cope of Heaven: Religion, Society, and Politics in Colonial America* (New York, 1986), 92–97. Jon Butler offers a less sanguine view of popular church adherence in his *Awash in a Sea of Faith: Christianizing the American People* (Cambridge, Mass., 1990), chap. 6. But see, in support of Bonomi, Richard W. Pointer, *Protestant Pluralism and the New York Experience: A Study of Eighteenth-Century Religious Diversity* (Bloomington, Ind., 1988).

10. The active participation of urban artisans in the religious controversies of the colonial era is recounted in Gary B. Nash, *The Urban Crucible: Social Change, Political Consciousness, and the Origins of the American Revolution* (Cambridge, Mass., 1979), 44–49, 50–52, 198–232.

11. The marriage figures were reached by comparing the recorded marriages for St. Michael's and Zion Lutheran churches, contained in *Pennsylvania Archives*, ed. Samuel Hazard (Philadelphia, 1852), vol. 9, ser. 2, 332–58, 414–40, with the 1797 city directory and 1798 city tax list. Presbyterian membership was similarly determined by comparing "Communicating Members of the First Presbyterian Church in 1802," "Pew Holders of the Second Presbyterian Church in 1798," and "Communicants of the Third Presbyterian Church, 1792–1804"—all at the Presbyterian Historical Society, Philadelphia—with the occupations listed in the 1797 city directory and 1798 city tax list. I am indebted to Billy Smith of Montana State University for use of his computer data base that has enabled me to make this comparison. The computations are my own.

12. Kenneth A. Lockridge, *Literacy in Colonial New England: An Enquiry into the Social Context of Literacy in the Early Modern West* (New York, 1974); Anne M. Boylan, *Sunday School: The Formation of an American Institution, 1790–1880* (New Haven, 1988), 15; Benjamin Rush to Jeremy Belknap, Jan. 5, 1791, *Letters of Benjamin Rush*, ed. L. H. Butterfield, 2 vols. (Princeton, 1951), 1:573.

13. On the reaction to Paine's *Age of Reason*, see Jerry W. Knudson, "The Rage around Tom Paine: Newspaper Reaction to His Homecoming in 1802," *New-York Historical Society Quarterly* 53 (1969): 34–63.

14. Doris Elisabett Andrews, "Popular Religion and the Revolution in the Middle Atlantic Ports: The Rise of the Methodists, 1770–1800" (Ph.D. diss., University of Pennsylvania, 1986), table 4, p. 281; Steffen, *Mechanics of Baltimore*, table 18, p. 258.

15. On the early history of Methodism in New England, see Emory Stevens Bucke, ed., *The History of American Methodism,* 3 vols. (New York, 1964), 1:409–16; and George Claude Baker Jr., *An Introduction to the History of Early New England Methodism, 1789–1839* (New York, 1941; reprint, New York, 1969). The rise of Methodism among the shoe-makers of Lynn is discussed briefly in Paul G. Faler, *Mechanics and Manufacturers in the Early Industrial Revolution, Lynn, Massachusetts, 1780–1860* (Albany, N.Y., 1981), 44–48. For working-class Methodism in the antebellum period, see Jama Lazerow, "A Good Time Coming: Religion and the Emergence of Labor Activism in Antebellum New England" (Ph.D. diss., Brandeis University, 1983); and Teresa Anne Murphy, *Ten Hours' Labor: Religion, Reform, and Gender in Early New England* (Ithaca, N.Y., 1992).

16. Quoted in Bucke, *American Methodism* 1:409.

17. Thomas Ware, *Sketches of the Life and Travels of Reverend Thomas Ware* (New York, 1839), 202.

18. It is noteworthy that the proportion of female congregants often exceeded that of male artisans in all the laboring-class evangelical churches investigated. While the at-traction of evangelical religion for eighteenth- and nineteenth-century middle-class women has been well documented, the relationship between working-class women and artisanal church membership remains almost unexplored.

19. Ronald Schultz, "God and Workingmen: Popular Religion and the Formation of Philadelphia's Working Class, 1790–1830," in *Religion in a Revolutionary Age,* ed. Ronald Hoffman and Peter J. Albert (Charlottesville, Va., 1993), table 1.

20. The classic statement of this view is Thompson, *Making of the English Working Class,* chap. 11; see also Anthony Armstrong, *The Church of England, the Methodists, and Society, 1700–1850* (Totowa, N.J., 1973), 199–213.

21. William Henry Williams, *The Garden of American Methodism: The Delmarva Penin-sula, 1769–1820* (Wilmington, Del., 1984), 105–7; Steffen, *Mechanics of Baltimore,* chap. 12; Bruce Laurie, *Working People of Philadelphia, 1800–1850* (Philadelphia, 1980), chap. 2. On the importance of respectability in defining the rising entrepreneurial class of master ar-tisans, see Gary John Kornblith, "From Artisans to Businessmen: Master Mechanics in New England, 1789–1850" (Ph.D. diss., Princeton University, 1983).

22. The clearest exponent of this view is Paul E. Johnson, *A Shopkeeper's Millennium: Society and Revival in Rochester, New York, 1815–1837* (New York, 1978). For similar views, see Faler, *Mechanics and Manufacturers;* and Anthony F. C. Wallace, *Rockdale: The Growth of an American Village in the Early Industrial Revolution* (New York, 1978).

23. Butler, *Awash in a Sea of Faith.* For another recent attempt to account for popular religion in the post-Revolutionary era, see Nathan O. Hatch, *The Democratization of American Christianity* (New Haven, 1989).

24. Hatch, *American Christianity.*

25. On the emergence of American Universalism, see Stephen A. Marini, *Radical Sects of Revolutionary New England* (Cambridge, Mass., 1982), 68–75.

26. Universalist Church in the U.S.A., *Hymns Composed by Various Authors* (Walpole, N.H., 1808), 80.

27. Elhanan Winchester, *Thirteen Hymns, Suited to the Present Times,* 2d ed. (Baltimore, 1776), 15.

28. Universalist Church, *Hymns,* 184–85.

29. On the connection between the workingmen's movement and Philadelphia Universalists, see Schultz, "God and Workingmen."

30. Max Weber, *The Protestant Ethic and the Spirit of Capitalism* (New York, 1958).

31. George Peck, *Early Methodism within the Bounds of the Old Genessee Conference from 1788 to 1828* . . . (New York, 1860), 44–45.

32. Ibid., 195, 200.

33. Ibid., 93. For a discussion of popular occultism in early America, see Jon Butler, "The Dark Ages of American Occultism, 1760–1848," in *The Occult in America: New Historical Perspectives,* ed. Howard Kerr and Charles L. Crow (Urbana, Ill., 1983), 58–78.

34. Peck, *Early Methodism,* 120.

35. Ibid., 73.

36. Ibid., 151, 167.

37. Robert Collyer, *Father Taylor* (Boston, 1906), 39.

38. For a discussion of Heighton's views on religion, see Schultz, "God and Workingmen."

39. [William Heighton], *An Address Delivered Before the Mechanics and Working Classes Generally, of the City and County of Philadelphia* (Philadelphia, 1827).

40. In this regard, early evangelicalism differed from its antebellum counterpart, which played a greater, if still limited, role in the working-class movements of the 1830s and 1840s. See Wilentz, *Chants Democratic,* 343–49; Murphy, *Ten Hours' Labor,* chaps. 3–4; and Jama Lazerow, "Religion and Labor Reform in Antebellum America: The World of William Field Young," *American Quarterly* 38 (1986): 265–86.

41. Enthusiastic religion and the union movement would join forces in the post–Civil War era, but by then evangelicalism was both less emotional and more open to outside influences. Late-nineteenth-century evangelicalism developed a social consciousness that had been altogether absent in its formative years. For the fate of religion and the working-class movement during the late nineteenth and early twentieth centuries, see Herbert G. Gutman, "Protestantism and the American Labor Movement: The Christian Spirit in the Gilded Age," *American Historical Review* 72 (1966): 74–101; Ken Fones-Wolf, "Religion and Trade-Union Politics in the United States, 1880–1920," *International Labor and Working-Class History,* no. 34 (1988): 39–55; and idem, *Trade Union Gospel: Christianity and Labor in Industrial Philadelphia, 1865–1915* (Philadelphia, 1989).

42. Laurie, *Working People,* chaps. 7–9.

43. Wilentz, *Chants Democratic,* 154–57.

44. Murphy, *Ten Hours' Labor,* chap. 4.

## Chapter 6 The Petitioning of Artisans and Operatives

1. *Mechanic* (Fall River), June 29, 1844. "All day" men were willing to work more than ten hours. The importance of Protestant religion and moral reform in the New England labor movement of the antebellum period is discussed in Jama Lazerow, "Religion and Labor Reform in Antebellum America: The World of William Field Young," *American Quarterly* 38 (summer 1986): 265–86; idem, "Religion and the New England Mill Girl: A New Perspective on an Old Theme," *New England Quarterly* 60 (Sept. 1987): 429–53; and Teresa Murphy, *Ten Hours' Labor: Religion, Reform, and Gender in Early New England* (Ithaca, N.Y., 1992).

2. *Mechanic,* Aug. 3, 1844.

3. *Mechanic,* Aug. 10, 1844. The article also criticizes the religious pretensions of the mill owner, probably Nathaniel Borden, who left a church because "there was some appearance of evil in it."

4. *Mechanic,* Oct. 12, 1844; ibid., Nov. 23, 1844; ibid., Nov. 30, 1844.

5. *Mechanic,* June 8, 1844; emphasis in original. As in many factory towns in New England, land development and textile production in Fall River were controlled by many of the same owners. See Murphy, *Ten Hours' Labor,* 16–19.

6. *Mechanic,* May 4, 1844.

7. *Mechanic,* May 11, 1844.

8. The circular was reprinted in the *Mechanic,* June 22, 1844. Hewitt was given money to travel throughout New England in July of that year, as reported in the *Mechanic,* July 27, 1844. His activities as a phrenologist were reported in the *Friend of Man,* Mar. 25, 1843, a reform newspaper published in Providence, when he appeared in that town in the spring of 1843.

9. Philip Foner has edited and published Hewitt's reports in "Journal of an Early Labor Organizer," *Labor History* 10 (1969): 205–27. The regionwide convention took place in the fall of 1844.

10. *Mechanic,* June 22, 1844. For a full discussion of the antebellum labor movement in Lynn see Alan Dawley, *Class and Community: The Industrial Revolution in Lynn* (Cambridge, Mass., 1976); Paul Faler, *Mechanics and Manufacturers in the Early Industrial Revolution, Lynn, Massachusetts, 1780–1860* (New York, 1981); and Mary Blewett, *Men, Women, and Work: Class, Gender, and Protest in the New England Shoe Industry, 1780–1910* (Urbana, Ill., 1988), 3–141.

11. *Mechanic,* Aug. 10, 1844.

12. Ibid.; emphasis in original.

13. *Awl,* (Lynn), Nov. 16, 1844; ibid., Nov. 23, 1844.

14. *Awl,* Mar. 1, 1845; emphasis in original.

15. Blewett, *Men, Women, and Work,* 68–96.

16. *Awl,* Aug. 21, 1844.

17. *Awl,* Sept. 18, 1844; emphasis in original.

18. *Awl,* Dec. 14, 1844; ibid., Dec. 21, 1844. Of the fifty-nine female supporters who were named in the *Awl,* twenty-six (44%) were married, eleven (18%) were unmarried, and twenty-two (37%) could not be identified either way. Of those women who were married, five were married to men who signed the ten-hour petition. The occupation of twelve husbands could be identified, and seven of them were cordwainers.

19. *Mechanic,* June 1, 1844. The group meeting at Lowell coalesced into the Lowell Association.

20. *Mechanic,* July 20, 1844; emphasis in original.

21. Ibid.; *Vox Populi* (Lowell), reported in *Manchester Operative,* Mar. 30, 1844. Further discussion of this wage cut may be found in Caroline Ware, *The Early New England Cotton Manufacture: A Study in Industrial Beginnings* (New York, 1966), 271–72.

22. *Mechanic,* Nov. 9, 1844.

23. *Mechanic,* Nov. 30, 1844.

24. *Operative,* Dec. 28, 1844, cited in Thomas Dublin, *Women at Work: The Transformation of Work and Community in Lowell, Massachusetts, 1826–1860* (New York, 1979), 116.

This split may have been the result of the political party involvement of workingmen in Lowell. According to Charles Persons, the workingmen ran a slate of candidates in the election that year. Charles Persons, "New England Workingmens Association, 1840–48," in Susan M. Kingsbury, ed., *Labor Laws and Their Enforcement, with Special Reference to Massachusetts* (New York, 1911), 23–54.

25. *Mechanic,* Apr. 2, 1845.

26. *Voice of Industry* (Lowell), Apr. 3, 1846; *Mechanic,* Dec. 28, 1844.

27. *Mechanic,* Aug. 3, 1844; ibid., Aug. 24, 1844; emphasis in original. For a different interpretation of these quotations see David R. Roediger and Philip S. Foner, *Our Own Time: A History of American Labor and the Working Day* (Westport, Conn., 1989), 43.

28. *Mechanic,* July 20, 1844.

29. *Mechanic,* June 1, 1844; emphasis in original.

30. Asa Bronson, *An Address on the Anniversary of the Fire Delivered in the Pearl St. Christian Chapel, July 2, 1844* (Fall River, Mass., 1844), 14; emphasis in original.

31. *Mechanic,* July 27, 1844.

32. *Mechanic,* Sept. 7, 1844; ibid., Sept. 14, 1844; emphasis in original.

33. *Manchester Operative,* May 18, 1844. This also may be the meeting described in the *Gleaner* (Manchester and Nashua), May 11, 1844—a meeting of day laborers who worked on the canal system and were concerned about low wages as well as long hours; the meeting adjourned to Wentworth Hall for a further meeting on Thursday evening, May 9. Hewitt's activities are reported in *Mechanic,* Aug. 3, 1844; ibid., Aug. 10, 1844; ibid., Aug. 17, 1844; ibid., Sept. 21, 1844; emphasis in original.

34. *Mechanic,* Aug. 31, 1844.

35. Ibid.

36. Ibid.; emphasis in original.

37. *Laborer* (Boston), reprinted in *Mechanic,* Sept. 21, 1844.

38. *Mechanic,* Sept. 14, 1844.

39. *Manchester Operative,* Sept. 7, 1844; ibid., Sept. 21, 1844. The peculiar make-up of the Dover Association may account for the criticisms made by their representative, Colby, at the fall meeting. Colby argued that laborers and employers, not the legislatures, should set laborers' hours, objected to setting capital and labor in opposition, and felt that his constituents "did not acknowledge themselves slaves." *Laborer* (Boston), Oct. 26, 1844.

40. *Woonsocket Independent,* reprinted in *Workingman's Advocate,* Sept. 28, 1844.

41. It was also stipulated that "all questions as to the merit of what may be called useful, productive industry shall be settled by a vote of the members present." *Awl,* Nov. 30, 1844.

42. *Manchester Operative,* Oct. 19, 1844.

43. Records of the Workingmen's Association of Fitchburg, 1844–45, Dec. 13, 1844, Manuscript Collection, Fitchburg Historical Society, Fitchburg, Mass.; emphasis in original.

44. *Mechanic,* Oct. 26, 1844; ibid., Nov. 2, 1844.

45. Linda Kerber, *Women of the Republic: Intellect and Ideology in Revolutionary America* (New York, 1986), 85–112; Angelina Grimké to Catherine Beecher, Alice S. Rossi, *The Feminist Papers: From Adams to de Beauvoir* (New York, 1973), 319; Lori Ginzberg, *Women*

*and the Work of Benevolence: Morality, Politics, and Class in the Nineteenth Century United States* (New Haven, 1990), 67–97.

46. *Weekly Bee,* Oct. 19, 1844.

47. *Mechanic,* Nov. 16, 1844; and Massachusetts House Document 1604; Massachusetts House Document 1587—both in Massachusetts State Archives, Boston, Mass. (hereafter cited as "MSA"); emphasis in original.

48. House Document 1587, MSA; emphasis in original.

49. Ibid. For a discussion of the language of petitions which focuses on the legal efficacy of these pleas, see Persons, "New England Workingmen's Association, 1840–48," 23–54.

50. *Awl,* Dec. 14, 1844.

51. *Mechanic,* Nov. 16, 1844; see also John Gregory's speech, ibid., Nov. 23, 1844.

52. Massachusetts House Document 1587/2, MSA.

53. Of the 23 foreign-born men who signed, 21 (91%) were born in Ireland, Scotland, or England. Of the 30 factory workers who signed the petition, birthplaces for 22 could be determined: 16 were foreign born, 15 (94%) of those were from those three countries. Of the 6 factory workers from the United States signing the petition, 4 were machinists. For a discussion of the attitudes of male workingmen in England toward the regulation of female labor during this period see Marianna Valverde, "'Giving the Female a Domestic Turn': The Social, Legal, and Moral Regulation of Women's Work in British Cotton Mills, 1820–1850," *Journal of Social History* 21 (1988): 619–34. For a discussion of the way in which the struggle for a shorter workday in the United States differed from that in England, see Kathryn Kish Sklar, "'The Greater Part of the Petitioners Are Female': The Reduction of Women's Working Hours in the Paid Labor Force, 1840–1917," in *Worktime and Industrialization: An International History,* ed. Gary Cross (Philadelphia, 1988), 106–7.

54. The numbers here are very small: occupations could be identified for only 6 percent (43 out of 725) of the female signatories to the large petition submitted from Lowell. However, given the newspaper accounts of female participation emanating from factory operatives, this small sample probably represents an accurate portrait of the women who signed this petition.

55. In addition to Blewett, *Men, Women, and Work,* see Christine Stansell, *City of Women: Sex and Class in New York, 1789–1860* (New York, 1986); and Ava Baron, "Women and the Making of the American Working Class: A Study of the Proletarianization of Printers," *Review of Radical Political Economics* 14 (1982), 23–42.

## Chapter 7 "Spavined Ministers, Lying Toothpullers, and Buggering Priests"

I would like to thank Paula Baker, David Montgomery, and Leonard Richards for their helpful comments on earlier drafts of this piece.

1. See, for example, Sean Wilentz, "On Class and Politics in Jacksonian America," *Reviews in American History* 10 (1982): 45–63. See also Geoff Eley and Keith Nield, "Why Does Social History Ignore Politics?" *Social History* 5 (1990): 249–71; and Iver Bernstein, "Expanding the Boundaries of the Political: Workers and Political Change in the Nineteenth Century," *International Labor and Working-Class History* 32 (1987): 59–75.

2. Iver Bernstein, *The New York City Draft Riots: Their Significance for American Society*

and Politics in the Age of the Civil War (New York, 1990); Amy Bridges, A City in the Republic: Antebellum New York and the Origins of Machine Politics (Cambridge, 1984); and John Brooke, The Heart of the Commonwealth: Society and Political Culture in Worcester County, Massachusetts, 1713–1861 (Cambridge, 1989). See also Ronald P. Formisano, The Transformation of Political Culture: Massachusetts Parties, 1790s-1840s (New York, 1983); and Richard B. Stott, Workers in the Metropolis: Class, Ethnicity, and Youth in Antebellum New York City (Ithaca, N.Y., 1990).

3. For more on the concept of a popular bloc, see Ernesto Laclau, Politics and Ideology in Marxist Theory: Capitalism, Fascism, Populism (London, 1977), esp. 143–98.

4. Among the better modern discussions of this process are Susan E. Hirsch, Roots of the American Working Class: The Industrialization of the Crafts in Newark, 1800–1860 (Philadelphia, 1978), 15–51; Steven J. Ross, Workers on the Edge: Work, Leisure, and Politics in Industrializing Cincinnati, 1788–1890 (New York, 1985), 94–140; and Sean Wilentz, Chants Democratic: New York City and the Rise of the American Working Class, 1788–1850 (New York, 1984), 3–19, 61–141. For the transition from shop to factory in a single-industry town, see Alan Dawley, Class and Community: The Industrial Revolution in Lynn (Cambridge, Mass., 1976), 11–41.

5. Herbert G. Gutman and Ira Berlin, "Class Composition and the Development of the American Working Class, 1840–1890," in Power and Culture: Essays on the American Working Class, by Herbert G. Gutman, ed. Ira Berlin (New York, 1987), 380–94. See also idem, "Natives and Immigrants, Free Men and Slaves: Urban Workingmen in the Antebellum South," American Historical Review 88 (1983): 1175–1200.

6. For a groundbreaking study of living standards in the late eighteenth century see Billy G. Smith, The "Lower Sort": Philadelphia's Laboring People, 1750–1800 (Ithaca, N.Y., 1990). See also Alfred F. Young, "George Robert Twelves Hewes (1742–1840): A Boston Shoemaker and the Memory of the American Revolution," William and Mary Quarterly, 3d ser., 38 (1981): 561–623.

7. Dawley, Class and Community, 11–41, quotation on 25.

8. I refer here to the proliferation of mobility studies which began in the late 1960s with Stephan Thernstrom, Poverty and Progress: Social Mobility in a Nineteenth-Century City (Cambridge, Mass., 1964), which not only changed academic thinking on the quality of social advancement but also encouraged a major reassessment of the thornier questions of status, occupational ranking, and so on. Some of the work inspired by Thernstrom and produced by such scholars as Theodore Hershberg, Michael Katz, and Clyde and Sally Griffen is cited in various notes below.

9. See, for instance, R. S. Neale, "Introduction," in Class and Ideology in the Nineteenth Century (London, 1972), 1–14; idem, "Class and Consciousness in Early Nineteenth-Century England: Three Classes or Five?" in ibid., 15–40; and Arno J. Mayer, "The Lower Middle Class as Historical Problem," Journal of Modern History 47 (1975): 409–36. See also Gary Kornblith, "The Craftsman as Industrialist: Jonas Chickering and the Transformation of American Piano Making," Business History Review 59 (1985): 349–68; Susan E. Hirsch, "From Artisan to Manufacturer: Industrialization and the Small Producer in Newark, 1830–1860," in Small Business in American Life, ed. Stuart Bruchey (New York, 1980), 80–99; and Ronald Schultz, The Republic of Labor: Philadelphia Artisans and the Politics of Class, 1720–1830 (New York, 1993).

10. See Neale, "Class and Class Consciousness."

11. The most comprehensive and stimulating treatment of class in nineteenth-century America is Stuart M. Blumin, *The Emergence of the Middle Class: Social Experience in the American City, 1790–1900* (New York, 1989).

12. What I am suggesting here is that studies of single-industry towns, centered as they are on factories, overlook the distinct possibility of an alternative industrial sector of smallish workshops specializing in repair work and light consumer goods. The consumer sector seems especially ripe for analysis given what we know about the forging of new consumption habits among early mill hands in places such as Lowell. Descriptive evidence indicates, for instance, that women from the countryside adopted urban ways with relative ease, exchanging simple rural dress and accessories for the more "modern" dress of the city and town. The likelihood is that such goods were locally produced. On such changing consumption habits see Thomas Dublin, *Women at Work: The Transformation of Work and Community in Lowell, Massachusetts, 1826–1860* (New York, 1979), 35–57.

13. See, for example, Blumin, *Middle Class*, 75; and Bruce Laurie, *Working People of Philadelphia, 1800–1850* (Philadelphia, 1980). See also Bruce Laurie, Theodore Hershberg, and George Alter, "Immigrants and Industry: The Philadelphia Experience, 1850–1880," in *Philadelphia: Work, Space, Family, and Group Experience in the Nineteenth Century,* ed. Theodore Hershberg (New York, 1981), 101 and table 5.

14. R. V. Robinson and C. M. Briggs, "The Rise of Factories in Indianapolis, 1850–1880," *American Sociological Review* 97 (1991): 622–56. I would like to thank Robert Robinson for sharing this manuscript with me.

15. See, for instance, Philip Scranton, *Proprietary Capitalism: The Textile Manufacture of Philadelphia, 1800–1885* (New York, 1983).

16. For a vivid account of different kinds of workshops and factories, see Blumin, *Middle Class*, 66–107. For a revealing look at a large employer with an entrepreneurial bent but a respect for craft, see George Henkels, *An Essay on Household Furniture . . .* (Philadelphia, 1850).

17. The best modern account of the early sweatshop is Christine Stansell, *City of Women: Sex and Class in New York, 1789–1860* (New York, 1986), 105–25. For the spread of sweating from a few crafts to nearly all, see Wilentz, *Chants Democratic*, 107–42.

18. See Bruce Laurie, *Artisans into Workers: Labor in Nineteenth-Century America* (New York, 1989), 15–46. See also Ross, *Workers on the Edge*, 94–140; and Hirsch, *Roots of the American Working Class*, 15–36.

19. Quoted in Blumin, *Middle Class*, 111.

20. See for instance, John Wood, ed., *The Daguerreotype: A Sesquicentennial Celebration* (Iowa City, 1989), esp. 15, 55, 83, 85, and prints numbered 45, 49, and 53. I would like to thank John Wood for making me aware of "occupational Daguerreotypes" and for sharing with me samples from his prodigious collection of this genre. See also Richard S. Field and Robin Jaffe Frank, eds., *American Daguerreotypes from the Matthew R. Isenberg Collection* (New Haven, 1990), 70–71, 79.

21. Scranton, *Proprietary Capitalism*, 68–71, 199–200, quotation on 69. For more on competence see Dawley, *Class and Community*, 151–56.

22. Laurie, *Artisans into Workers*, 57–61. See also Blumin, *Middle Class*, 138–91; Wilentz, *Chants Democratic*, 117–19; and Laurie, Hershberg, and Alter, "Immigrants and Industry," 104–5, and tables 10, 14.

23. Blumin, *Middle Class,* 116.

24. Ibid, 109–21. See also Clyde Griffen and Sally Griffen, *The Ordering of Opportunity in Mid-Nineteenth-Century Poughkeepsie* (Cambridge, Mass., 1978), esp. 55–60; and Peter Knights, *The Plain People of Boston, 1830–1860: A Study in City Growth* (New York, 1971), 98–99.

25. See chap. 9, below.

26. See chap. 8, below. According to the 1860 Manuscript Census for Cambridge, at his death in 1860 Buckingham had twenty-five hundred dollars in real property.

27. Michael B. Katz, Michael J. Doucet, and Mark Stern, *The Social Organization of Early Industrial Capitalism* (Cambridge, Mass., 1982), 376. See also Blumin, *Middle Class,* 115; and Stuart M. Blumin, "Mobility and Change in Antebellum Philadelphia," in *Nineteenth-Century Cities: Essays in the New Urban History,* ed. Stephan Thernstrom and Richard Sennett (New Haven, 1969), 164–208. See also Griffen and Griffen, *Ordering of Opportunity,* 103–17.

28. See below, chap. 8. For more on Buckingham see Gary J. Kornblith, "From Artisans to Businessmen: Master Mechanics in New England, 1789–1850," 2 vols. (Ph.D. diss., Princeton University, 1983), 2:291–349; and Joseph T. Buckingham, *Personal Memoirs and Recollections of Editorial Life,* 2 vols. (Boston, 1852).

29. Kornblith, "Artisans to Businessmen," 2:291–349.

30. See, for example, Wilentz, *Chants Democratic,* 23–42, 145–53. See also Mary Ryan, *The Cradle of the Middle Class: The Family in Oneida County, New York, 1790–1865* (Cambridge, 1981), 145–85; and Rex Burns, *Success in America: The Yeoman Dream and the Industrial Revolution* (Amherst, Mass., 1976).

31. See Edwin T. Freedley, ed., *Leading Pursuits and Leading Men* (Philadelphia, 1854); idem, *Philadelphia and Its Manufactures . . .* (Philadelphia, 1858); Isaac Vansant, ed., *Royal Road to Wealth: An Illustrated History* (Philadelphia, n.d.)

32. Suzanne Lebsock, *The Free Women of Petersburg: Status and Culture in a Southern Town, 1784–1860* (New York, 1984), 84. See also Mary P. Ryan, *Womanhood in America from Colonial Times to the Present* (New York, 1975), 102; and Steven Mintz and Susan Kellogg, *Domestic Revolutions: A Social History of American Family Life* (New York, 1988), 60–62.

33. Lydia Maria Child, *The American Frugal Housewife, Dedicated to Those Who Are Not Ashamed of Economy,* 16th ed. (Boston, 1835). For more on Child see Edward T. James, Janet W. James, and Paul S. Boyer, eds., *Notable American Women: A Biographical Dictionary,* 3 vols. (Cambridge, Mass., 1971), 1:330–33; Helene B. Gilbert, *The Heart Is Like Heaven: The Life of Lydia Maria Child* (Philadelphia, 1964); and William Osborne, *Lydia Maria Child* (New York, 1980).

34. Child, *Frugal Housewife,* 5.

35. Ibid., 4.

36. Blumin, *Middle Class,* 108–37.

37. See, for example, Philip Scranton, "Varieties of Paternalism: Industrial Relations and the Social Relations of Production in American Textiles," *American Quarterly* 36 (1984): esp. 248–57, on what Scranton calls "fraternal paternalism." See also Bridges, *City in the Republic,* 154–61, in which Bridges explains how the "mutualism" of the small workplace carried over into politics.

38. Quoted in Edward Pessen, "The Working Men's Party Revisited," in *New Perspectives on Jacksonian Parties and Politics,* ed. Edward Pessen (Boston, 1970), 210.

39. See, for example, Henry Brokmeyer, *A Mechanic's Diary* (Washington, D.C., 1910). See also Herbert G. Gutman, "Work, Culture, and Society in Industrializing America, 1815–1919," in *Work, Culture, and Society in Industrializing America: Essays in American Working Class and Social History* (New York, 1977), 3–78; Paul Faler, "Cultural Aspects of the Industrial Revolution: Lynn, Massachusetts, Shoemakers and Industrial Morality, 1826–1860," *Labor History* 15 (1974): 367–94; and Bruce Laurie, "'Nothing on Compulsion': Lifestyles of Philadelphia Artisans, 1820–1850," ibid., 15 (1974): 91–120. For a different interpretation of early industrial discipline see Stott, *Workers in the Metropolis*, 123–61; and David Brody, "Time and Work during Early American Industrialism," *Labor History* 30 (1989): 5–46.

40. Graphic evidence offers some of the most revealing views of "the street" in the mid–nineteenth century. As an example, see Mary Black, ed., *Old New York in Early Photographs, 1853–1901* (New York, 1973), esp. 69.

41. See Scranton, "Varieties of Paternalism," 248–57. See also Wilentz, *Chants Democratic*, 316–24; and Anthony F. C. Wallace, *Rockdale: The Growth of an American Village in the Early Industrial Revolution* (New York, 1978), 55–56, 459–71.

42. The best overview of the early labor movement is Edward Pessen, *Most Uncommon Jacksonians: The Radical Leaders of the Early Labor Movement* (Albany, N.Y., 1967).

43. See ibid. See also Formisano, *Transformation of Political Culture*, 27–236, quotation on 230.

44. Bridges, *City in the Republic*, 50.

45. Robinson, "Rise of Factories," table 7. The one notable exception to this pattern in Indianapolis in 1850 was the large factory, which paid the highest wages of all. But the rather small number of observations casts some doubt on this finding. For Philadelphia see Laurie, Hershberg, and Alter, "Immigrants and Industry," 103–4 and table 8.

46. Ibid.

47. See Stansell, *City of Women*, 105–25.

48. Child, *Frugal Housewife*, 99.

49. Neale, "Class and Class Consciousness," 15–40. It is interesting to note that Jacksonian artisans themselves used this terminology as well. The preamble of the Mechanics' Union of Trade Associations spoke of "capitalists," "mechanical and productive classes," and "middling classes." See John R. Commons et al., *Documentary History of American Industrial Society* 10 vols. (reprint, New York, 1958), 5:88–89.

50. Susan G. Davis, *Parades and Power: Street Theater in Nineteenth-Century Philadelphia* (Philadelphia, 1986). See also Sean Wilentz, "Artisan Republican Festivals and the Rise of Class Conflict in New York City, 1788–1837," in *Working-Class America: Essays in Labor, Community, and American Society*, ed. Michael Frisch and Daniel Walkowitz (Urbana, Ill., 1983), 37–77; and Wilentz, *Chants Democratic*, 87–89.

51. See Laurie, *Artisans into Workers*, 58–61.

52. Whitney Cross, *The Burned-Over District: The Social and Intellectual History of Enthusiastic Religion in Western New York, 1800–1850* (Ithaca, N.Y., 1950).

53. Ian Tyrrell, *Sobering Up: From Temperance to Prohibition in Antebellum America, 1800–1860* (Westport, Conn., 1979), 159–90. See also Ruth M. Alexander, "'We Are Engaged as a Band of Sisters': Class and Domesticity in the Washingtonian Temperance Movement, 1840–1850," *Journal of American History* 75 (1988): 763–85.

54. Brian Greenberg, *Worker and Community: Response to Industrialization in a Nine-*

*teenth-Century American City, Albany, New York, 1850–1884* (Albany, N.Y., 1985), 101. For basic works on fraternalism see Albert C. Stevens, *The Cyclopedia of Fraternities* (New York, 1907); Charles W. Ferguson, *Fifty Million Brothers* (New York, 1937); and Jack C. Ross, *An Assembly of Good Fellows: Voluntary Associations in History* (Westport, Conn., 1976).

55. Mary Ann Clawson, *Constructing Brotherhood: Class, Gender, and Fraternalism* (Princeton, 1989).

56. Richard L. McCormick, *The Party Period and Public Policy: American Politics from the Age of Jackson to the Progressive Era* (New York, 1986), 279.

57. Michael Holt, *The Political Crisis of the 1850s* (New York, 1978), 60; and Formisano, *Transformation of Political Culture*, 19. Formisano here draws on William G. Shade, "Political Pluralism and Party Development: The Creation of a Modern Party System, 1815–1852," in *The Evolution of American Electoral Systems*, ed. Paul Kleppner et al. (Westport, Conn., 1981), 77–111. Of course, third parties were even more unstable than mainstream parties, but that was their nature.

58. Carl Siracusa, *A Mechanical People: Perceptions of the Industrial Order in Massachusetts, 1815–1880* (Middletown, Conn., 1979), 118.

59. Bridges, *City in the Republic*, 149.

60. Holt, *Political Crisis of the 1850s*, vii. One can cite numerous studies that share this perspective. See, for instance, William E. Gienapp, *The Origins of the Republican Party, 1852–1856* (New York, 1987).

61. The most persuasive argument for the relative weakness and superficiality of the "first party system" by comparison to the second is Formisano, *Transformation of Political Culture*, 3–170.

62. This process of adjustment, or perhaps more accurately of negotiation and give-and-take, between the political center and the margin is still not well understood. It is especially murky at the local level, where much of the negotiation seems to have taken place.

63. Wilentz, "Class and Politics," 45–63.

64. See Richard L. McCormick, "The Social Analysis of American Political History—After Twenty Years," in *Party Period and Public Policy*, 108–15, for a heady critique of those historians who seek to integrate economics and politics but wind up equating social class with ideology, and republicanism in particular.

65. Edward Pessen, "Did Labor Support Jackson? The Boston Story," *Political Science Quarterly* 67 (1949): 263.

66. William A. Sullivan, "Did Labor Support Andrew Jackson?" *Political Science Quarterly* 62 (1947): 569–80; Lewis H. Arky, "The Mechanics' Union of Trade Associations and the Formation of the Philadelphia Working-Men's Movement," *Pennsylvania Magazine of History and Biography* 76 (1952): 142–76; Formisano, *Transformation of Political Culture*, 222–44; and Pessen, *Most Uncommon Jacksonians*, 9–33.

67. See n. 3, above.

68. See Kathleen Smith Kutolowski and Ronald Formisano, "Antimasonry Re-examined: Social Bases of the Grass-Roots Party," *Journal of American History* 71 (1984): 269–93. See also Kathleen Smith Kutolowski, "Freemasonry and Community in the Early Republic: The Case of Antimasonic Anxieties," *American Quarterly* 34 (1984): 534–61. The literature on Antimasonry is reviewed in Michael F. Holt, "The Antimasonic and Know

Nothing Parties," in *History of U.S. Political Parties,* ed. Arthur Schlesinger Jr., 4 vols. (New York, 1973), 1:575–737.

69. Formisano, *Transformation of Political Culture,* 198.

70. Compare, for example, Kutolowski and Formisano, "Antimasonry Re-examined"; Paul Goodman, *Towards a Christian Republic: Antimasonry and The Great Transition in New England, 1826–1836* (New York, 1988), 180–88; and Brooke, *Heart of the Commonwealth,* 386–87.

71. See Cross, *Burned-Over District.* Much of the recent work on Antimasonry is dedicated to disproving Cross's thesis that the movement represented a revolt of the lower middle class against the village aristocracy. While the evidence indicates a fairly diverse movement, I continue to believe that Cross basically had it right.

72. For a similar argument see John Jentz, "The Antislavery Constituency in Jacksonian America," *Civil War History* 27 (1981): 101–22. Magdol and Jentz elaborate what Leonard L. Richards initially argued in "'*Gentlemen of Property and Standing': Antiabolitionist Mobs in Jacksonian America* (New York, 1970). For a review of the literature on the social basis of abolitionism see Magdol, *Antislavery Rank and File,* 143–55.

73. Reinard Johnson, "The Liberty Party in Massachusetts, 1840–1848: Antislavery Third Party Politics in the Bay State," *Civil War History* 28 (1982): 237–65. See also Brooke, *Heart of the Commonwealth,* 368–69; and Reinard Johnson, "The Liberty Party in New England: The Forgotten Abolitionists" (Ph.D. diss., Syracuse Univ., 1976).

74. Johnson, "Liberty Party in Massachusetts," 256 and n. 54. See also Brooke, *Heart of the Commonwealth,* 368–83. For a general history of antislavery parties see Aileen S. Kraditor, "The Liberty and Free Soil Parties," in Schlesinger, ed., *History of U.S. Political Parties,* 1:741–882.

75. John R. Mulkern, *The Know-Nothing Party in Massachusetts: The Rise and Fall of a People's Movement* (Boston, 1990), 75.

76. Holt, *Political Crisis of the 1850s,* 161. See also Michael Holt, "The Politics of Impatience: The Origins of Know Nothingism," *Journal of American History* 60 (1973): 309–32. For a review of the literature on Know-Nothingism see Holt, "Antimasonic and Know Nothing Parties."

77. Mulkern, *Know-Nothing Party,* 67.

78. This assumes, of course, that nativism enjoyed the deep base in factory labor that Mulkern claims. It would appear, however, that the Know-Nothings ran only slightly better in manufacturing towns than in the state as a whole. In addition, since a good proportion of the factory workforce consisted of women, who could not vote, and Irish immigrants, who were underregistered, it is likely that a good proportion of the Know-Nothing vote came from outside the factory, possibly from small shops. On the artisanal base of urban nativism see Wilentz, *Chants Democratic,* 315–24; Bridges, *City in the Republic,* 83–98; and Laurie, *Working People,* 168–77, and table 11, 170–71.

79. The older literature tends to make a distinction between urban and rural parties. See, for example, Nathan Fine, *Labor and Farmer Parties in the United States, 1828–1928* (New York, 1961). More recent work draws any number of distinctions between insurgencies. For instance, Brooke, *Heart of the Commonwealth,* places them within the ideological context of Haringtonianism or Lockeanism; Formisano, *Transformation of Political Culture,* describes different expressions of populism; and though not directly concerned with political insurgency, Wilentz, *Chants Democratic,* stresses class distinc-

tions between the Working Men of the 1830s and the nativists of the 1840s. Like Wilentz, Mulkern, *Know-Nothing Party*, underlines the class distinctions, but unlike Wilentz, Mulkern treats nativism as a sort of working-class movement.

80. See, for example, Laurie, *Working People*, 67–83; and Wilentz, *Chants Democratic*, 172–216.

81. Mulkern, *Know-Nothing Party*, 79–86.

82. Compare, for example, Brooke, *Heart of the Commonwealth*, 344–52, with Goodman, *Towards a Christian Republic*, 54–79.

83. Wilentz, *Chants Democratic*, 77–87; and Laurie, *Working People*, 64–84. The strong association between labor leaders and rationalism held largely for the 1830s, though some workers, chiefly millhands in the 1830s, were clearly evangelicals. See Wallace, *Rockdale;* and Cynthia Shelton, *The Mills of Manayunk: Industrialization and Social Conflict in the Philadelphia Region, 1787–1837* (Baltimore, 1986). The leadership generation of the 1840s showed a strong revivalist influence. See Jama Lazerow, "Religion and Labor Reform in Antebellum America: The World of William Field Young," *American Quarterly* 38 (1986): 265–86. See also Teresa A. Murphy, *Ten Hours' Labor: Religion, Reform, and Gender in Early New England* (Ithaca, N.Y., 1992).

84. Johnson, "Liberty Party in Massachusetts," 252–53. Formisano, *Transformation of Political Culture*, 287–88, also draws attention to the Liberty party's growing strength in a factory district, though the district was previously Whig.

85. On the Free Soil vote see Frederick J. Blue, *The Free Soilers: Third Party Politics, 1848–54* (Urbana, Ill., 1973), 141–51; and Joseph G. Rayback, *Free Soil: The Election of 1848* (Lexington, Ky., 1970), 279–87. See also Brooke, *Heart of the Commonwealth*, 372–73.

86. See, for example, Commons, *Documentary History*, vol. 5, pt. 1, 93–107, 114–23, 149–54, 157–64, 188–91. See also Pessen, *Most Uncommon Jacksonians*, 173–96.

87. See, for example, John Higham, *Strangers in the Land: Patterns of American Nativism* (New Brunswick, N.J., 1955); and Ray Allen Billington, *The Protestant Crusade, 1800–1860: A Study of Origins of American Nativism* (New York, 1938); Blue, *Free Soilers;* and Rayback, *Free Soil.*

88. Kirk H. Porter and Donald Bruce Johnson, eds., *National Party Platforms, 1840–1960*, 2d ed. (Urbana, Ill., 1961), 4–8, 13–14.

89. Ibid., 22–23.

90. Mulkern, *Know-Nothing Party*, 112; and Formisano, *Transformation of Political Culture*, 335–39. Mulkern offers no explanation for the failure of these bills. Formisano shows how the secret ballot and the ten-hour day were linked, and attributes the failure of the latter to bribery of legislators; to the commitment of some nativists to the doctrine of freedom of contract; and to some factory owners' voluntary reduction of mill hours, which "reduced some of the momentum the ten-hour movement had built." Formisano, *Transformation of Political Culture*, 339. While this argument makes some sense, much work needs to be done on this phase of the ten-hour movement.

91. Mulkern, *Know-Nothing Party*, 108–13; and Formisano, *Transformation of Political Culture*, 331–39.

92. See, for instance, Richard H. Sewell, *Ballots for Freedom: Antislavery Politics in the United States, 1837–1860* (New York, 1976), 117–37; James Brewer Gilbert, *Holy Warriors: The Abolitionists and American Society* (New York, 1976), 74–123; Gerald Sorin, *Abolitionism: A New Perspective* (New York, 1972), 77–98; and Bertram Wyatt-Brown, *Lewis Tappan and the Evangelical War against Slavery* (Cleveland, Ohio, 1969), 276–82.

93. A number of recent scholars—including Formisano and Mulkern, cited above—underline the reformist thrust of third parties. See especially Kevin Sweeney, "Rum, Romanism, Representation, and Reform: Coalition Politics in Massachusetts, 1847–1853," *Civil War History* 6 (1976): 116–37, for one of the first such interpretations.

94. On Wright see Johnson, "Liberty Party in Massachusetts," 247–48; Dumas Malone, ed., *Dictionary of American Biography* (New York, 1936), 20:548–49; and Lawrence B. Goodheart, *Abolitionist, Actuary, Atheist: Elizur Wright and the Reform Impulse* (Kent, Ohio, 1990).

95. Johnson, "Liberty Party in Massachusetts," 256. See also Formisano, *Transformation of Political Culture*, 287–88.

96. Quoted in Siracusa, *Mechanical People*, 186. See also Sweeney, "Rum, Romanism, Representation, and Reform."

97. Siracusa, *Mechanical People*, 187.

98. [William Heighton], *An Address to the Members of Trade Societies, and to the Working Classes Generally* (Philadelphia, 1827), 14.

99. Ibid., passim.

100. Quoted in Blumin, *Middle Class*, 35.

101. The claim that immigrants were a source of cheap labor that would drive down wages and displace American-born tradesmen constituted one of the major themes of nativism. See Laurie, *Working People*, 173–74; Wilentz, *Chants Democratic*, 266–69; and Bridges, *City in the Republic*, 69–90. Bridges astutely notes that the skilled worker's aspiration to respectability exacerbated hostility to the Irish, who were associated with "dissolute character." Quoting Joseph R. Gusfield, she argues that the nativist worker would "not risk the possibility that he might be classed with the immigrants." Bridges, *City in the Republic*, 89.

102. See, for example, Holt, *Political Crisis of the 1850s*, 173–74; and Mulkern, *Know-Nothing Party*, esp. 118–33.

103. See Formisano, *Transformation of Political Culture*, esp. 245–67.

104. Ibid. See also Davis, *Parades and Power*; and Wilentz, "Artisan Republican Festivals."

105. On the fortunes of small businessmen see Michael B. Katz, *The People of Hamilton, Canada West: Family and Class in a Mid-Nineteenth-Century City* (Cambridge, Mass., 1975), 176–89; and Griffen and Griffen, *Ordering of Opportunity*, 105–12. I have just begun to read this autobiographical literature. For examples of what such work can reveal, see chaps. 8 and 9, below.

## Chapter 8 Becoming Joseph T. Buckingham

The author wishes to acknowledge the help of Jeff Blodgett, Carol Lasser, Bruce Laurie, Sean Wilentz, Michael Zuckerman, the editors of this volume, and the anonymous reader and copyeditor for the Johns Hopkins University Press.

1. According to Sean Wilentz, "Artisan independence conjured up, not a vision of ceaseless, self-interested industry, but a moral order in which all craftsmen would eventually become self-governing, independent, competent masters—an order to match the stonemason's ditty that they would 'steal from no man.' Men's energies would be devoted, not to personal ambition or profit alone, but to the commonwealth; in the workshop, mutual obligation and respect—'the strongest ties of the heart'—would prevail; in

more public spheres, the craftsmen would insist on their equal rights and exercise their citizenship with a view to preserving the rule of virtue as well as to protecting their collective interest against an eminently corruptible mercantile and financial elite." Sean Wilentz, *Chants Democratic: New York City and the Rise of the American Working Class, 1788–1850* (New York, 1984), 102. For a general discussion of the shifting meaning of "independence" as an American ideal in the late eighteenth and early nineteenth centuries, see Rowland Berthoff, "Independence and Attachment, Virtue and Interest," in *Uprooted Americans: Essays to Honor Oscar Handlin,* ed. Richard L. Bushman et al. (Boston, 1979), 97–124.

2. Joseph T. Buckingham, *Personal Memoirs and Recollections of Editorial Life,* 2 vols. (Boston, 1852), 1:3–40.

3. Ibid., 1:51–52.

4. Petition of Joseph B. Tinker to Massachusetts General Court, June 8, 1804, Acts 1804, 31, Archives of the Commonwealth, Boston.

5. Buckingham, *Personal Memoirs* 1:51–52.

6. [Joseph T. Buckingham], "Croaker No. XXVI," *Boston Courier,* Sept. 22, 1849.

7. Buckingham, *Personal Memoirs* 1:53–54.

8. Ibid., 1:59, 61–62.

9. Ibid., 1:62; J.T.B. [Joseph T. Buckingham], "The Faustus Association," *Boston Daily Evening Transcript,* Oct. 1, 1859.

10. Joseph T. Buckingham, comp., *Annals of the Massachusetts Charitable Mechanic Association* (Boston, 1853), 123, 125.

11. *Comet,* Oct. 19, 1811, 2; Buckingham, *Personal Memoirs* 1:59–60.

12. B[uckingham], "The Faustus Association," *Boston Daily Evening Transcript,* Sept. 16, 1859; Rollo G. Silver, *The American Printer, 1787–1825* (Charlottesville, Va., 1967), 88–89; Record Books 1, 2, Boston Association of Booksellers Collection, American Antiquarian Society, Worcester, Mass.

13. Buckingham, *Personal Memoirs* 1:60.

14. [Joseph T. Buckingham], "Croaker No. XLVIII," *Boston Courier,* Mar. 23, 1850.

15. Buckingham, *Personal Memoirs* 1:63.

16. Ibid., 1:63–64.

17. Ibid., 1:73–78; *New-England Galaxy and Masonic Magazine,* Oct. 10, 1817.

18. [Joseph T. Buckingham], "Croaker No. LI," *Boston Courier,* Apr. 13, 1850.

19. Ibid.

20. [Joseph T. Buckingham], "Croaker No. LII," *Boston Courier,* May 25, 1850; Buckingham, *Personal Memoirs* 1:81–82.

21. "To Patrons," *New-England Galaxy,* Apr. 10, 1818.

22. Ibid., 1:101.

23. "Nobility of Wealth," *New-England Galaxy,* Sept. 29, 1820.

24. "Mr. Otis and the Middling Interest," *New-England Galaxy,* May 17, 1822.

25. Buckingham, *Personal Memoirs* 2:5–10.

26. *Boston Courier,* May 9, 1825.

27. *Boston Courier,* Sept. 3, 1827.

28. Buckingham, *Personal Memoirs* 2:64.

29. *New-England Galaxy,* July 25, 1828.

30. While the final terms of their agreement are unknown, Buckingham's asking price was six thousand dollars, one-third payable at the time of purchase and the rest

due in biannual installments of five hundred dollars each. This did not include the sale of "the printing apparatus," which Buckingham chose to retain for use "in printing the Courier and . . . for some trifling job work." Joseph T. Buckingham to Theophilus Parsons, n.d., Ch.D.10.29A, Rare Book Room, Boston Public Library, Boston, Mass.; Buckingham, *Personal Memoirs* 1:256.

31. *Boston Courier*, May 10, 1828.

32. Buckingham, *Personal Memoirs* 2:67.

33. *Boston Courier*, June 16, 1831; ibid., June 30, 1831; Buckingham, *Personal Memoirs* 2:76–77 n.

34. Buckingham, comp., *Annals of Charitable Mechanic Association*, 228–64.

35. Buckingham also presented himself as a spokesman for Boston's emerging middle class, as Anne C. Rose points out in *Transcendentalism as a Social Movement, 1830–1850* (New Haven, 1981), 22–24.

36. Joseph T. Buckingham, *An Address Delivered before the Massachusetts Charitable Mechanic Association at the Celebration of their Eighth Triennial Festival, October 7, 1830* (Boston, 1830), [5]-10.

37. Ibid., 12–14. Note that Buckingham deliberately blurred the distinction between manual and nonmanual labor which Stuart M. Blumin argues was fundamental to the development of middle-class identity. Stuart M. Blumin, *The Emergence of the Middle Class: Social Experience in the American City, 1760–1900* (New York, 1989), chap. 4.

38. Buckingham, *Address before Charitable Mechanic Association*, 18–19.

39. Ibid., 23. On the growing middle-class concern for character in a mobile society, see especially Mary P. Ryan, *Cradle of the Middle Class: The Family in Oneida County, New York, 1790–1865* (New York, 1981), chap. 4.

40. *Boston Courier*, Sept. 24, 1830.

41. Ibid.

42. *Boston Courier*, Oct. 21, 1830.

43. *Boston Courier*, Oct. 28, 1830.

44. *Boston Courier*, Oct. 25, 1830.

45. Buckingham, *Personal Memoirs* 2:231–34.

46. *Boston Courier*, Sept. 15, 1834; ibid., Oct. 27, 1834.

47. *Boston Courier*, Nov. 3, 1834.

48. *Boston Courier*, Oct. 27, 1834.

49. Buckingham, *Personal Memoirs* 2:74.

50. Joseph T. Buckingham to Nathan Appleton, Apr. 17, 1834, Appleton Family Papers, box 5, folder 8, Massachusetts Historical Society, Boston.

51. Ibid.

52. Buckingham, *Personal Memoirs* 2:74.

53. "A New Year," *Boston Courier*, Jan. 1, 1835.

54. Buckingham, *Personal Memoirs* 2:103–5.

55. On the myth of the self-made man in Jacksonian America, see Rex Burns, *Success in America: The Yeoman Dream and the Industrial Revolution* (Amherst, Mass., 1976); John William Ward, *Andrew Jackson: Symbol for an Age* (New York, 1955); and Irvin G. Wyllie, *The Self-Made Man in America: The Myth of Rags to Riches* (New York, 1954), chap. 1. On the anxieties underlying the apparent optimism of the era, see especially Marvin Meyers, *The Jacksonian Persuasion; Politics and Belief* (Stanford, Calif., 1957); Lawrence Frederick Kohl, *The Politics of Individualism: Parties and the American Character in the Jacksonian*

*Era* (New York, 1989); and Charles Sellers, *The Market Revolution: Jacksonian America, 1815–1846* (New York, 1991).

56. On the bourgeois fear of deception in urban society, see Karen Halttunen, *Confidence Men and Painted Women: A Study of Middle-Class Culture in America, 1830–1870* (New Haven, 1982).

## Chapter 9 From Artisan to Alderman

I wish to thank Alfred F. Young, Bruce Laurie, and Fannia Weingartner for their camaraderie and incisive commentary; the editors for their encouragement and helpful criticisms; and David Yntema and Francis Bogess for research assistance.

1. W. W. Moore Papers (hereafter cited as WWM Papers), Obituary File, folder 1, MSS. 188, Historical Society of Washington, D.C., Washington, D.C. The basic facts of Moore's biography are contained in the articles in this file.

2. Here, I am attempting to place special emphasis on the way in which artisanal notions of respectability, mutuality, and independence among what Stuart Blumin calls the "nonmanual sector" affected the emerging class relations of antebellum America. Along with Blumin, I feel that recognizing the early importance of the social relations and management strategies of foremen, clerks, and petty proprietors will help us understand both early trade union development and class development. Stuart Blumin, *The Emergence of the Middle Class: Social Experience in the American City, 1760–1900* (Cambridge, 1989), 66–78. More narrowly, this essay amends the position—first articulated by Elizabeth Baker and followed by Benson Soffer—that foremen were not common or important in the printing trade until the 1850s. In fact, my research indicates that foremen and clerks were common in large newspaper and book printing offices as early as the 1820s. See Elizabeth Baker, *Printers and Technology: A History of the International Printing Pressmen and Assistants' Union* (New York, 1957), 18; and Benson Soffer, "The Role of Union Foremen in the Evolution of the International Typographical Union," *Labor History* 2 (1961): 62–81.

3. Bruce Laurie, comments on papers delivered at the Second Labor History Symposium, "The American Artisan," held at the George Meany Memorial Archives, Silver Spring, Md., Oct. 11–12, 1990.

4. WWM Papers, Obituary File, folder 1.

5. Charles Steffen, *The Mechanics of Baltimore: Workers and Politics in the Age of Revolution, 1763–1812* (Urbana, Ill., 1984), esp. 209–84; Paul A. Gilje, "The Baltimore Riots of 1812 and the Breakdown of the Anglo-American Mob Tradition," *Journal of Social History* 13 (1980): 547–64.

6. Handwritten note on envelope back signed by Mrs. M. McFarland (Moore's daughter, Mary), WWM Papers, Obituary File, folder 1. When Benjamin Edes died in 1832, Moore reluctantly refused the family's request that he return to Baltimore to assume control of the office, saying that he owed allegiance to his current employer. Moore (hereafter cited as "WWM" in archival references) to Samuel Edes, Oct. 14, 1832, in W. W. Moore Letter Book (hereafter cited as Moore Letter Book), *National Intelligencer* Papers, MSS. 196, Historical Society of Washington, D.C.

7. On apprenticeships in general, see W. J. Rorabaugh, *The Craft Apprentice: From Franklin to the Machine Age in America* (New York, 1986); for other examples of men just out of their apprenticeships being promoted, see Rollo Silver, *The American Printer,*

*1787–1825* (Charlottesville, Va., 1967), 5, 12; on tramp printers, see William S. Pretzer, "Tramp Printers: Craft Culture, Trade Unions, and Technology," *Printing History* 12 (1984): 3–16.

8. Columbia Typographical Society, *Protest of the Columbia Typographical Society against the Washington Institute* (Washington, D.C., 1834).

9. WWM to Duff Green, Feb. 26, 1834, in Moore Letter Book; emphasis in the original.

10. The petition and letter (dated Feb. 28, 1834) are in WWM Papers, folder 3; Moore's reply is contained in WWM to Thomas T. Sloan, Feb. 28, 1834, Moore Letter Book.

11. For printers' festivals, see Rollo Silver, "The Convivial Printer: Dining, Wining, and Marching, 1825–1860," *Printing History* 4 (1982): 16–25; the symbolism of printers' festivals, toasts, and iconography is related to artisanal republicanism in William S. Pretzer, "The Iconography of the Printing Trade," in *Travail et loisir dans les sociétés pré-industrielles,* ed. Barbara Karsky and Elise Marienstras (Nancy, France, 1991), 133–43.

12. William S. Pretzer, "'The British, Duff Green, the Rats, and the Devil': Custom, Capitalism, and Conflict in the Washington Printing Trade, 1834–36," *Labor History* 27 (1985–86): 5–30. Other versions of the Duff Green affair, each with a different emphasis, appear in Rorabaugh, *Craft Apprentice,* 91–95; Bruce Laurie, *Artisans into Workers: Labor in Nineteenth-Century America* (New York, 1989), 38; and Ava Baron, "An 'Other' Side of Gender Antagonism at Work: Men, Boys, and the Remasculinization of Printers' Work, 1830–1920," in *Work Engendered: Toward a New History of American Labor,* ed. Ava Baron (Ithaca, N.Y., 1991), 47.

13. WWM to Duff Green, July 9, 1835, Moore Letter Book.

14. In this complex swirl of events and issues, it seems to me impossible to conflate all the points of contention to a matter of gender. Thus, I believe that Ava Baron overstates the impact of gender in labor relations in "An 'Other' Side of Gender Antagonism at Work"; and in idem, "Questions of Gender: Deskilling and Demasculinization in the U.S. Printing Industry, 1830–1915," *Gender and History* 1 (summer 1989): 178–99. However, Moore's suggestion that women be employed in place of boys demonstrates how gender was one of the categories of labor manipulated by business innovators, a point that Baron makes most persuasively in "Contested Terrain Revisited: Technology and Gender Definitions of Work in the Printing Industry, 1850–1920," in *Women, Work, and Technology: Transformations,* ed. Barbara Drygulski Wright (Ann Arbor, Mich., 1987), 58–83. In this instance, Moore pitted women against untrained boys, not skilled workers, and eventually contributed to establishing an unskilled job category specifically for women, one that did not exist before the introduction of power presses. Deskilling and feminization of skill existed in a dialectical relationship, but the threat of women compositors was only one of many attacks on the privileged position of nineteenth-century printers.

15. WWM to the Committee of the Columbia Typographical Society, Jan. 30, 1835, Moore Letter Book.

16. WWM to John Heart, Columbia Typographical Society, Feb. 23, 1837, Moore Letter Book; Minutes of the Columbia Typographical Society, Apr. 1, 1837, in the possession of the Columbia Typographical Union no. 101, Washington, D.C.

17. See Moore Letter Book, various letters dating from 1829 to 1835, especially WWM to Richard Ronaldson (a typefounder), Sept. 9, 1829; WWM to R. B. Spaulding (a print-

ers' supply firm), Sept. 15, 16, 28, Oct. 5, 9, 17, 1829; WWM to R. Hoe and Company (a press manufacturer and supplier), Oct. 24, Dec. 26, 1829, Oct. 4, 1830.

18. Moore's testimony is reported in House Select Committee on Printing, *Public Printing*, House Report 298, 26th Cong., 1st sess., Mar. 26, 1840, 110–18; and House Committee on Public Expenditures, *Public Printing*, House Report 249, 36th Cong., 1st sess., Mar. 26, 1860, 85–90. His testimony is suggestive of his ideological consistency in the face of changing conditions. In 1840, he advocated a government-owned and -operated printing office because it would prevent abuses by private printers who received favors from public officials. In 1860, he still felt that a government office run by practical printers independent of political influence would save money and produce good work. However, an additional twenty years' experience in Washington led him to fear that a government office would be more open to political influence than were the private offices that had traditionally done government printing. On both occasions, Moore advocated fair dealing and equal opportunity, government efficiency through economic activity, and the independence of trained printers.

19. *A Record of the First Exhibition of The Metropolitan Mechanics' Institute* (Washington, D.C., 1853).

20. Of course, technology alone did not initiate or drive the reorganization of the trade, but the introduction of power presses did have specific results. For discussions of the division of labor and deskilling in the printing trade in this era, see Sean Wilentz, *Chants Democratic: New York City and the Rise of the American Working Class, 1788–1850* (New York, 1984), 112, 129–31; and Steven J. Ross, *Workers on the Edge: Work, Leisure, and Politics in Industrializing Cincinnati, 1788–1890* (New York, 1985), 38–39, 107–12.

21. Moore explains that Green is about to purchase two power presses "competent to execute nearly all of the presswork, with the aid of girls only and consequently the number of persons to be engaged will be considerably lessened" in WWM to James L. Peterson, Sept. 21, 1831, Moore Letter Book.

22. WWM to George Harris, Apr. 20, 1830, Moore Letter Book.

23. Ibid.

24. WWM to Thomas Kennedy, Mar. 29, 1832, offering "Smith" presses for sale; WWM to Thomas C. Hambly, June 11, 1832, making a similar offer; WWM to Greele and Willis, Apr. 5, Aug. 8, 1831, asking in the first letter for information regarding "Adams Patent Printing Machines"; and WWM to R. Hoe and Co., Oct. 24, 1832, regarding a chase for the double "Napier Press"—all in Moore Letter Book.

25. WWM to William Kerr Jr., July 2, 1830, Moore Letter Book.

26. WWM to Samuel Edes, Oct. 14, 1832, Moore Letter Book.

27. WWM to William Kerr Jr. and Sr., July 2, 1830, Moore Letter Book; W. W. Moore, *United States Telegraph*, "extra" edition, June 12, 1835.

28. *National Intelligencer*, Jan. 1, 1865; *The Compact Edition of the Oxford English Dictionary* (Oxford, 1971), s.v. "esteem."

29. WWM to Duff Green, Sept. 15, 16, 1837, Moore Letter Book.

30. WWM to Thomas Lucas, Jan. 1, 1838, Moore Letter Book.

31. For skill as capital, see Committee of Correspondence to Duff Green, Apr. 17, 1834, printed with Columbia Typographical Society, *Protest against the Washington Institute*.

32. Receipts for school tuition and expenses paid to Joanne McLeod, Apr. 22, 1845, and Apr. 29, 1846; receipts for school tuition and expenses paid to Miss Lalarme, July 2,

1847, and July 29, 1848; Davis and Garrett, invoice and accounts for construction of a house for W. W. Moore at Sixth and F Streets, Jan. 1, 1856—all in WWM Papers, folder 10.

33. On the rise of salaried, nonmanual workers in artisanal trades, see Blumin, *Middle Class,* 66–107; for the importance of lower-middle-class moral values, personal respectability, and independence in the context of nineteenth-century American labor and ideology, see Christopher Lasch, *The True and Only Heaven: Progress and Its Critics* (New York, 1991), 177–225, 483–96; for the European petty bourgeoisie, see Geoffrey Crossick and Heinz-Gerhard Haupt, eds., *Shopkeepers and Master Artisans in Nineteenth-Century Europe* (London, 1984).

34. Receipt from Samuel Walker for payment "in full for portraits of himself and wife," dated Nov. 29, 1854, WWM Papers, folder 10; for the bourgeois symbolism and commercial importance of portraits commissioned by nineteenth-century "middling sorts," see David Jaffee, "'One of the Primitive Sort': Portrait Makers of the Rural North, 1760–1860," in *The Countryside in the Age of Capitalist Transformation: Essays in the Social History of Rural America,* ed. Steven Hahn and Jonathon Prude (Chapel Hill, N.C., 1985), 103–38.

35. James Henretta, "The Study of Social Mobility: Ideological Assumptions and Conceptual Bias," *Labor History* 18 (1977): 166–78.

36. For a description of the shifting residential patterns of Washington's printers, see William S. Pretzer, "The Printers of Washington, D.C., 1800–1880: Work Culture, Technology, and Trade Unionism" (Ph.D. diss., Northern Illinois University, 1986), 22–27.

37. Davis and Garrett, invoice and accounts for construction of a house for W. W. Moore at Sixth and F Streets, Jan. 1, 1856; tax bills dated Aug. 31, 1852, Sept. 9, 1856, and Nov. 1871—all in WWM Papers, folder 10.

38. Various invoices for house repairs dating from the 1880s; W. O. Berry and Co., invoice for New Style Baltimore Stove and Parris Range, and "bricking up the fireplace," Mar. 1, 1884; Hooe, Brother and Co., invoice for ingrain carpet, Mar. 7, 1885—all in WWM Papers, folder 10.

39. Bureau of the Census, schedule of the census of population of Washington, D.C., for 1830, microfilm, p. 105; idem, schedule of the census of population of Washington, D.C., for 1840, microfilm, p. 91; idem, schedule of the census of population of Washington, D.C., for 1850, microfilm, p. 267.

40. The ratio of free blacks to slaves grew from nearly 1:1 in 1830 to 2.72:1 in 1850. Letitia Woods Brown, *Free Negroes in the District of Columbia, 1790–1846* (New York, 1972), 11, table 1.

41. *The Presbytery of Washington City: Prepared for the Centennial of the General Assembly, 1880* (Washington, D.C., 1880); John C. Smith, *Historical Discourse Commemorative of the 27th Anniversary of the Fourth Presbyterian Church* (Washington, D.C., 1855); receipt for pew rent, Sept. 30, 1886, WWM Papers, folder 10.

42. George M. Marsden, *The Evangelical Mind and the New School Presbyterian Experience* (New Haven, 1970), 231–41.

43. WWM Papers, Obituary File, folder 1; William M. Marine, *The British Invasion of Maryland, 1812–1815* (Baltimore, 1913), 384.

44. John Naylor to WWM, Nov. 5, 1832; WWM to William B. Lewis, Nov. 26, 1833; W. W. Seaton to WWM, Apr. 11, 1833; Friendship Literary Debating Society to WWM, Aug. 28, 1834; WWM to the National Cadets, Sept. 25, 1834—all in WWM Papers, folder 9.

45. "Capt. Moore's Reply," undated, WWM Papers, folder 3; Sean Wilentz, "Artisan Republican Festivals and the Rise of Class Conflict in New York City, 1788–1837," in *Working-Class America: Essays on Labor, Community, and American Society,* ed. Michael H. Frisch and Daniel J. Walkowitz (Urbana, Ill., 1983), 37–77.

46. Independent Order of Odd Fellows, Grand Encampment of the District of Columbia, *Proceedings, 1846–67* (Washington, D.C., 1867), 3, 34, 172–75, 504–11.

47. Brian Greenberg, *Worker and Community: Response to Industrialization in a Nineteenth-Century American City, Albany, New York, 1850–1884* (Albany, N.Y., 1985), 90. Steven Ross is more critical of the role of fraternal organizations, asserting that "although they perceived themselves as classless organizations, voluntary associations such as the Odd Fellows, Masons, and Red Men, which were invariably dominated by their well-to-do members, nevertheless served as social mechanisms for inculcating men with the dominant ideals of hierarchy, deference, temperance, and self-discipline." Ross, *Workers on the Edge,* 165–66.

48. Mary Ann Clawson, *Constructing Brotherhood: Class, Gender, and Fraternalism* (Princeton, 1989); see also Blumin, *Middle Class,* 225; and Mark C. Carnes, *Secret Ritual and Manhood in Victorian America* (New Haven, 1989).

49. W. W. Moore, quoted in an undated clipping of a newspaper article entitled "I.O.O.F. / Honors to a P.G.S. and a Worthy Citizen and Odd Fellow / Unveiling of the Picture of Capt. W. W. Moore—Interesting Exercises," WWM Papers, folder 9.

50. Grand Sire F. D. Stuart, quoted in "I.O.O.F. / Honors to a P.G.S. and a Worthy Citizen and Odd Fellow."

51. *Oxford English Dictionary,* s.v. "esteem."

52. "I.O.O.F. / Honors to a P.G.S. and a Worthy Citizen and Odd Fellow."

53. The history of Moore's terms in elected office and the list of printers' names are reconstructed from H. W. Crew, *Centennial History of the City of Washington, D.C.* (Dayton, Ohio, 1892), 298–316.

54. This summary of his career is based on a sample of city council proceedings published in the *National Intelligencer* for 1856–57, 1863–67, and 1870.

55. *National Intelligencer,* June 6, 1857.

56. *National Intelligencer,* Jan. 10, 1865; ibid., Jan. 11, 1865; ibid., Jan. 16, 1865.

57. *National Intelligencer,* July 12, 1870; William Tindall, *Standard History of the City of Washington* (Knoxville, Tenn., 1914), 231.

58. WWM Papers, Obituary File, folder 1.

59. The Metropolitan Railway was the second urban transportation company incorporated in the District of Columbia, chartered by Congress on July 1, 1864. It operated small cars, each of which was drawn by a single horse. Its lines ran from the Capitol to the railroad station, the Post Office, the Patent Office, the War Department, the Navy Department, Ebbitt House, Willard's Hotel, and the Arlington Hotel. It provided transportation diagonally across the city, from the northeastern part to the west. This route went close by the major commercial center as well as the concentration of workers' housing just north of Pennsylvania Avenue near Judiciary Square. *Boyd's Washington and Georgetown Directory for 1871* (Washington, D.C., 1871), 47; William Tindall, "Beginnings of Street Railways in the District of Columbia," *Records of the Columbia Historical Society* 21 (1918): 24–87.

60. "A Model Officer," newspaper clipping, n.d. [internal evidence dates it to about Nov. 29, 1877], WWM Papers, folder 3.

61. Unidentified newspaper obituary, WWM Papers, Obituary File, folder 1.

62. WWM to William Kerr Jr. and Sr., July 2, 1830, Moore Letter Book.

## Chapter 10 "All Her Sons Join in One Social Band"

1. For background on New York's artisanal societies see Howard B. Rock, *Artisans of the New Republic: The Tradesmen of New York City in the Age of Jefferson* (New York, 1979), chap. 5; idem, *The New York City Artisan, 1789–1825: A Documentary History* (Albany, 1989), 3–34, 199–241; Sean Wilentz, "Artisan Republican Festivals and the Rise of Class Conflict in New York City, 1788–1837," in *Working Class America: Essays on Labor, Community and American Society,* ed. Michael H. Frisch and Daniel J. Walkowitz (Urbana, Ill., 1982), 37–79; and idem, *Chants Democratic: New York City and the Rise of the American Working Class, 1790–1865* (New York, 1984), chap. 2.

2. William Herbert, *The History of the Twelve Great Livery Companies of London,* 2 vols. (London, 1834, 1837; reprint, New York, 1968); P. H. Ditchfield, *The City Companies of London and Their Good Works: A Record of Their History, Charity, and Treasure* (London, 1904); William F. Kahl, *The Development of the London Livery Companies* (Boston, 1960); George Unwin, *The Gilds and Companies of London* (London, 1908).

3. Herbert, *History of the Twelve Great Livery Companies* 1:1–132; Kahl, *Development of the London Livery Companies,* 1–32.

4. Kahl, *Development of the London Livery Companies,* 15–26; George Rudé, *Hanoverian London, 1715–1830* (Berkeley and Los Angeles, 1971), chaps. 2, 3, 5.

5. Unwin, *Gilds and Companies of London,* 252; Herbert, *History of the Twelve Great Livery Companies* 2:531; John Bromley and Heather Child, *The Armorial Bearings of the Guilds of London* (London, 1960), 46, 158.

6. Robert Withington, *English Pageantry: An Historical Outline,* 2 vols. (Cambridge, Mass., 1918; reprint, 1968), i-ii, 68, 91, 116; Frederick W. Fairholt, *Lord Mayors Pageants* (London, 1843); Unwin, *Gilds and Companies of London,* 272.

7. Ditchfield, *City Companies of London,* 22. Unwin, *Gilds and Companies of London,* 190, 214, 349; B.W.E. Alford and T. C. Baker, *A History of the Carpenters Company* (London, 1968), 105, 168.

8. Kahl, *Development of the London Livery Companies,* 27–30.

9. Rock, *Artisans of the New Republic,* 128–35, 272–77.

10. Ibid., chaps. 1–5; Wilentz, *Chants Democratic,* chaps. 1–2.

11. Bromley and Child, *Armorial Bearings,* 190.

12. Sidney I. Pomerantz, *New York: An American City, 1783–1803* (New York, 1938), 95–97; Thomas Earle and Charles T. Congdon, eds., *Annals of the General Society of Mechanics and Tradesmen of the City of New York, 1775–1880* (New York, 1882).

13. Arthur Adams, *The History of the Worshipful Company of Blacksmiths from Early Times until the Year 1785* (London, 1951), 87; Bromley and Child, *Armorial Bearings,* 14.

14. Rock, *Artisans of the New Republic,* 90–91, 136–38, 166–69.

15. Shane White, "'We Dwell in Safety and Pursue Our Honest Callings': Free Blacks in New York City, 1783–1810," *Journal of American History* 75 (1988): 445–70.

16. Rock, *Artisans of the New Republic,* 272–73; idem, *New York City Artisan,* 205–8; Bromley and Child, *Armorial Bearings,* 283.

17. Rock, *New York City Artisan,* 144–45; Bromley and Child, *Armorial Bearings,* 96.

18. Rock, *Artisans of the New Republic,* 135–43; idem, *New York City Artisan,* 3–15; Wilentz, *Chants Democratic,* 87–97.

19. Cadwallader D. Colden, *Memoir Prepared at the Request of a Committee of the Common Council of the City of New York* (New York, 1825), 228–29, 372.

20. Ibid., 378–79.

21. Ibid., 226–27, 372; Bromley and Child, *Armorial Bearings,* 182.

22. Colden, *Memoir,* 214; Bromley and Child, *Armorial Bearings,* 5; Rock, *Artisans of the New Republic,* 184–97.

23. Colden, *Memoir,* 215; Bromley and Child, *Armorial Bearings,* 46.

24. Joyce Appleby, *Capitalism and a New Social Order: The Republican Vision of the 1790s* (New York, 1984).

25. Among the important works for this discussion are J.G.A. Pocock, *The Machiavellian Moment: Florentine Political Thought and the Atlantic Republican Tradition* (Princeton, 1976); idem, "Virtue and Commerce in the Eighteenth Century," *Journal of Interdisciplinary History* 3 (1972): 119–34; Lance Banning, *The Jeffersonian Persuasion: Evolution of a Party Ideology* (Ithaca, N.Y., 1978); idem, "Jefferson Ideology Revisited: Liberal and Classical Ideas in the New American Republic," *William and Mary Quarterly,* 3d ser., 43 (1986): 3–19; Appleby, *Capitalism and a New Social Order;* Joyce Appleby, "Republicanism in Old and New Concepts," *William and Mary Quarterly,* 3d ser., 43 (1986): 20–34; idem, "The Social Origins of American Revolutionary Ideology," *Journal of American History* 64 (1978): 935–78; and Isaac Kramnick, "Republican Revision Revisited," *American Historical Review* 87 (1982): 629–64.

26. David J. Saposs, "Colonial and Federal Beginnings (to 1827)," in *History of Labour in the United States,* ed. John R. Commons et al. (1918; reprint, New York, 1966), 1:25–165; Rock, *Artisans of the New Republic,* 237–94; Wilentz, *Chants Democratic,* 23–48; Paul A. Gilje, *The Road to Mobocracy: Popular Disorder in New York City, 1763–1834* (Chapel Hill, N.C., 1987), 188–97, 253–64; W. J. Rorabaugh, *The Craft Apprentice: From Franklin to the Machine Age in America* (New York, 1986).

27. Rock, *Artisans of the New Republic,* chap. 10.

28. This is seen most clearly in the arguments presented at the 1809 conspiracy trial of New York's organized cordwainers. The transcript is reprinted as *People vs. Melvin* in *A Documentary History of American Industrial Society,* ed. John R. Commons et al., 10 vols. (Cleveland, 1910–11), vol. 3; pertinent sections are reprinted in Rock, *New York City Artisan,* 201–3, 247–51.

29. Wilentz, *Chants Democratic,* 13–18 and *infra.* Richard Twomey, *Jacobins and Jeffersonians: Anglo-American Radicalism in the United States, 1790–1820* (New York, 1989), chap. 6.

30. Rock, *New York City Artisan,* 249–50, 252–53.

## Chapter 11 With Hammer in Hand

The author is greatly indebted to Nancy Bercaw, Peter Liebhold, Ellen Miles, and Anne L. Pierce for their insights and generous assistance.

1. Ellen G. Miles, "The Portrait in America, 1750–1776," in *American Colonial Portraits, 1700–1776,* ed. Richard H. Saunders and Ellen G. Miles (Washington, D.C., 1987), 44–45; Wayne Craven, *Colonial American Portraiture: The Economic, Religious, Social, Cultural, Philosophical, Scientific, and Aesthetic Foundations* (Cambridge, 1986), 126–38.

2. Miles, "Portrait in America, 1750–1776," 45.

3. Hedy Monteforte Da Costa Nunes, "Iconography of Labor in American Art, 1750–1850" (Ph.D. diss., Rutgers University, 1983), 52–56.

4. Miles, "Portrait in America, 1750–1776," 61–65. For several examples of non-occupational artisan portraits see Helen Comstock, "Portraits of American Craftsmen," *Antiques* 76 (1959): 320–23.

5. Although the painting has often been described as Revere posed at his workbench, the well-polished surface should not be confused with an artisan's workspace. Copley often used reflective tabletops in his portraits as a device for playing off light and shadows. While the surface might have been part of a sales counter, it also might have had no connection with Revere's shop.

6. Craven, *Colonial American Portraiture*, 334.

7. Jules David Prown, *John Singleton Copley in America, 1738–1774* (Cambridge, Mass., 1966), 20.

8. Deborah A. Federhen, "From Artisan to Entrepreneur: Paul Revere's Silver Shop Operation," in *Paul Revere—Artisan, Businessman, and Patriot: The Man behind the Myth* (Boston: 1988), 68–69.

9. Several very good studies have been written on the meaning and history of artisanal parades and celebrations. These works include Sean Wilentz, "Artisan Republican Festivals and the Rise of Class Conflict in New York City, 1788–1837," in *Working-Class America: Essays on Labor, Community, and American Society*, ed. Michael H. Frisch and Daniel J. Walkowitz (Urbana, Ill., 1983); Howard Rock, *The New York City Artisan, 1789–1825: A Documentary History* (Albany, 1989); Susan G. Davis, *Parades and Power: Street Theatre in Nineteenth-Century Philadelphia* (Philadelphia, 1986); Dirk Hoerder "Some Connections between Craft-Consciousness and Political Thought among Mechanics, 1820s to 1840s," *Amerikastudien* 30 (1985): 328–51.

10. Whitfield J. Bell Jr., "The Federal Processions of 1788," *New-York Historical Society Quarterly* 46 (1962): 5–39.

11. For a full account of the procession see Robert H. Babcock, "The Decline of Artisan Republicanism in Portland, Maine, 1825–1850," *New England Quarterly* 63 (1990): 3–34.

12. Cadwallader D. Colden, *Memoir, Prepared at the Request of a Committee of the Common Council of the City of New York, and Presented to the Mayor of the City, at the Celebration of the Completion of the New York Canals* (New York, 1825); John Bromley and Heather Child, *The Armorial Bearings of the Guilds of London* (London, 1960); Sean Wilentz, *Chants Democratic: New York City and the Rise of the American Working Class, 1788–1850* (New York, 1984), 87–97; Rock, *New York City Artisan*, 3–34.

13. Ransom R. Patrick, "John Neagle, Portrait Painter, and Pat Lyon, Blacksmith," *Art Bulletin* 33 (1951): 188.

14. Ibid., 191; the National Numismatic Collection at the National Museum of American History, Washington, D.C., has numerous examples, usually on small denominations, of these notes. The image, not surprisingly, was particularly popular among Pennsylvania banks. Another example of the wide use and appeal of this image can be seen in parade items. Illustrated in Jean Lipman, Elizabeth V. Warren, and Robert Bishop, *Young America: A Folk-Art History* (New York, 1986), 78, is a fireman's leather parade hat with Lyon's portrait painted on it, from an unidentified mechanic fire company from the 1840s.

15. Patricia Hills, *The Working American* (Washington, D.C., 1979), 34–34.

16. Franklin B. Hough, *The New York Civil List from 1777–1855 Prepared from the Official Records* (Albany, 1855), 253.

17. For published examples of Lincoln's and Grant's use of artisanal imagery see Keith Melder, *Hail to the Candidate: Presidential Campaigns from Banners to Broadcasts* (Washington, D.C., 1992), 106–7; and Bernard F. Reilly Jr., *American Political Prints, 1766–1786: A Catalog of the Collections in the Library of Congress* (Boston, 1991), 424, 602.

18. Beaumont Newhall, *The Daguerreotype in America* (New York, 1976), 15, 67–69; Robert Taft, *Photography and the American Scene: A Social History, 1839–1889* (New York, 1938), 63–77.

19. Taft, *Photography and the American Scene*, 81–82; William C. Darrah, *Cartes de Visite in Nineteenth Century Photography* (Gettysburg, Pa., 1981), 4–6; Handbills Collection, Photographic Collections, George Eastman House, Rochester, N.Y.

20. Papineau and Thomas, handbill, Handbills Collection, Photographic Collections, George Eastman House. Cabinet cards were photographs mounted on a heavy paper stock, approximately 4.5 inches by 6.5 inches in size.

21. Broadside from J. D. Well's Daguerrian Gallery, Handbills Collection, Photographic Collections, George Eastman House.

22. Handbill for J. H. Hero and Company, Mrs. Ralph Mackay Collection, Photographic Collections, George Eastman House.

23. Handbills Collection, Photographic Collections, George Eastman House.

24. *How to Sit for Your Photograph, By Chip* (Philadelphia, [c. 1850]), in the Richard and Ronay Menschel Library, George Eastman House.

25. Brooks Johnson, "The Progress of Civilization: The American Occupational Daguerreotype," in *America and the Daguerreotype*, ed. John Wood (Iowa City, 1991), 112.

26. Ibid., 112–15.

27. For further information on popular labor imagery see Harry R. Rubenstein, "Symbols and Images of American Labor: Dinner Pails and Hard Hats," *Labor's Heritage* 1 (1989): 34–49.

28. Richard Oestreicher, "From Artisan to Consumer: Images of Workers, 1840–1920," *Journal of American Culture* 4 (1981): 53.

29. Ibid., 62–64. In a survey of the National Museum of American History's tintype collection of occupational portraits the ratio between skilled workers and workers ranging from semiskilled to unskilled was also about two to one.

30. It should also be noted that women workers' incomes were considerably less than those of their male counterparts, and this might also help to explain the tendency toward group photographs.

31. For a good summation of the literature on the changing attitudes towards manual work and class transformation see Stuart M. Blumin, *The Emergence of the Middle Class: Social Experience in the American City, 1760–1900* (Cambridge, 1989), 108–37; Sean Wilentz, "The Rise of the American Working Class, 1776–1877: A Survey," in *Perspectives on American Labor History: The Problems of Synthesis*, ed. J. Carroll Moody and Alice Kessler-Harris (DeKalb, Ill., 1990); and Bruce Laurie, *Artisans into Workers: Labor in Nineteenth-Century America* (New York, 1989).

# Contributors

**Robert Asher** is professor of history at the University of Connecticut and is author and editor of numerous books on labor history

**Christine Daniels** is assistant professor of history at Michigan State University. She has published articles in the *William and Mary Quarterly* and *Labor History* and is preparing a book on artisans in the colonial Chesapeake.

**Paul A. Gilje** is professor of history at the University of Oklahoma. His works include *The Road to Mobocracy: Popular Disorder in New York City, 1763–1834* (1987) and the forthcoming *Rioting in American History*, and he co-edited *Keepers of the Revolution: The Working People of New York in the Early Republic* (1983).

**Michele K. Gillespie** is assistant professor of history at Agnes Scott College. She is currently preparing a book on artisans and workers in antebellum Georgia.

**Gary J. Kornblith** is associate professor of history at Oberlin College and is working on a book-length study of Joseph T. Buckingham. His articles on New England artisans have appeared in *Business History Review, Journal of the Early Republic, Massachusetts Review,* and other journals.

**Bruce J. Laurie** is professor of history and chair of the department of history at the University of Massachusetts at Amherst, and author of *Working People of Philadelphia, 1800–1850* (1980) and *Artisans into Workers: Labor in Nineteenth Century America* (1989). He is currently working on the development of popular antislavery politics in nineteenth-century Massachusetts.

**Teresa A. Murphy** is associate professor of history at George Washington University. She is the author of *Ten Hours' Labor: Religion, Reform, and Gender in Early New England* (1992).

**William S. Pretzer** is a member of the Education Program Team at Henry Ford Museum and Greenfield Village, Dearborn, Michigan. He has published several articles on printing labor and technology and edited a volume of essays on Thomas Edison's invention process, *Working at Inventing: Thomas A. Edison and the Menlo Park Experience* (1989).

**Howard B. Rock** is professor of history at Florida International University. He is the author of *Artisans of the New Republic: The Tradesmen of New York in the Age of Jefferson* (1979), *The New York City Artisan, 1789–1825: A Documentary History* (1989), and co-editor of *Keepers of the Revolution: New Yorkers at Work in the Early Republic.*

**Harry R. Rubenstein** is a museum specialist in the Division of Political History, National Museum of American History. He is the author of several articles and exhibitions on American labor material culture and history.

**Ronald Schultz** is associate professor of history at the University of Wyoming. He is the author of *The Republic of Labor: Philadelphia Artisans and the Politics of Class, 1720–1830* (1993).

**Tina H. Sheller** is lecturer in history at the University of Maryland, College Park and is the author of several articles and associate editor of *Latrobe's View of America, 1795–1820* (1985). She is currently enlarging her study of Baltimore artisans into a comprehensive examination of the Revolutionary movement in Baltimore.

**James Sidbury** is an assistant professor of history at the University of Texas at Austin and is currently completing a book on the development of urban slavery in Richmond, Virginia, from 1750 to 1810.

# Index

Library of Congress Cataloging-in-Publication Data

American artisans : crafting social identity, 1750–1850 / edited by Howard B. Rock,
    Paul A. Gilje, and Robert Asher.
    p.    cm.
ISBN 0-8018-5029-0. — ISBN 0-8018-5030-4 (pbk.)
    1. Artisans—United States—History.    I. Rock, Howard B., 1944– .
    II. Gilje, Paul A., 1951– .    III. Asher, Robert.
HD2346.U5A74    1995
331.7'94-dc20          95-1296

                                                            CIP